THE ALLERGY

Did you know that smokin   ne
instigators of migraine? Th   , ougar,
chocolate, tea, coffee, even ora. ., could each be a root cause
of apparently unrelated illnesses? Or that reactions to many
everyday chemicals – gas, insecticides, petrol fumes – can
produce a wide range of symptoms, from rashes to arthritis to
depression?

Discover how GPs, specialists, nutritional physicians and
others are today tracking down the hidden causes of a huge
range of illnesses, and read the moving stories of patients who
have been given a new lease of life.

If in the past you too have been told 'You'll just have to put up
with it,' *The Allergy Connection* may be able to demonstrate that
you don't.

THE ALLERGY CONNECTION

BARBARA PATERSON

THORSONS PUBLISHING GROUP
Wellingborough * New York

Published in the UK by Thorsons Publishers Ltd.,
Denington Estate, Wellingborough, Northamptonshire NN8 2RQ,
and in the USA by Thorsons Publishers Inc., 377 Park Avenue South,
New York, NY 10016. Thorsons Publishers Inc. are distributed to the
trade by Inner Traditions International Ltd., New York.

First published June 1985
Second Impression July 1985

British Library Cataloguing in Publication Data

Paterson, Barbara
    The allergy connection.
    1. Allergy
    I. Title
    616.97   RC584

    ISBN 0-7225-0984-7

Printed and bound in Great Britain

To Pam and Pat
twin fighters in a common cause

The Vikings knew how to stay healthy on long sea voyages. Every ship carried a large barrel of apples.

The Middle Ages forgot. As a result, more seamen died of scurvy than from all other causes, including battle and shipwreck.

In 1747 Dr James Lind carried out the first clinical trial on the warship Salisbury, and in *A Treatise of the Scurvy* demonstrated the vital importance of lemon juice.

In 1795, in the Royal Navy, the daily issue of lemon juice was made compulsory.

It was not until early this century that scientists could distinguish and isolate the essential element, and label it Vitamin C.

In the history of human effort, effective arts have always preceded correct explanatory hypotheses. Thus, an art of metallurgy existed for several thousands of years before the formulation, in the present century, of satisfactory hypotheses to account for the phenomena of tempering and alloying . . . The incorrectness of their hypotheses should have made it impossible for the old smiths and founders to possess an art of metal working . . . Our knowledge of the human mind-body is limited and patchy, and our theories about it are admittedly inadequate. Nevertheless, an effective art of medicine exists, in spite of the fact that many medical hypotheses will be formulated of which contemporary physicians cannot even dream.

Aldous Huxley, *The Art of Seeing*
© Mrs Laura Huxley

Contents

'A good book with a wealth of information. It will be most useful for anyone wanting to do research into what is happening in the world of allergies, as well as help allergic patients to choose what to do and where they can go when no help is forthcoming from their doctors.' *Amelia Nathan Hill of Action Against Allergy.*

The Case of Julie R

May 1982

Patient No.6: Julie R
Before she arrives at the surgery, her doctor reads out her notes.

'Julie is a seriously ill eleven-year-old. Bottle-fed; childhood history of swollen glands, chestiness, hayfever. Was seriously ill after Christmas – very weak, with pains in knees and wrists – and in hospital for five weeks. Doctor diagnosed depression. Later went into hospital again: still no diagnosis. Tachycardia: pulse rate of 120 – characteristic of food allergy. All routine checks were done at the hospital six weeks ago. She's been on a diet of five foods for five days. (In the hospital she ate virtually nothing, and they kept pushing milk down her.) This is her second visit.'

Julie comes in supported by her parents. She is very thin, very weak, very pale. She hasn't even the strength to undo her shoe-laces. She speaks only to whisper 'Yes' or 'No' when asked a direct question.

Her parents say she is sleeping better. Her hayfever has improved. She's perhaps a little more awake. Mentally there's no change.

Another physical check shows only one marked difference: her pulse is now down to 96.

Her parents listen carefully to the explanation of the next stage of her treatment, the reintroduction of different foods.

Suddenly her mother starts talking. 'She's usually so active, doing so many things. She's got so many interests. When she comes back from school she chatters non-stop. We have to ration her or the others don't get a chance. Now it's like talking to a brick wall. She just sits. All she does is look at mail order catalogues. Before, she'd read a book a day.

'We've not known what to do for the best. At the hospital one doctor said she must walk every hour. They'd get her up and drag her along – she hadn't any strength in her. Then a second doctor came in while they were walking and felt her pulse, picked her up and carried her back to bed, said she mustn't be moved.'

Her doctor adds to Julie's notes, 'Already we have a good idea as to the cause. We're sure we'll be able to help her.'

From a letter, dated 28 August 1982:
'. . . Julie R is now fully recovered, and I had a post card from her when she was on holiday recently.'

She had proved to be food-allergic (notably to dairy products), and on eliminating the suspect foods she lost all her previous symptoms.

She has remained well ever since.

How This Book Came to be Written

Three years ago a neighbour – a young woman I'd known since she was five – collapsed at work. Since she had been suffering from a whole series of illnesses for some time, she was taken into hospital for tests and observation. Finally, still undiagnosed, she was sent home. Over the next few months I was kept informed of her progress – or, rather, continued lack of it – and witnessed the strain her condition was having on her immediate family and all her relatives.

Diagnosis: food and chemical allergies
It was five months before I was told that at last the true cause had been found. She had been diagnosed as highly allergic to foods and chemicals.

I was astonished: and, frankly, more than a little sceptical. Though I come from an allergic family, knew about strawberries and shellfish, and have a friend who can't eat cheese or drink red wine, it was a big leap from that kind of experience to being ready to believe the things I was now being told.

Eggs could cause migraines. Squashes could provoke asthma. Cheese could produce hallucinations. Oranges could cause rashes. Milk could produce ulcers. Gas could affect joints. Tap water could bring about convulsions. Tea could cause violent indigestion. Bread could cause depression. Even plastics and electrical equipment could produce reactions in certain sensitive individuals.

Initially I had to struggle to conceal my disbelief, but the more I learned the more open-minded I became. I found that my neighbour's experiences corresponded closely with those of other patients I also began to meet. The books and medical papers I read, the speakers I heard at seminars, the doctors I questioned, were all making similar statements.

I learned:
– that allergies were not, as I had previously thought, comparatively rare and comparatively trivial, but common, persistent, and often serious in their effects;

– that some doctors with experience of food and chemical allergies estimated *at least* one in twenty of the population to be affected;

– that it was everyday foods and chemicals which could cause the greatest problems: dairy products, grains, tea, coffee, sugar, gas, formaldehyde, phenol;

– that reactions could produce very many common symptoms which orthodox medicine frequently dismissed or mis-diagnosed;

– that both foods and chemicals could react on the central nervous system, thus producing *mental* as well as physical symptoms.

I heard of the patients crowding into the few clinics which take this approach into consideration, and of recoveries after years of illness. I found that Action Against Allergy, the National Society for Research into Allergy, and the Hyperactive Children's Support Group were receiving, between them, at least 25,000 letters of enquiry each year. Even the smallest mention in a local paper or on local radio would bring many requests for help.

Allergy and traditional medicine
Yet if it was true that so much ill health was directly attributable to individual reactions to a range of common foods, drinks and chemicals, how was it that the medical profession almost entirely ignored this vital connection?
I was told there were four main reasons:
1. Clinical medicine has for years been moving towards treating symptoms rather than investigating causes.
2. Hospital medicine has become compartmentalized. Patients are treated for different symptoms in different clinics; there is virtually no co-ordination between different departments, and therefore no recognition that apparently disparate symptoms may be connected.
3. During their medical training, doctors have in the past been

taught little about nutrition and its basic role in illness and health. Even today this aspect is the exception rather than the rule.

4.   'Allergy' is not a recognized specialization, and thus does not fit into the medical career structure.

Some harmful effects of lack of awareness

Conviction came only gradually, but the more I learned the more convinced I became that food and chemical allergies were indeed realities.

Other disquieting thoughts followed. Most of the patients I was meeting were not suffering from one isolated symptom, but from several. While some of these symptoms were visible (skin problems, arthritis), most were not (stomach pains, migraines, depression, exhaustion). It was hardly surprising that their GPs, faced with patients complaining of a wide range of symptoms for which they could find no cause, had often concluded that these were either non-existent or 'psychosomatic', and dealt with them by prescribing tranquillizers (or anti-depressants or sleeping-tablets), often in massive doses.

Was it not at least possible that a proportion of patients currently on similar drugs were also suffering from undiagnosed allergies? In 1982 21 million tranquillizers were prescribed, 50% of which were unseen repeats; even though, as the recent Medical Research Council Report states: 'They are often prescribed in situations in which the medical problem, if it exists at all, is only a minor component of the patient's total predicament.'

If only a modest percentage of these could be helped by the gentle methods I was discovering, how much unhappiness patients could be spared – and how effectively the NHS drugs bill could be cut.

A potentially even more serious consideration was the close connection between allergy and certain forms of severe mental illness. A cross-section of the patients I was seeing had previously been admitted to psychiatric hospitals, often more than once, for symptoms which were subsequently discovered to have been of allergic origin. Again, was it not reasonable to suppose that there might be, in psychiatric hospitals across the country, other patients whose mental illness was caused or aggravated by food or chemical allergies?

If what these doctors were saying was correct, then thousands upon thousands of ill people were being dismissed as neurotic, sent off on endless rounds of consultants, subjected to unnecessary operations, and even committed to long stays in hospitals, simply because the root *causes* of their symptoms went unrecognized.

The evidence indicated that too many ill people were being told: 'You'll just have to put up with it – there's nothing more we can do.' I wanted to pass on the message that sometimes – not always, but quite often – there *was* something they could do. They could look at how they ate and drank and how they lived and – like the patients I was meeting – perhaps discover why they were ill and how to recover their health.

Blue-print for a book

I began to plan a book which would pick up from where Dr Richard Mackarness's *Not All In the Mind* (Pan, 1976) and *Chemical Victims* (Pan, 1980) left off, and which would, in particular, look at subsequent developments here in the field of clinical ecology (environmental medicine: see page 21).

I decided to tackle the problem from two different angles: by examining the work of a core of doctors who had been interested in aspects of food and chemical allergies for several years; and by describing the experiences of sufferers.

The Allergy Connection, then, describes the background, methods and views of nineteen medical practitioners in different parts of the country; of a clinical psychologist; and a lay healer. I am most grateful for the help I have received, and for the patience with which innumerable questions have been answered.

I am also grateful to the many patients who were willing to share their experiences with others. Some contacted me direct; others were met by chance in clinics; others were suggested as illustrating the effects of certain substances, or as presenting unusual combinations of symptoms.

I interviewed over eighty during a period of two years: mainly in their own homes, and on their own. Each story was individual and absorbing, and I wish there was space enough to use them all.

I have tried to make a selection which illustrates the extent of the problem of allergy. Some stories are long and complex, others short and straightforward; there are multiple symptoms and single symptoms; physical and mental; affecting people of all ages, from infants to the retired.

There is, however, a high ratio of females to males. This accurately reflects the statistic that more females than males are affected; but I also suspect that women are more aware of health problems, and more attuned to the possible involvement of allergy.

Shortly before completing the book, I contacted again all the selected patients I had not spoken to in the preceding six months. Where two (or more) interviews thus took place, this is indicated by [†] at the end of each account. Where the patient's condition had already been stable at the first interview, and the follow-up confirmed this, any subsequent information is merely incorporated into the text. However, when, at the time of the first interview, the patient had been still suffering from symptoms, or was only starting on treatment – i.e., neither patient nor doctor could be sure of the outcome – and when the following interview demonstrated a marked change, I have indicated this by dividing the account into two parts. Where patients have preferred to use a pseudonym, this is shown by an asterisk.

These are *their* stories, told in their own words.

With hindsight it seems clear that my young neighbour – whose experiences triggered off this book – had been suffering for years from a long list of symptoms clearly indicative of allergy. While she has made a good though still precarious recovery, it has been at enormous cost. If the true cause of her ill health had been picked up much earlier, she and her family would have been spared great pain and anguish.

It is my hope, as it is hers, that *The Allergy Connection* will help many others to be healthier – and perhaps happier – than they ever thought possible.

The publishers regret that in no circumstances can they refer readers seeking medical advice to any of the medical practitioners or specialists mentioned in this book; or to the author.

An Immunologist Looks at Allergy

David Freed, MB, ChB, MD, qualified from Manchester Medical School in 1968, having been appointed Prosector in Anatomy in 1964, and gaining both the Undergraduate Prize in Ophthalmology and the Undergraduate Prize in Paediatrics in 1968. From 1968 to 1969 he was house physician and surgeon at Withington Hospital, and then became first Assistant Lecturer and then Lecturer in the Department of Bacteriology and Virology at Manchester University. He became an MD in 1977 and in 1983 Lecturer in Immunology.

Immunology and allergy are intimately connected, in ways which are not, as yet, fully understood. Dr David Freed is an immunologist who does not confine his interest in their relationship to laboratory research work, but is also ready to exchange views with practising doctors and indeed laymen, and to listen to and consider their experience. The result, as he explains, is that 'in the mid 70s I thought I knew all about allergies. Now I know less and less. I feel totally incompetent.'

The first immunologist
The very first immunologist was Mithradates, a king of Pontus in Asia Minor in the first century BC. To avert the possibility of being poisoned, he took daily minute doses of all known poisons, no doubt basing this practice on experiments carried out on slaves. In this way he eventually made himself immune – rather unfortunately, since when the Romans finally arrived he was unable to kill himself with a massive dose of poison and had instead to fall on his sword.

Immunity

Nearly two thousand years later Pasteur and his fellow-scientists began investigating the mechanisms linking immunity and infectious disease. It was found that if an animal contracted a disease and survived, and if subsequently this animal's blood serum was injected into another, that animal would not contract the illness. This immunity could similarly be transferred from one human being to another. The germ which caused the initial infection was termed 'antigen'; and the element in the blood serum which counteracted it was termed 'antibody'.

Doctors began to use these 'antibodies' against infection. This method – known as 'passive immunotherapy' – is still used in certain infections, such as acute severe diphtheria.

Immunity or anaphylaxis

At the turn of the century two French physicians, Paul Portier and Charles Richet, went on a Mediterranean cruise where they embarked on immunological experiments. They mashed up a jelly-fish, extracted the poison, and injected it into a dog. The dog fell ill, but recovered. They presumed that the dog was now immune: instead, when they injected a second dose of poison, the unfortunate animal died. They termed this reaction 'anaphylaxis'.

Back on dry land they repeated similar experiments with other dogs. They discovered that some died very suddenly; while others, on being given the second injection, would react by falling ill but would recover very quickly. In other words, the initial injection would produce *either* immunity *or* anaphylaxis.

The Viennese paediatrician von Pirquet found that the same reactions could happen in humans. He was using immunotherapy to treat children by injecting anti-toxins to various illnesses. He discovered that on subsequent exposure to the antibodies the children either recovered very quickly, or died. (The same severe reaction which was called anaphylaxis in animals was then termed 'serum sickness' in humans.)

Changed reactivity = allergy

Von Pirquet realized that it was strange indeed that the same conditions could produce two apparently opposite results. All that was clear was that the patient's initial pre-injection reactions had undergone a change. 'For this general concept of a changed reactivity,' he said, 'I propose the term *allergy*.'

Among the conditions he listed as examples of allergy were: repeated smallpox vaccinations; re-inoculations in syphilis;

anaphylaxis; hayfever; and tuberculosis. The term 'allergen' – an as yet undefined element which produced an 'allergy' – he saw as being more far-reaching than 'antigen', and one which might include substances which, while not producing antibodies, might yet lead to supersensitivity.

In 1919 R A Cooke, in the *Journal of the American Medical Association*, stated that 10 per cent of all human beings manifested some form of hypersensitivity. He went further than von Pirquet and distinguished positively between an 'antigen' – something which produced measurable antibodies in the blood – and an 'allergen', which did not. (Though the example he gave was misleading: the antibodies did exist, but his tests were at that time unable to detect them. They were found two years later.)

Professor R R A Coombs later went on to re-define allergy as 'an altered state of potential responsiveness',* a definition which Dr Freed finds ambiguous.

Allergy: the immunologists' definition
Today, classical immunologists, including Dr Freed, reserve the term 'allergy' to mean a self-damaging immunological response brought about by antibodies or lymphocytes. If the mechanism is unknown, they and he use less precise words such as 'intolerance' or 'sensitivity'.

Dr Freed feels that it is important to try to retain a distinction between the two terms, because in the future it may be possible to distinguish between 'allergy' and 'intolerance' and hence choose between different kinds of treatment for often identical symptoms.

It is also important to bear in mind that what appears to be 'allergy' may be due to any one of a number of causes. An individual made ill by milk, for example, may be suffering through any one of the following causes (among others): acute IgE allergy (causing asthma, diarrhoea etc.); infection (TB, Q fever etc.); toxins and pesticides; bovine hormones; phytoestrogens; milk-alkali syndrome; inappropriate fatty acids and minerals; or lactase deficiency.

Dr Freed considers that at present there is no clear indication, in most cases, whether food allergy is caused by immunology or not. Some people can have food antibodies without being ill; while others can be ill without having the antibodies.

Clinical Aspects of Immunity by P G H Gell and R R A Coombs, 2nd Ed., Blackwell, 1966; with von Pirquet's original paper.

It is a pity, he believes, that scientists and members of the general public cannot agree on some neutral all-inclusive term. Since this is unlikely to happen, it is particularly important that anyone who uses the word 'allergy' makes sure that the listener understands it in the same sense. Otherwise, as he points out, patient, GP and specialist may all be using it in different senses; talk at cross-purposes; and mutually arouse unnecessary antagonism.

As Dr Freed has pointed out, there is no one accepted term which includes both the narrow classical immunologist's definition of 'allergy' (a self-damaging immunological response) and 'allergy' as an altered reaction, whether or not the mechanism is known. Some of the doctors in this book are careful to reserve 'allergy' for the first category, while using 'masked allergy' or 'allergic-type response' or 'idiosyncrasy' or 'hypersensitivity' for the second. Where this is so, I have followed suit. Otherwise, 'allergy' is used throughout to include both definitions.

Glossary

Anaphylaxis An extreme allergic reaction which can result in death.

Atopic Used loosely to describe a person with a tendency to allergy. A stricter definition would indicate someone who has two or more positive reactions to skin tests; and/or has a genetically determined (susceptibility) trait which may lead to excess production of IgE on exposure to potentially allergenic substances; and/or presents two or more of the symptoms asthma, eczema, hayfever, urticaria.

Clinical ecology 'Environmental' medicine: assessment of the whole patient primarily from the clinical picture, taking into consideration diet, background, personal relationships, and exposure to environmental hazards.

Coca's pulse test In 1942, Dr Arthur Coca, an American professor of pharmacology, discovered that many reactions to food allergens were accompanied by a marked rise in the pulse-rate. A rise (or, very occasionally, a fall) of ten beats or more per minute is considered significant. (See *The Pulse Test* by Dr A Coca.)

Elimination/exclusion diets These take various forms, but all have the same aim: to cut out a range of commonly eaten foods and drinks which frequently cause allergic reactions.

Enzyme Potentiated Desensitization (EPD) A treatment in which a small cup containing specially treated solutions of specific foods is placed on the scarified skin, generally on the arm, of the patient, retained there for a period, and the process repeated at intervals. (See Chapter 9.)

Food families People allergic to one food are often allergic to others which are closely connected. Those who react to dairy produce, for example, may also react to beef or veal. People who react to wheat may also react to any other member of the gramineae (grasses) family: corn, rice, oats, barley or rye. Potatoes and tomatoes belong to the same family, and so on.

IgE test A laboratory test, obtainable through the NHS, which measures the amount of immunoglobulin E (one of the five types of proteins which show antibody activity) present in the blood. A raised level indicates a susceptibility to allergy as defined by classical immunologists (see page 19).

Intradermal skin test (also called provocative skin test; serial dilution test; titration) Suspected allergens are injected (not pricked) just beneath the skin. Reactions (flare and weal) are measured and used, together with the observation of any accompanying symptoms, as an indication of allergy. (See Vaz G A and others, *Lancet*, 1978, 1066, for a comparison of the relative effectiveness of skin prick tests, intradermal testing, and RAST.)

Mansfield diet Lamb, pears and spring water.

Neutralization The intradermal method is also used to establish the appropriate dilution of an allergen for treatment. By injecting progressively weaker solutions of a substance, it is possible to observe when no further reactions (or symptoms) are caused. This is known as the turn-off point. The concentration which produces this nil effect is then made up into a solution to be used either as drops to be taken under the tongue, or by injections, to neutralize an individual's reactions to that substance. (See Joseph B Miller, *Annals of Allergy*, 3, 38, 1977, A Double-Blind Study of Food Extract Injection Therapy.)

> Some doctors and patients refer to this process as 'desensitization'. However, this latter term is more properly reserved for the process used in the orthodox treatment of allergy, where progressively *stronger* solutions are used to build up the patient's defences.

RAST (Radioallogosorbent test) A blood test which measures specific IgE levels in response to a suspected allergen. Obtainable through the NHS for those who have already been shown to have raised IgE levels. In normal circumstances, only four foods per patient are tested. (See also p. 114.)

Rotation or rotary diet A diet in which no food or family of foods is eaten more than once every four days, and which thus limits exposure to potentially harmful elements.

Skin-prick and patch tests   Conventional skin tests available through the NHS. A drop of allergen is placed on the skin, which is then either scratched or pricked: sensitivity is indicated by a flare (redness) and weal (swelling) reaction within 10-15 minutes. Sometimes the substances are left for a longer period under a large plaster: these are known as patch tests. The results are far more accurate for inhalants than for foods, which produce a high rate of both false positives and false negatives. (See Aas, K, *Clinical Allergy*, 8, 39-50.)

Stone Age diet   Recommended by Dr Mackarness, this is based on the hypothetical primitive human diet. It permits all fresh meat, fish, vegetables, fruit, nuts, pulses, olive oil, spring waters; eliminating all dairy produce, eggs, cereals, sugar, tea, coffee, alcohol, and all packaged and processed foods. There are various more limited versions of this diet: some also rule out beef and veal; or pork; or citrus fruits.

Withdrawal symptoms   Reactions which may occur when an allergic food or chemical is withdrawn, as, for example, in the first few days of an elimination diet. These may be mild or extremely severe: including headaches, extreme fatigue, flu-like symptoms, hallucinations, aching joints, depression etc.

Chapter 1

A Brief Background to Food and Chemical Allergy

Food allergy is not a novel medical fad. Observant doctors from Hippocrates on – and their patients – have noted that certain individuals are unable to eat food which is perfectly acceptable to others. In the seventeenth century Bonnie Prince Charlie suffered from a 'bloody flux' (haemorrhagic diarrhoea) until he stopped drinking milk, whereupon, as the diarist Sullivan put it, 'he lived upon watter and was parfectly well.'

It is, however, true to say that it is only very recently and very gradually that the topic has aroused any kind of general interest, and even today the average GP is unlikely to bear the possibility of food allergy in mind as he records his patients' symptoms. As for chemical allergy, this is considered – when it is considered at all – as a rare and exceptional hazard. Yet it seems probable that over the past thirty years the incidence of both food and chemical allergies has increased dramatically for two main reasons: changes in diet, and the enormous increase of chemicals in our environment.

1. WHO DEVELOPS ALLERGIES?
Clinical ecologists have evolved a concept, 'total overload', to describe an individual's vulnerability – how likely he or she is to become allergic. They recognize that there are a number of factors which help to determine an individual's responses to potential allergens. Among these are:

a. Inherited predisposition Allergies tend to run in families. The reactions may cause different symptoms in different individuals, but there will be a common factor of genetic susceptibility.

b. Whether breast-fed or bottle-fed An infant's immune system develops only slowly, and a breast-fed baby is helped by antibodies present in its mother's milk. Breast-fed babies are less likely to develop allergies either in infancy or in later life.

c.   Quality of diet   A good and varied diet (see below) helps to prevent both food and chemical allergies.

d.   Stress   Emotional problems, work difficulties, physical overwork, infectious illness, accident, pregnancy: any of these can overburden the body's capacity to cope with potential allergens.

e.   Susceptibility to seasonal allergens   People who react to flowers, pollens etc. may also be susceptible to food and chemical allergies, and most particularly at the time when they are reacting most severely to their known allergens.

f.   Repeated exposure to foods or drinks hazardous for that individual   Though some foods and drinks are more likely to cause reactions than others, any individual may be allergic to any one. The more often an 'allergic' food or drink is taken, the greater the demands on the body's capacity to deal with it. Sufferers are often addicted to the foods and drinks which are causing them most harm.

g.   Individual susceptibility to chemicals   Individual responses to exposure to chemicals can vary enormously.

These are only general indications. It is possible, for example, to develop allergies without any family tendency, and a breast-fed infant may react to allergens present in the mother's milk. Nonetheless, these remain useful pointers.

2.   THE IMPORTANCE OF THE RIGHT DIET
Of all the factors which affect allergy – and our whole capacity to become and remain well – the one most likely to be under specific and individual control is the choice of food and drink.

When doctors themselves fail to appreciate the direct link between diet and health, it can hardly be surprising that their patients should also fail to make the connection. Moreover, studies reveal a wide discrepancy between even the broadest concept of a 'good diet' and what people actually eat. This is particularly true of certain groups such as teenagers, the elderly and single working people.

Yet evidence of the vital importance of nutrition is available, and has been for many years.

A nutritional pioneer
At the turn of the century, Francis Hare – a British psychiatrist

practising in Australia – observed that his patients were adversely affected by starchy and sugary foods, and that their symptoms (bronchitis, asthma, migraine, arthritis, etc.) were radically reduced when carbohydrates were removed and substituted by proteins. His long book expounding these observations and conclusions, *The Food Factor in Disease* (Longmans; see the BMA Library), was first heavily criticized and then ignored.

McCarrison's experiments with different diets

Some years later Sir Robert McCarrison, Director of Research on Nutrition in India, was to arrive at similar conclusions after pursuing a different line of approach. Travelling through the sub-continent, he was struck by the marked differences between the health and physique of different races in different parts. To start with, he was uncertain whether these differences could be attributed to genetic background, local climate and conditions, or simply to very different diets.

Over a period of years he carried out a series of experiments on groups of rats. Keeping them in the same excellent conditions, but giving them different diets, he was able to demonstrate that their health – both physical and mental – corresponded directly with the quality of their food. At one end of the scale, those rats fed on wholefoods, fresh fruits and vegetables, some dairy products plus a little meat, were disease-free and lived harmoniously together. At the other end, rats fed on white bread, sweet tea, tinned meat and a few overcooked vegetables were stunted in growth, prone to illness, and so ill-adapted to social co-existence that the stronger began to kill and eat the weaker.

McCarrison went on throughout the rest of his working life to study the connection between diet and disease: by continued experiments with animals, by altering and improving diets for both them and humans, by personal observations on his travels, and by collecting, collating and analysing relevant statistics in India, the UK and the USA. He demonstrated the connection between illnesses and food deficiencies, the importance of a balanced diet, and the significance of vitamins, minerals and trace elements. He showed that people fed on the average British diet were likely to suffer from a wide range of symptoms.

In 1936 a summary of his work and conclusions was printed in the *British Medical Journal** to be greeted, as Dr W W Yellowlees put it in his 1978 James Mackenzie lecture, by 'a deafening silence'.

*His papers are available through the McCarrison Society: see p. 247

McCarrison and the Cheshire doctors

Three years later, however, his views were endorsed by a committee representing six hundred Cheshire GPs, who pointed out the direct parallels between McCarrison's experience and their own. 'Our daily work brings us repeatedly to the same point: ... illness results from a life-time of wrong nutrition .... We are called upon to cure sickness. We conceive it to be our duty in the present state of knowledge to point out that much, perhaps most, of this sickness is preventable and would be prevented by the right feeding of our people.'

Good food and farming

The serious recommendations of the Cheshire doctors were largely overlooked with the onset of war. It was not until 1951, with the publication of Eve Balfour's *The Living Soil* (Faber, 1951), that this aspect of nutrition was again re-considered. Beginning by examining McCarrison's work afresh, she went on to study the whole process of agriculture, producing convincing evidence of the superiority of organic farming. She based her views not on the analysis of different crops but rather on the results of feeding tests.

Pottenger's cats

During these same years, in the States, Dr Francis Marion Pottenger, Jr, was also concerned to discover and demonstrate the effects of different diets. His feeding experiments with cats (*Pottenger's Cats*: Price-Pottenger Nutrition Foundation) showed, as had McCarrison's, that changes in diet produced changes in health. Cats fed primarily on raw meat and untreated milk thrived; cats fed on cooked meat and treated milk suffered from various illnesses and allergies, were more vulnerable to fleas and parasites, more prone to irritability, and had less healthy offspring. Pottenger went on to propose that humans too must be similarly affected by the kind and quality of their food.

Cleave and the Saccharine Disease

Shortly afterwards, in 1956, T L Cleave published a paper which was to be the genesis of his important book *The Saccharine Disease*, published ten years later (Wright, Bristol 1966). Like McCarrison, Cleave derived his theories both from his own experiences – as a surgeon-captain in the Navy – and from his analyses of illness and diet in various parts of the world. Like McCarrison too, he demonstrated that many symptoms of illness were due to diet, but he went on to emphasize the negative side: the consequences of a bad diet.

Cleave demonstrated how a wide range of illnesses which had previously been rare but were becoming increasingly common – ulcers, diverticulitis, constipation, diabetes, coronary diseases – stemmed from one single cause, which he named the Saccharine Disease: the consumption of refined carbohydrates, and in particular of sugar and white flour.

Despite his careful observations and meticulous analyses, Cleave's work too went largely unrecognized at the time. It is only recently that his basic message, along with McCarrison's, Balfour's and Pottenger's – that many illnesses are *caused* and not inflicted – has begun to receive the interest and understanding it deserves.

3. FOOD ALLERGIES

As Pottenger demonstrated with his cats, and as has since been confirmed by other doctors' observations, a good diet – one rich in a variety of fresh wholefoods, and low in refined sugars, starches and processed foods – offers considerable protection against the development of allergies. However, this only means that people are *less* likely to become allergic, not that they become immune. Allergy remains an *individual* reaction.

Idiosyncrasy and illness

Already in 1873 Dr Charles Blackley had shown that 'hayfever' was caused by idiosyncratic reactions to pollens: elements which were harmless to most people could produce illness in some. In the early years of the century, isolated papers were published both here and in the USA associating certain symptoms with similarly idiosyncratic reactions to foods.

Rowe, Rinkel and allergy

Then, in 1926, Dr Albert Rowe in America produced his first paper on elimination dieting, which was amplified eleven years later in his book *Clinical Allergy*. Like McCarrison, and later Cleave, he linked many common symptoms with diet; but he also went one stage further and showed how these symptoms could result from *individual* reactions.

Rowe's work inspired another doctor, Herbert Rinkel, to experiment with his own diet. He had been ill throughout his medical training, with sore throats, running nose and ear troubles, and had been unable either to find a cause or to cure his problems. By a combination of experiment and lucky chance, Rinkel discovered that food allergy (in his case, to eggs) was indeed the cause of his illness: but it was not the straightforward strawberry-rash kind of allergy.

In his case, his egg allergy acted like low-key alcoholism. Provided he continued to have his regular doses of eggs – which he had eaten daily for years – his condition was stable, although his overall health was indifferent. When he stopped having eggs, he would feel better after the first two or three egg-free days; then if he then tried eggs again, he found he would have an acute reaction and became very ill indeed. Rinkel did not know the mechanism behind this type of allergy; he merely observed that it happened.

'Masked allergy'

He called this reaction 'masked allergy', observing that it was – not surprisingly – difficult to detect. Far from the guilty food or drink causing an unpleasant reaction, it would appear to produce a pleasurable boost.

Rinkel's initial paper was rejected by the American *Annals of Allergy*. Over the next eight years he carried out over twenty thousand individual food tests on patients, before finally publishing his report in 1944 ('Role of food allergy in internal medicine', *Annals of Allergy*, 2, 1944).

Masked allergy, adaptation, and stress

At this time his views were heard by Dr Theron Randolph of Chicago, who went on to carry out further investigations in his own practice. It took another ten years to work out fully the theory of masked allergy, assisted by the findings of Professor Hans Selye at the University of Montreal on adaptation and stress. Selye distinguished three stages: initial exposure to the substance, followed by repeated doses at regular intervals; increased doses, leading to a stable level of apparent health and well-being; and exhaustion, when the body ceased to attempt to adapt. At this point the patient would begin to suffer from one or several symptoms.

Mackarness's personal experiences

Although both Rinkel and Randolph went on to publish a succession of medical papers and books in the States, their work met with little general recognition in their own country and was virtually unknown in the UK. Then, in 1958, Dr Richard Mackarness, a British physician who later also qualified in psychiatry, met Randolph in Chicago. As a result Mackarness discovered that his own long-term symptoms were allergically caused, and could be banished by eliminating the incriminated substances. His personal experience endorsed the success he observed that Randolph was having with his patients, and the importance of the work Randolph had published.

His work in Britain
On his return to Britain, Mackarness successfully used the dietary approach with some of his patients, and wrote an initial paper for *Medical World* in 1959. For many years he went on to combine his routine work with his growing interest in allergy, examining potentially allergic cases at his local district hospital, and later establishing a clinic specifically oriented to the treatment of such allergies.

The Clinical Ecology Group
At the same time, during the 1960s and 70s, a handful of doctors in Britain had also independently begun to investigate the role of diet as a cause of illness. The publication in 1976 of Mackarness's *Not All in the Mind* greatly stimulated this line of enquiry. By 1979 a number of like-minded doctors had joined together to form the Clinical Ecology Group (now the British Society for Clinical Ecology), which held its first international meeting in London.

In May 1984 the Royal College of Physicians and the British Nutrition Foundation published *Food Intolerance and Food Aversion*, the first official recognition that food allergy (intolerance) exists.

4. CHEMICAL ALLERGIES AND THE TOTAL ENVIRONMENT
Newspapers report the effects of drug-sniffing. Schools shut because pupils react to cavity insulation. Drugs are withdrawn following side-effects and deaths. There are public protests over the dangers of pesticides. There is growing awareness that chemicals have their dangers; yet it remains unusual for environmental factors to be considered as a potential cause of illness.

Even those doctors who were the first to be concerned about food allergies took some while to look at the effects of chemicals. Not until the late 1940s and early 1950s were the first papers published linking them with illness.

In the years since then, as the use of chemicals has escalated, so too have the problems they can cause. Doctors and scientists have become increasingly concerned about their effect on health. With the ever-growing involvement of chemicals in agriculture and the food-manufacturing industry, it has also become increasingly difficult to distinguish between food and chemical allergies.

Growing awareness of chemical hazards

In the 1930s Rowe had already discussed the possibility of chemical allergy; in 1948 Dr Stephen Lockey, a leading Pennsylvania allergist, produced the first of several papers in reactions to dyes in medicines and foods, and in the late 1950s and early 1960s Randolph began to publish examples of many illnesses caused by reactions to chemicals. In 1962 *Silent Spring* by Rachel Carson (Houghton Mittlin Co., Boston) conclusively demonstrated the devastating effects of chemical agriculture, and in the following year appeared Randolph's *Human Ecology and Susceptibility to the Chemical Environment* (Charles C Thomas).

Since then, Randolph's experience with patients in the States – and that of other doctors following his example – indicates that exposure to chemicals in food, water and the air is rapidly becoming a major cause of illness.

Potential hazards

It is only possible here to indicate briefly some of the potential hazards:

Agricultural spraying of pesticides and herbicides   There are at present no statutory controls over their use. Some chemicals are permitted here which are banned in other countries (e.g. 2-4-5-T and dioxin). Others have been cleared for use here following invalid safety studies. The sprays themselves (especially aerial sprays), and the vaporization which can occur, can drift considerable distances.

Fertilizers   Nitrates are washed off into rivers and sink down through the soil towards the water table. At least a hundred groundwater sources already exceed the EEC 50mg per litre limit (itself thought by some to be too high).

Traces of chemicals in foods and drinks   According to a recent survey (August 1984) by the Association of Public Analysts, one third of a sample of 165 different fruits and vegetables in Britain contained chemical residues, including DDT and Lindane (both banned in the States). Meat and poultry may also retain traces of hormones and antibiotics.

Additives and preservatives   Three thousand additives are in current use: these include several permitted here but forbidden abroad. Only four of the seventeen permitted UK colourants are considered safe both by the EEC and the USA. Surveys in the USA have shown that additives can affect susceptible individuals.

Industrial waste and effluents   Chemical discharges from factories and waste-disposal plants may affect both air and water; some pollutants are thought to be carried thousands of miles.

Chemicals in the home   These include treatments for dry and wet rot, gas, aerosol sprays, fly-killers, detergents, and the 'out-gassing' from plastics, especially soft plastics. Garden weedkillers and insecticides can contain the same dangerous chemicals as agricultural sprays. Formaldehyde, which is contained in many different substances from adhesives to wallpaper, and from foam insulation to curtains, has been shown to be a major source of symptoms in sensitive people. A recent Canadian report states that: 'There is a growing population of chemically susceptible persons for whom present residential air quality standards are totally unacceptable.'

Chemicals at work   Chemicals used in manufacturing processes, photocopiers, carbonless copy paper, heating systems, modern furniture using man-made substances, fumes from carpets; all can provoke reactions. Architects know of the dangers of what they term 'the tight office syndrome'; and in a recent letter to the World Health Organisation Environmental Health Service, an independent environmental chemist (Baskerville Technical Services) describes the effects on health of the presence of solvent vapours.

Medical drugs   All drugs carry the risk of adverse reactions: one survey (*British Medical Journal*, 2, 1979) showed that 41% of patients studied in one general practice showed a reaction to a drug prescribed for the first time. Research indicates that the Pill affects the immune system (see Chapter 6).

Ubiquitous chemicals   Petrol and diesel fumes, chlorine (present in tap water and elsewhere), phenol (used in plastics, disinfectants, preservatives in drugs etc.); ethanol (ethyl alcohol); cigarette smoke; deodorants, after-shaves, all scented toiletries: all these can cause severe reactions.

In addition, there are the unquantified hazards of both direct and indirect contamination arising from the generation of nuclear energy.

Unappreciated dangers

Faced with such a formidable array of everyday hazards, why do so few people seem to be affected? Doctors aware of these dangers believe there are three main reasons for this apparent immunity.

1. Since the danger is largely unsuspected by patients themselves or their doctors, most chemically-caused illnesses remain undiagnosed or mis-diagnosed.

2. As with pure food allergies, individuals respond individually: Dr Roger Williams, of the University of Texas, in his book *Biochemical Individuality* (published 1956) discusses this in detail. Two people exposed to the same chemical may therefore react quite differently.

3. The effect of chemicals is cumulative; there can also be a synergistic effect, when different chemicals act together to produce an additional result. Thus two people exposed to the same chemical, but with different backgrounds and histories, may respond very differently.

Growing acceptance of the existence of environmental hazards

When the whole area of food and chemical allergy is so vast and complex, and when reactions can affect both mind and body, it is hardly surprising that it has taken so many years for medical science to begin to come to terms with its existence.

Today, eighty years since Dr Hare published his pioneering work, it seems that he and his colleagues may at last be on the verge of being cautiously admitted into polite medical society.

The 1984 international meeting of the British Society for Clinical Ecology and the Society for Clinical Ecology was not only addressed by the President and Fellows of the Royal College of Physicians, but was reported in notably sympathetic terms in the *Lancet*. Its correspondent accepted that the kind of environmental hazards discussed by the speakers, and outlined above, do indeed exist. In concluding with a call for 'an objective assessment of the prevalence of these adverse effects' the report does no more than echo the repeated wishes of the clinical ecologists: recognition from their colleagues of the reality of these problems, more research to qualify and quantify their existence, and more NHS help to assist those patients diagnosed as sufferers.

Chapter 2

The Many Symptoms of Allergy

'I had two peppermints and went berserk': Julie McKinnon, age 40

When I left school at fifteen I got an apprenticeship, icing wedding cakes. I used to get headaches. I'd feel cold, and always lethargic. When I got back home I'd slump in a chair and fall asleep. My mother would get very cross. The fire would be blazing away and I'd be sitting there wrapped in cardigans. By the time I was seventeen my headaches were becoming agonizing. I was sent for eye-tests, and then head X-rays: but there was nothing wrong.

I got married at 23, and we moved away. I got more and more depressed – in fact, suicidal. We thought it was because I was missing my family. I started eating a lot of sweet things to try to cheer myself up. All it did was put on weight.

I began to lose blood from my back passage. My GP said I was constipated. Then on one occasion, when I was 25, to be frank I filled the loo with blood. I was very weak and frightened, but the doctor wouldn't come. He prescribed some tablets. We didn't know what to do.

We moved soon after and found a very good woman GP, who listened. She sent me to a specialist. When I got into hospital they all insisted that I'd aborted. They told me there was no way I could have lost blood like that unless I'd done something to myself. I kept explaining that we desperately wanted a child and we'd been trying for years. They wouldn't believe me.

Back home again I became very depressed. I couldn't walk. I couldn't bend down to clean the bath because of the headaches. I became very weak – I collapsed in the road and couldn't even get up. I began hallucinating. I'd cry in the morning when I woke up: *because* I'd woken up. I couldn't bear to comb my hair because I'd see images in the mirror and couldn't break away from them.

I was sent to hospital for tests – all sorts of tests. I was there for ten days, hallucinating all the time: seeing a tree coming through the window and plucking me out of bed – things like that.

Finally they discovered what was wrong: pernicious anaemia. They gave me injections. My hair returned to its normal colour, black; it had faded to brown. I started to pick up. Every day I could do a bit more.

In 1973 our daughter was born. Then over the years, again I began to feel more and more depressed – without any apparent reason. I thought I was going crazy. I didn't want to see any more doctors because I thought they'd only give me tranquillizers.

About three years ago I really started to lose control. I was flaring up before my daughter, and taking a hundred painkillers a week. My speech started to come out back to front. I was a danger on the road. I'd walk out in front of cars without seeing them. Finally I went to my new GP – we'd moved again – and he told me : 'Pull yourself together and control your temper.'

I couldn't.

Then I read an article about allergies. My husband went out and bought books. I was past caring. One of them was Mackarness's *Not All in the Mind*.

We started working out the foods. I completely cut out all sweet stuff, and we got in touch with Dr H through Action Against Allergy. Then, before I managed to get to the clinic, my husband took us to see the start of the Transatlantic Yacht Race. While we were waiting I was offered two peppermints and ate them without thinking.

I went berserk. I nearly walked straight off the quay. I was violent. I began to fight. I saw things zooming out of proportion towards me. The words that came out! It wasn't me at all.

My husband got me to the car and said 'This is the end.' He drove me straight to the clinic. I wouldn't move. My husband went in, and came back and said: 'Do come. All the people waiting in the clinic say "*Please do come in.*"' In the end I did.

Dr H put me on a five-day distilled water fast. The first two days were terrible. I had a splitting headache and was laid out on the settee, feeling very cold and sick. On the third day I started to feel better, and in the afternoon I really improved and even did some housework. On the fourth and fifth day I felt marvellous – *no headaches*! I went out and worked in the garden, spring-cleaned the house and did some painting. My husband was amazed; normally I never felt like doing anything. The food addiction also explained the weight problem I had been battling with in vain for years and years. Oh, how wonderful it was to wake up without a headache, not to need to take all those pills!

Over the next few months I found that I was allergic to all foods, quite a few moulds, some chemicals, and tree and grass pollens. Now I have my drops I can eat small amounts of my allergic foods. I've been taking them for three years, and now I only need to take them once and not four times a day. For chemicals and pollens I still need the drops four times a day if I go outside.

National Health doctors just tell you to snap out of it. I wish their medical school professors would wake up to the fact that food allergies are real! I have thank goodness not known what depression is since I started taking my drops. Oh, I still get fed up with myself at times, but that deep depression has gone. It's just lovely to be alive now. I wake up feeling fantastic. My whole fanily life has changed.

The discovery of allergies has been my salvation. All I want now is to make up for all those wasted years. If it hadn't been for my husband I don't know where I'd have been. I always felt I would end locked up. Now I have a new life ahead. †

'I'd been dreading the winter': Derek Lilley, age 54

As a young man I was always under the weather. There were occasions when I didn't feel so bad, but they never lasted long. I was always constipated.

In 1971 I lost 1½ stone – through over-working I thought, but it turned out that I had an over-active thyroid. I had an operation. A couple of years later it began to play up again, and in 1974 I went back for radioactive treatment.

I still didn't feel well. I had tests done for gallstones and ulcers, then X-rays. The doctor could see nothing, so they kept telling me I was a fit man. I told them *no*, they were wrong. They gave me tablets.

About three years ago I saw a programme on TV about food allergies. That made me think hard. Already I'd been beginning to reject foods one after the other. And alcohol – I'd never drunk much, but now if I went out with my mates and had a half I'd get an instant reaction. The muscles in my back and stomach would go into a spasm. I'd feel a burning sensation which would take hours to fade.

It was probably three months later that my muscles started

aching all over. My bones creaked in bed. 'This is the last straw!' I thought. Because I'm in the building trade, and I do a lot of physical work, I could see myself out of a job. I didn't want to go to a doctor. I thought I'd just be put on one drug after another.

My wife bought magazines about homoeopathic medicine, and she wrote to them. That's how I got in touch with Dr H. I was tested for a whole range of foods, and I got reactions to all of them in various degrees. When I started with the drops there was only a gradual improvement, but then it speeded up and soon I felt really well. All my aches and pains disappeared. I'd been dreading the following winter, but I just sailed straight through it. †

Dr E C H, MB, ChB, was formerly a medical paratroop officer with a field ambulance in the Indian Airborn Divison. He qualified in 1944 after training in Bristol, and spent 25 years in general practice in Plymouth.

Dr D W, MRCS, LRCP, MFHom, trained at University College Hospital and qualified in 1956. She went into general practice – part-time from 1960 while bringing up a family.

Together Dr H and Dr W gave up orthodox medicine 'in disgust' in 1973. After training in homoeopathy at the Royal Homoeopathic Hospital in London, under the Queen's physician Dr Marjorie Blackie, they established – in 1975 – a homoeopathic clinic in Devon.

The main stimulus for the departure of Dr H and Dr W from orthodox medicine was their growing disenchantment over what they felt was its distorted sense of priorities: too much emphasis on drugs to treat symptoms, and too little on understanding or dealing with causes. They felt that many of these drugs were dangerous, yet they were pressured by patients to supply them. They found new patients arriving already addicted and demanding fresh supplies – this was particularly the case with tranquillizers – and some consultants to whom they referred patients would insist on prescribing similar drugs. Instead of relying on these to pacify their patients, Dr H and Dr W wished to change the whole orientation of medical treatment.

The prevalence of masked allergy

Today their clinic treats over five hundred new patients a year: mostly from the south-west, but also from all over the country. Virtually all have previously been investigated – often over many years – by both GPs and specialists. Dr H and Dr W believe that the commonest form of illness which defeats both GPs and specialists is caused by masked allergy; and most patients who come seeking homoeopathic treatment – to which they often turn in desperation when all else has failed – are found to be suffering from unsuspected allergy to food or chemicals. They estimate that well over 50% of their patients turn out to have allergy-based problems.

Diagnoses through case-histories

For eight out of ten suspected allergy patients, a careful history is sufficient on its own to establish a correct diagnosis. Allergic problems frequently start in infancy with colic, eczema or asthma, often coinciding with the introduction of bottle feeding or weaning. In childhood there may be frequent bouts of tonsillitis or earache, running nose, skin troubles, bed-wetting, wheeziness or asthma, constipation or diarrhoea. There may also be apparently psychological disturbances: sleep-walking, head-rolling, hyperactivity, tantrums and learning difficulties.

Later in life, the most common symptom of masked allergy is probably lack of energy. As Dr H explains, 'These patients have all the symptoms associated with anaemia, but are rarely found to be anaemic.' There may be inexplicable fevers, enlargement of the lymph glands, headaches, attacks of migraine. 'In short, any bizarre or inexplicable symptoms in any part of the body may be caused by masked allergy. That is why it has been called the unsuspected enemy.

'Typically, patients with masked allergy are those who have nothing apparently wrong with them, but have never been consistently well. In our experience, the three commonest symptoms of allergy are: lack of energy; tension and discomfort in the muscles of the neck; and disturbances of sleep. There are also three symptoms which are almost diagnostic of masked allergy: tiredness on waking; feeling ill with hunger; and variations in the acuity of vision.'

These are only three of an astonishingly wide range of symptoms which could be caused by allergies. From Dr H's clinical experience of hundreds of allergic patients, most with several different symptoms, he has worked out a comprehensive list. He points out that each could have many other different causes; but that, when a patient has a multiplicity of symptoms deriving from a variety of different systems in the body, the likelihood that this indicates masked allergy must be considered. A life history of a catalogue of complaints, none of which adds up to any one specific illness, endorses the probability of this being the correct diagnosis.

'The importance of considering masked allergy when any unusual pattern of symptoms occurs is that, provided the diagnosis is made early, it is so easy to cure the patient's symptoms. If this opportunity is missed and the patient given the wrong treatment, the condition can become intractable. What is essential is *not to treat apparently inexplicable symptoms with drugs*. It is not safe to give patients with masked allergy tranquillizers, sleeping-pills, painkillers, hormones and so on.'

Symptoms found in masked allergy syndrome

HAIR
> Greasy hair
> Dry hair
> Early greyness
> Early loss of hair
Dandruff may also be a manifestation of masked allergy

EYES
> Photophobia: a very common symptom. ('Headlights worry these patients;' says Dr H, 'some experience pain in the eyes when facing a bright light.')
> Fluctuations of vision: it gets bad, improves, and then deteriorates again ('There is no other cause that I know of for this phenomenon')
> Bags under the eyes (known in America as 'allergic shiners')
> Dark shadows under the eyes
> Sore eyes
> Dry eyes
> Feeling of grit in the eyes

EARS
> Hearing may become hypersensitive
> The patient may become relatively deaf
> 'Glue ear' ('Patients who need grommets in their ears almost certainly have a masked allergy.')

MOUTH
> Bad breath
> Bad taste
> Loss of taste
> Sore tongue
> Bleeding gums

Dry and cracked lips
Dry tongue and mouth
Mouth ulcers

THROAT

Recurrent sore throats ('Patients with masked allergy almost always lose their tonsils and adenoids.')
Continuous and unremitting dry cough

NOSE

Snuffling
Catarrh
Constantly runny nose ('The child who rubs the end of the nose with the palm of the hand almost certainly has an allergy: this has been called the allergic salute.')
Acute sense of smell
No smell at all

CHEST

Recurrent bronchitis and asthma
A choking, suffocating feeling, especially at night ('Patients feel they can't get enough air into the lungs, and tend to over-breathe. Over-breathing can itself trigger a whole new series of symptoms.')

STOMACH

Perversion of appetite – cravings for some foods, distaste for others
Loss of appetite (anorexia nervosa) which can swing to bingeing (bulimia)
Stomach pains
Ulcers ('One of the commonest causes of stomach and duodenal ulcers is milk, and by encouraging people to drink more milk you can almost guarantee they'll never get better.')
Tremendous weight problems ('These patients often have a weight problem. They may be unable to gain weight, or be tremendously overweight. There are often marked fluctuations in weight over a short period. Some patients are totally unable to lose weight, but as soon as you take them off the food to which they have a masked allergy the fat melts away like butter in the sun.')
Bilious attacks
Wind both up and down ('This can be very embarrassing.')
Bloating of the stomach

Mesenteric adenitis – swollen abdominal glands

COLON

The irritable bowel syndrome in all its forms
Piles (possibly)
Chronic constipation ('Almost certainly a manifestation.')

GENITO-URINARY SYSTEM

Persistent and unexplained cystitis, with nothing abnormal traceable in the urine
Bed-wetting
Loss of sexual desire
Impotence ('Reversible when allergy is diagnosed'.)
Prostatis
Recurrent thrush
PMT (pre-menstrual tension)
Heavy periods ('I believe that a fantastic number of women have to have hysterectomies because of food allergies.')

SKIN

All sorts of rashes, including acne and eczema
Weals, such as urticaria or hives
Hypersensitivity to the touch of clothing
Very dry flaking skin
Very greasy skin

NAILS

Nail-biting is probably a manifestation of masked allergy

JOINTS

Painful and aching joints
Audible clickings in the joints
Arthritis ('Some cases are certainly due to food allergy.')

HEART

Pulse may be speeded up
Pulse may be slowed down ('I've now seen two patients who had had a pacemaker fitted for a slow pulse which was due to a masked allergy. In my opinion it is very dangerous in such circumstances to put patients on drugs to speed up or slow down the pulse rate.')
Coronary thrombosis ('Food allergy has been a proven cause in some cases.')

MISCELLANEOUS

Excessive sweating, without apparent cause

Abnormal thirst

Catarrh: not just nasal catarrh; any secretory function of the body may be implicated

Inexplicable fevers ('This is the case of glandular fever that isn't, or brucellosis that isn't.')

Sensations of extreme heat or extreme cold

Premature ageing: patient looks and feels old ('This is the patient who feels old in middle age. In my opinion food and chemical allergy could be the cause of the increasing number of cases of pre-senile dementia. If this is so it is a preventable condition.')

CENTRAL NERVOUS SYSTEM

Extreme exhaustion

Headaches

Migraines

Violent mood swings from elation to deep depression

Aggression

Sleep disorders and nightmares

Snoring

Grinding of teeth

Panic attacks

Lack of concentration

Incoherence

Difficulties in reading and comprehension

Writing can deteriorate and even change to mirror-writing; spelling becomes difficult

Impairment of memory

Clumsiness and proneness to accidents

Facial tics

Trembling in the body; tingling all over

Pins and needles in hands and feet; restlessness; inability to stay still in bed; fidgety legs

Loss of balance; giddiness

Weakness which becomes almost paralysis

Total lack of energy

Symptoms affecting the mind

Of this long list of symptoms, those affecting the central nervous system can be the most distressing for both the patients themselves and for their families. In most cases, they are subjective and not objective: neither doctors nor relatives can see visual evidence that they do in fact exist. Very often the patients are told that the illness is all in the mind.

At the same time, they may give every appearance of psychological disturbance. They can have hallucinations or think they hear voices. 'They're not themselves, and they *know* they're not themselves. They can become vicious, cruel, bloody-minded, quite unable to control themselves: a danger to themselves and others.' This is frequently combined with an inability to sleep, nightmares, sleep-walking, and inexplicable feelings of terror and anxiety.

Dr H believes that investigation might show that allergic illness accounts for some cases of baby-battering, where a badly affected parent is confronted by an infant who is also food-allergic, hyperactive and screaming.

It is particularly unfortunate when, as frequently happens, such patients enter mental hospitals. There their problems are likely to be compounded. In the first place, if an allergy is not suspected, the foods they are given are likely to exacerbate their condition. In addition, these allergic patients are very liable to suffer from severe side-effects to drugs. Many are given ECT, which is, in Dr H's words, 'a total disaster'. Even ordinary hospitals present hazards for allergic patients because the wards are contaminated with sprays, bleach, cleansers and polishes.

Dr H explains that many patients who have a masked allergy problem may remain free of symptoms for long periods, and it is not until times of stress (bereavement, pregnancy, an accident, illness) that the body's adaptive powers become exhaused and symptoms appear or reappear. These are often mistakenly ascribed to the stress itself, whereas this has merely lowered the capacity of the system to deal with potential allergies. Once again, patients are in grave danger if they are prescribed tranquillizers or sleeping tablets as the best way of dealing with this situation.

Diagnosis and treatment
Sometimes the case history – together with the patient's account of way of life and eating habits – not only indicates the diagnosis of allergy, but pinpoints the allergen, particularly when addiction is involved. Dr H recalls the patient who ate 5lbs of cheese a week, another who had tomato ketchup with every meal, and a third who never went out without taking a flask of tea. Such straightforward solutions, though, are relatively rare. 'Patient awareness is increasing all the time. These glaring examples get spotted and dealt with, so that we now rarely meet them at all.

'Even when the clues are less obvious, it's possible to make a tentative estimate of the cause or causes of allergy by bearing in mind that the two groups of foods most commonly involved are *dairy products* and *grains*. It's a simple matter to remove milk, grains and their products from the diet for two or three weeks to see how much improvement is attained. It's wise also for patients to omit caffeine, nicotine and alcohol, sugar, all food additives, and all processed foods.

'In about 20% of cases a simple elimination diet fails to solve the problem, and we then proceed to intradermal skin testing (see page 22), both to diagnose the allergens and then to work out their correct neutralizing dilutions. We do our best to avoid testing because it's time-consuming and expensive, but it can be a useful short cut, especially for patients in a great deal of trouble.'

Following from the results of the testing, individually devised oral drops are made up for each patient. Dr H describes this whole procedure as 'a labour of love', and is not surprised that it is not widely available. The basic concentrates (of lettuce, rye, tomato, etc.) are commercially produced, both in America and Britain, and are the same as those used in hospitals for prick testing. The specific allergens indicated by the tests are then diluted to their correct turn-off level, and combined into one solution. This is so calculated that one drop, taken four times a day, can protect a patient against a maximum of 26 different foods.

Chemical allergies
The most difficult cases of all are those which involve chemical allergies. When one of these is suspected, it is possible for a patient to be tested for reactions to the combustion products of petrol, North Sea gas, Calor gas, diesel, and tobacco; and also for such ubiquitous chemicals as phenol, formaldehyde and alcohol. Some chemicals remain very elusive. Dr H and Dr W believe that among the handful of obstinate cases who, sadly, they are unable to help, are those with as yet undiagnosable chemical allergies.

'Fortunately, these very difficult cases remain a very small minority. It is rare to find a patient who is allergic *only* to chemicals. Often, by diagnosing and removing food allergies, we cut down the total burden on the system to a level where it can then cope with the attacks of chemicals that before it could not handle. Candidiasis (see Index), the result of a yeast takeover in the intestine, is a further complication which can bedevil the allergic syndrome. Treatment of this condition often brings a difficult case under control.

'We find we can help almost all the patients who come to us, but not always. We have to admit that we too sometimes have our failures. We give no drugs or antibiotics. We believe that the treatments we supply can do no harm. The human body has enormous powers of self-recovery; our role is to help patients draw on this essential reserve. Once off allergens, and stabilized, patients can recover full health – and even, with caution, reintroduce the foods to which they were once allergic.'

The key issue of our time

'I believe that the pattern of illness in society has changed. Whereas in previous eras germs were the determining factor, today pollution is the major source of trouble. Much of modern illness is man-made, and much is iatrogenic – actually *caused* by medically-prescribed treatments.

'Pollution attacks the immune system, and people become allergic. This acquired form of allergy may then become hereditary. The incidence of allergy in both partners of a marriage – itself a random pairing – indicates how prevalent this problem has become.

'An understanding of the nature of masked allergy, its link with pollution, and its great importance as the successor to the germ theory of disease, makes this whole subject the key issue of our time.'

Chapter 3

A GOOD DIET = HEALTH
A FAULTY DIET = DISEASE

'I'm glad we discovered it early':
Anita Houlson, age 35, talks about her daughter Sally,
age 4

I've never had allergic problems myself, but my husband has had a skin complaint for ages, and reacts to detergents. My father's had to have injections for dust mites, and my grandmother was brought up on goat's milk – presumably because she couldn't take cow's milk.

Sally began getting eczema-ish patches in the creases of her elbows and knees when she began going onto ordinary foods. It was just a little to start with. The doctor gave us lotions and creams. Then the rash got worse and worse. She went crackers with the itching. She was bad-tempered all the time. She wasn't sleeping. She'd get us up three or four times a night. She screamed and wouldn't let us put her in the bath because the water hurt her.

After six months of this I made an appointment to see Dr Breakwell. I had to wait a fortnight and I thought I wouldn't last that long!

Dr Breakwell discussed everything with me, and from then on it was plain sailing. I was lucky, because when he explained about the Stone Age diet I said: 'Well, that's almost what she's eating already!' Since my husband's a farmer, we had our own meat, our own fruit and vegetables, and our own well-water. Apart from that Sally didn't really have any extras except squashes, a few sweets and some biscuits. So it was easy to narrow things down. It would have been much harder for anyone else.

With Sally, the main trouble is colourings, especially tartrazine.

She can't have lemon or orange squash, coloured fizzy drinks, salad cream, fish pastes, anything in coloured breadcrumbs, coloured crisps, lemon or orange or green sweets or jellies or lollies, bought biscuits or cakes. It's hard to work out sometimes whether it's the additive, or the food, or a combination of food plus additive.

I was trained as a home economist, which is useful, because it means I've plenty of books at home I can refer to. Interestingly enough, a 1962 book mentions specifically that chemical colourings were then banned in foods – only natural colourings were permitted. It's obviously changed since then, but I don't know when. Although of course we were taught basic nutrition – vitamins, proteins, carbohydrates and so on – there was never any mention that some foods could be harmful for some people.

We had a set-back recently when Sally had an ear infection and I gave her junior aspirin. Sally didn't improve, and it was only when I began to look for relevant pieces in *Chemical Victims* that I discovered that tartrazine was an 'aspirin-related coal-tar compound'.

After that episode Sally's skin was terrible, and we had to start all over again. I was angry with myself for giving her the aspirin. Still, to look at her now no one would think that anything had happened. Her skin is clear again after lots of hard work.

Sally knows what makes her poorly, and she's sensible about it even at her age. The rewards of our hard work are enormous. She's just taken her first ballet examination and was awarded a 'highly commended' mark. She adores the water and swimming, and can somersault into the water and dive.

I'm so grateful that we found out the trouble while Sally was still so young. I often wonder whether her confidence would have been shattered if her skin had remained an eyesore. She would just have gone on getting worse and worse. It doesn't bear thinking about! †

From invalid to cricket captain:
Marilyn Hughes, age 31, talks about her son Jason, age 12

He was a premature baby. I fed him to start with, then the nurses began giving him supplementary feeds, and when I got home I couldn't breast-feed him any more and he went on to cow's milk plus sugar. I think at that time they said to add a teaspoon to every feed. The moment he started on this he got constipation.

At twelve days he got a bad attack of what they called the

snuffles. He kept on being ill and fretful. They said it was teething. I kept on seeing different doctors. At two he got pneumonia – that was the first time I saw Dr Breakwell – and he was admitted to hospital.

He went on being ill. When he started school he was away from it more often than he was there. His work suffered. He kept getting throat infections. He never had a sense of smell. His nose ran all the time, and he kept getting asthma attacks. He was always wheezing, especially at night. We'd be up and down getting him glasses of water at two and three in the morning.

He was using a spinhaler regularly, a dose of Intal four times a day. It helped, but it didn't put him right. If you listened to his chest, you could still hear him wheeze.

In September 1981 Dr Breakwell suggested that he went on a diet. Within two days his streaming nose had gone. He smelt the dustbin for the first time! His asthma simply disappeared, and since then he's gone from strength to strength.

Orange squash is the most drastic of all. And Coke. Funnily enough, I'd already noticed that he was starting to wheeze after drinking Coke, and I'd stopped it immediately. Apart from that, he mustn't eat any white bread or sugar.

He never used to be able to play soccer with his mates, and now he plays football at school. He's done cross-country runs. He's cricket captain. When he got a cold last winter it was all gone in a week. Before, he'd have needed drugs and cough stuff and heaven knows what.

I'm ready to help anybody in a similar position, because when you've got problems like this you need support. You need someone to say: 'Yes, it works. Keep on going.' †

Dr John Breakwell, MB, ChB, DRCOG, qualified in Birmingham in 1970. After two years' hospital work in Worcester as house surgeon, house physician and senior house officer in paediatrics, he spent six months in Hull in an obstetric post. In 1973 he returned to Worcester to start in general practice. He has been there ever since.

Dr Breakwell has been interested in the dietary approach to illness all his practising medical life. Initially he was inspired in his student days by the lectures and writings of Professor McKeown, of Birmingham University's Social Medicine Department. 'The wisdom of it struck me: the emphasis on the *causes* rather than the treatment of illness.'

Cleave and the saccharine disease

Then in his final year he read *Diabetes, Coronary Thrombosis and the Saccharine Disease*, by Surgeon-Captain T L Cleave, with G D Campbell and N S Painter (John Wright & Sons, second edition, 1969). Here he found a simple and convincing demonstration that a good diet could produce health, and a faulty diet, disease. (See p. 28.)

Dr Breakwell was convinced by Cleave's meticulous demonstrations of the links between the increased consumption of refined carbohydrates, notably sugar and white flour, and the increased incidence of many illnesses, which produced different symptoms and were given different labels, but which all sprang from the same basic source. He was also struck by Cleave's analysis of the three principal effects of this over-consumption of refined foods:

1. The physical effect caused by the loss of fibre;
2. The damage caused by the concentration of highly-concentrated substances;
3. The lack of protein following from the over-eating of foods possessing little protein.

The first effect is now widely known and accepted; the other two are still not appreciated.

'I was convinced by the evidence given by Cleave that these refined foods could produce, first, constipation, and secondly diverticular diseases; also diabetes, hypertension, coronary disease and so on. Where a large residue is left in the bowel, bacteria which in moderation are necessary and friendly thrive and multiply and do harm, leading to cholecystitis, appendicitis and so on. Doctors know that children may get appendicitis after a birthday party, due to the surge growth of bacteria. These are local diseases due to proliferation, but there are also more distant diseases of the urinary tract, such as pylonephritis. The increase of toxins can also lead to ulcerative colitis. Those patients with "allergies" who eat many refined foods *may* be suffering from true allergies, or from toxins released from the bowel.

'Two chapters which I then read least assiduously – on *peptic ulcers* and *a different type of over-consumption* – I now consider among the most important.'

Dr Breakwell was able to put part of his beliefs into practice in his paediatric house job. He interested one of his consultants in the role played by fibre, and so was able to issue a diet sheet and work out individual diets for patie... ts. On starting general practice he continued to adopt a wholefood approach whenever this seemed suitable.

McCarrison: nutrition and health

In 1972 he read the writings of Sir Robert McCarrison for the first time (see p. 27). Again, these were a revelation; and after studying the evidence of McCarrison's observations and the results of his experiments, he wholeheartedly agreed with his conclusion that 'The greatest single factor in the acquisition and maintenance of good health is perfectly constituted food.' This was endorsed by his reading of Lady Eve Balfour's *The Living Soil* (Universe Books, New York, 1975) and Dr Lionel Picton's *Thought on Feeding* (Faber & Faber). Yet another element was added when he read Dr Richard Mackarness's *Not All in the Mind* shortly after its publication, with its suggestion that specific foods – not simply refined carbohydrates – could be harmful to specific individuals.

Three months later his eldest son, then eight, was admitted to hospital with a rash, high fever, swollen glands, and painful swollen joints. Aspirin and an antibiotic were implicated. Dr Breakwell, already worried about his son's illness and alerted by Dr Mackarness's book, began to consider what a profound effect salicylates could have, and to what extent major symptoms could spring from apparently minor causes.

Clinical ecology in a general practice

It was about this time that he began to introduce the clinical ecological approach into his practice. In a personal diary he wrote at the end of the year: 'There have been times during the past months when I have felt at the frontiers of knowledge . . . It is a sign of the sluggishness, conservatism and entrenched attitudes of the majority of my professional colleagues that they have not been similarly stirred . . . There is a growing awareness not only of the inadequacy, but, at times, of the actual danger to health and to life of some modern treatments.'

From the end of 1979 he began to use the Stone Age diet for selected patients. Following some successful results, he gave a talk on its effects to post-graduates at Ronkswood Hospital: finding that while junior house doctors were interested, 'consultants were either scathing or asleep.' Since then, very gradually, he has found an increasing interest in this approach.

He is now one of eight Health Centre doctors, six full-time and two part-time, caring for 14,500 patients. He is still the only one to adopt the dietary approach. His colleagues are now tolerant: one or two are actively interested, but feel they lack the time to follow suit. Dr Breakwell feels this is a sign of failure on his part. 'I haven't got the message across that this is *not* an extra.

This is basic to understanding and treating illness.'

Patients attending the Centre at short notice will be seen by whoever is on duty. If they wish to consult one specific doctor they must make an appointment. Dr Breakwell finds that, now his approach is becoming widely known, he tends to get booked up well in advance. This means that he treats mainly regulars and chronic attenders; not the acute, and fewer children – which he regrets.

Of the patients he sees, he treats those with obvious and identifiable causes in the orthodox way. Of the others, he tries clinical ecological methods in 75% of the cases. (The other 25% might also benefit, but he believes that for various reasons they either can't or won't respond.) Of those on whom he tries this approach, he finds that '30-40% of patients with chronic relapsable conditions have allergies.' Of these, possibly ⅓ have true allergies potentially identifiable by blood tests, while the other ⅔ show 'intolerance' or 'allergy-type reactions'. This is, as he points out, only an *estimate* based on his clinical experience; but he believes that it errs on the side of caution, and that the true rate may be far higher.

He has now tried his diets on 'literally hundreds and hundreds of patients,' with marked success. He has successfully treated eczema (particularly in infants, and often linked with milk); ulcerative colitis (several patients perfectly well, and others improved but not completely cured – the prime culprit again being milk); migraines; rapid and irregular heart-beat in the absence of organic heart-disease; anxiety states and panic attacks; behavioural disturbances, especially in children (apart from intolerances, a prime cause here may be lead); and asthma. This last he finds especially satisfying to treat, as results are so soon observed. The most common cause is junk food: sugar, cola, soft drinks, and foods with additives.

Teaching and learning he sees as a two-way process. 'Doctors can learn much from their patients – or they should.' He has been on the Stone Age diet himself, and found he felt 'terrific' after leaving off cheese, tea, coffee and beer. He most laments having to abstain from cheese sandwiches when he returns from a late night call: 'very comforting, a cheese sandwich.' He feels it helps his patients to know that he has similar problems.

Mind, body and health

Dr Breakwell is convinced that the mind and body are related, and that the psyche enters into illness. The health of the body is affected by emotions, psychological reactions, surgical interventions, and drugs. 'Cartesian philosophy, the separation of mind and matter, has influenced medical thinking ever since the eighteenth century. We're only just breaking free of it.' He is also interested in other approaches to medicine. 'In the West we are too ready to feel that life should always be pleasant. If something goes wrong, our response is to look to drugs. Instead, we should consider that when something's wrong it's there to teach us. We should search for *why*, and then put it right.'

Compatible eating

A further contribution to his views on nutrition was added when, in 1983, Doris Grant introduced him to Dr William Howard Hay's work on compatible eating, which explains how 'incompatible eating' – carbohydrates and protein eaten at the same meal – might lead to food allergies. Dr Breakwell is now researching this hypothesis in general practice. (See *Food Combining For Health* by Doris Grant and Jean Joice, Thorsons, 1984.)

Patients, pre-conception and pregnancy

Attitudes of patients vary enormously. Some are frankly sceptical. As one of his earliest patients, with ulcers, palpitations and panic attacks left his surgery, he heard her tittering to her husband: 'As if all my illnesses could be due to milk!' (On subsequent investigation, however, this proved to be the case.)

Among those most open to persuasion are those attending ante-natal clinics; ideally, as Dr Breakwell points out, ante-natal care would start with pre-conception. He recommends, as does Foresight (see p. 248), a whole-food diet with a total avoidance of junk foods, sweets, crisps and squashes with additives; no smoking; and no superfluous drugs. The Pill, if used, should be stopped at least three months before conception. The father's role too is important, not least in sharing the diet and abstaining from smoking. This approach, combined with breast-feeding, will protect the infant's immune system and help to prevent the later development of food intolerances.

Dr Breakwell would very much like to be able to branch out and offer other services such as skin-testing, which he feels would be particularly useful in cases where he suspects, but cannot prove, the effects of chemicals in the environment. However, he feels that this would take time away from his general practice, and at present he believes that he can be of more use to more patients by concentrating on his dietary approach.

The way forward in general practice

'I would like to see more GPs adopt this very basic way of looking at illness. You feel diffident to start with, but confidence comes with experience. Asthma is particularly satisfactory, as the results are so clear-cut – and the results of succumbing to temptation are so clear-cut too. Ideally of course we all need more time, and I think practitioner nurses could help here. By seeing patients – with their consent – with minor problems, they could free doctors for the work for which they've been trained. Working together, GPs and nurses could then have the time to concentrate on the role of preventive medicine, and thus reduce illness and the subsequent need for medical and surgical intervention.

'This is for the future; but meanwhile there is still much that can be done. It's rarely possible to fit in an hour-long interview with patients, but a ten-minute consultation once a month can produce excellent results over a period. It allows a patient to absorb a new approach a little at a time, and gradually adopt a new way of eating thinking about health.

'Doctors like us, who are trying a new approach – though it's an old approach really – have to move slowly. If we move too fast, orthodox medicine will either pooh-pooh us or just turn away. We have to avoid giving them a culture shock.

'I respect my fellow-doctors, and surgeons with their extraordinary skills; but one thing I hope most profoundly is that we shall soon see a synthesis between alternative medicine and orthodox medicine, to get the best of what's right with each.

'I do see encouraging trends, and I believe this change must come.'

Dr Breakwell has written articles on nutrition and preventive medicine for *Modern Medicine* and *General Practitioner*; he is also Editor of the McCarrison Society's *Newsletter*. He broadcasts regularly on local radio about positive aspects of health.

'He went into screaming withdrawals'
Marilyn Walker,* age 32, talks about Alan,* age 5

The only allergy I knew I had was to penicillin, but my husband always suffered from them and so did his family. When I married at nineteen – he was a year older – he was getting bad asthma and often had a runny nose.

Alan was born when I was twenty-seven, and it was then that I began to wheeze for the first time. I began reacting to dust – I had injections against it.

I very much wanted to breast-feed. Alan was born three weeks early, an induced birth, and I was given Pethidine. It affected him: he was too sleepy to suck. I wouldn't let them feed him, and for three days and nights he had nothing but glucose and water. Then I found the nurse, in spite of my objections, giving him a milk feed. After that I breast-fed him. At four months I gave him cereal and boiled diluted milk feed. At five months he wheezed.

At eight months he got terrible croup. For the next five months he was constantly ill. Once he was prescribed an antihistamine which was bright orange, and one night when he was particularly bad they told me to increase the dose to two teaspoons. We had a terrifying night. He was hallucinating all the time. He was crying, pushing me away, and begging for his mummy. He had eight different courses of antibiotics before he was fourteen months old.

He was wheezing all the time. You could hear him in the kitchen from the living-room. He was drinking 1½ pints of milk a day and loving it.

Then, when I finally went to see Dr M when Alan was fourteen months old, the first thing he suggested was taking him off the milk.

Alan went into screaming withdrawals. We were very upset, because he was normally such a placid child. After the screaming fits, he got what we thought was a cold, but it was probably part of the reaction. He was still wheezing, but the cough he'd been having every night was much better.

When we went back to the hospital Dr M was away, and we saw his assistant, who didn't know about allergies. Because of what he said, and because we'd become confused by Alan's 'colds', we put the milk back in. Alan started screaming all night long. A fortnight later, on our next visit, Dr M prescribed a four-day rotation diet 'for the mother's sanity!'

Alan began to be *much* better. Every morning there'd be a tiny wheeze after toast and honey. I thought it must be the honey, but Dr M said it was more likely to be the grains. I didn't want to have to come to terms with it, but after several weeks I did. I took him off all grains. The wheeze, diarrhoea, tetchiness, cough, running nose – all went. We'd never been able to go out without taking Piriton and a bronchaldilator with us. Now we didn't need them any more.

Alan has started school now. When he began taking school dinners he had problems, but now he takes his own lunches he's well. Coping with the diet and the restrictions isn't easy: but it's so well worth it. †

'Perhaps symptoms themselves could be removed': Jim Kenningham, age 53

In 1965 I had testicular cancer. I was cured with surgery and radiation. Then in 1970 I entered teacher training college, and found I had neurotic problems such as agoraphobia.

When I qualified, in 1973, I found I couldn't cope with teaching. I was still getting agoraphobia, suffering from nausea, and vomiting. In 1974 I joined a tutorial therapy group as a patient. The method is a sort of behavioural therapy: training you to get rid of the symptoms if you can, but learning to live with them if you can't.

By 1976, with the help of the group, I thought I'd really sorted myself out. I was coping with teaching, and I could handle the social side of life. Then in 1980 I found I was having difficulty in writing, and I couldn't play the piano properly. I got pins and needles in my hands and feet. I was very weak. I could hardly walk.

I was diagnosed as a classic case of Guillain Barre disease, a viral infection which indirectly brings about destruction of the nervous tissue: but apparently caused *directly* by the individual's own immune system – triggered by the virus – going berserk and destroying this in error. I was told I'd gradually improve. After nine months' illness I went back to work in September.

My wife went to see Dr M that October, and he suggested that it might be worthwhile for me to try the exclusion diet. I said I was positive I was *not* allergic, but I agreed to try.

Well, I was astounded!

As soon as I introduced different foods I could see *immediately* what caused what reaction. I'd get stomach cramps, painful wind, nausea, and an overriding feeling of fatigue and malaise, with definite psychological feelings of depression, inadequacy and irritability, wanting to crawl into a corner and get away from reality. Some of the symptoms were really unpleasant. Sometimes my face ached everywhere – round the eye sockets, round the nose, round my teeth. It wouldn't come and go – it would be a solid pain that lasted for a whole day.

After just six weeks I was feeling better. My sickness went. The pains were easing off. I could sleep the whole night without waking. After three months I was feeling well. No aches in my joints, and none of my other symptoms.

My ideas kept changing. I hadn't felt before that there could be a direct link between food and my mental state. I'd been taught that mental states are the result of training patterns from the past. But sometimes I'd feel perfectly normal, and sometimes I didn't. There had to be something else as well. Perhaps allergies could be the trigger.

I'd been a lay psychiatrist for six years with the Lamont Clinic group, under close supervision by a consultant. GPs and hospital specialists would refer to us what were loosely described as neurotics. They were people who had problems with everyday life that no one had successfully helped them to deal with: agoraphobics; people who couldn't walk yet no physical cause had been found; alcoholics; people who got panic attacks; some with learning problems; the very obese – I remember one woman of 28 stone; almost anyone with any sort of problem.

For years I'd been telling people like this to put up with their symptoms, to try to see beyond them. I know we helped many. But now I wonder if some of those symptoms mightn't have been caused by allergies, and whether, instead of teaching people to tolerate them, the symptoms themselves could have been removed. I'm thinking of problems like balance difficulties, physical sickness, stomach trouble – especially gasto-enteritis, difficulties in writing, learning problems. Many suffered from visual distortion, where they saw things growing enormously large and then small, as though their eyes were becoming zoom lenses. Once I would have put it down to tension, but now I wonder.

If only some of these symptoms could be due to allergies, then I believe we should start looking at them in a different way. †

'Georgina might be crippled by now':
Susan Binns, age 39, talks about her daughter Georgina, age 7

When Georgina was thirteen months old, they diagnosed rheumatoid arthritis. Her index finger was swollen, and she was always clumsy, always falling. She had a biopsy at the hospital. One day, when she was eighteen months old, I got her up in the morning and found she couldn't walk. Her knee was all swollen.

Back we went to the hospital. She was kept in, given bed rest for a week, and put on a high dose of soluble aspirin. Her knee went down, and we took her home. About six weeks later the other knee swelled up. We were very worried. Both her knees were growing deformed. Her finger was purple. Her knees were purple. She was in a lot of pain, but I didn't want her on drugs.

My cousin, a physiotherapist, said we should go and see

arthritis specialists in Leeds. They confirmed that she had hardly any movement in her knees. She was put in splints, which we had to leave on her all night long, and she had to keep on doing exercises.

Then one day I saw a programme on Pebble Mill where a woman who'd had arthritis had been cured by diet – well, not cured, but without any symptoms any more. She'd written a book about it called *Diet for Life* (Mary Laver and Margaret Smith Pan, 1981). I asked my GP about it and he said to go ahead.

So I set to and got organized. I noticed signs of improvement within the first two weeks. She wasn't in so much pain. I didn't have to get up so often. Gradually I took her off aspirin. In five months she had full movement in all her joints, and no pain. In herself she was quite different – she'd been an awkward child.

When I went back to Leeds I was a bit anxious about what they might say, but in fact everyone was interested. I told them everything and they were amazed. Apparently they knew nothing then about this approach, and they asked me if I could find out more about what foods Georgina was reacting to. Since I was seeing Dr M at the time, I asked for his help. In a short time we had her diet sorted out. She can tolerate more foods now than she did, but definitely no dairy produce.

The arthritis is still active. If she comes off her diet, it comes back. Otherwise she's fine, and her normal height and weight. There's been no long-term damage. When she was at play-school she found it hard to join in. She couldn't kneel down on the floor. One finger is still a bit bent, but no longer lumpy. She's just won her first swimming certificate. And running – you should see her run!

I'd do anything I could to let other people know about this. To see all those little ones at the hospital, all crippled. And their poor faces. If we hadn't found out about this, Georgina could be crippled too by now. They say her arthritis is in remission, but I don't believe that. I think that as long as she sticks to her diet, she will remain well. And maybe one day she will grow out of her arthritis altogether. †

DR J M, MB, BSc, MRCP, FRCP, *member of the British Society of Clinical Ecology, trained at St Thomas's and qualified in 1962. After house jobs in Plymouth, he travelled abroad with his wife Elaine (a physiotherapist who is also keenly interested in allergies), and their first child for 4½ years, including a year in the United States at the George Washington University Hospital, and 2½ years in New Zealand. On his return, he spent one year in*

Watford followed by two years in St Thomas's as Medical Registrar. He then moved to Hammersmith Hospital for 2½ years as Lecturer and Senior Medical Registrar, and then to the Middlesex for one year. Finally, in 1974, he came to Airedale General Hospital as a Consultant with an interest in chest diseases.

Dr M's interest in allergies started in Hammersmith Hospital in 1971, where he was asked to set up an asthma register. This involved visits to St Mary's, Paddington, and Brompton Hospital, a Hospital for Diseases of the Chest. Here he met many of those working in the asthma field. Among them, at St Mary's, was Dr William Frankland – now retired, but still working in an honorary capacity at Guy's Hospital – who had been studying allergies for forty or fifty years.

Asthma and diet
At Hammersmith Dr M began to detect a relationship between asthma and diet. 'I never believed that asthma was all psychological. At the same time, conventional skin tests to detect allergens could prove negative and still the patient would get asthma.' Using Dr L M's exclusion diet (see page 137), he began to find some patients who responded well. His interest, first in allergies and then in the close connection between food and disease, developed steadily from this point.

In 1978 he read *Not All in the Mind*. 'I only believed half of it to start with. Then in May 1979 I went to the initial meeting of the Clinical Ecology Group (now the British Society of Clinical Ecology) when several American specialists came over here, and as a result of what I heard there, and my own experiments later, I became convinced that if anything Mackarness didn't go far enough.'

Before this crucial meeting he had already been trying out various diets on some of his Airedale patients; he now felt that a more radical approach was needed. Depending on individual case-histories, he started prescribing either complete fasts on spring water, or a version of Dr Mansfield's lamb and pears diet (see p. 105). With the co-operation of the hospital pharmacist, he also began to use intradermal skin testing.

Patients
At present 50% of Dr M's patients are NHS seen at the hospital clinic, and 50% are private patients seen in his consulting rooms. Initially almost all of his patients had chest problems, but

now he increasingly sees people with a wide range of symptoms. They are also coming from further afield. He see approximately two new NHS and three to four new private patients each week. He has an NHS waiting-list of six weeks; the private list is somewhat shorter. With only a few exceptions, he expects GP referrals.

'It's very time-consuming. I have to see each at least three times, and each appointment takes about thirty minutes; this is on top of my other practice. But once they're sorted out they stop bothering you – or their GPs!'

Among adult patients, women outnumber men three to one – possibly four to one. Among children, the proportion is more nearly equal. Formerly, the majority had been to many doctors, some to dozens: a few had seen as many as fifteen different specialists. As his reputation for treating allergies becomes known, he now sees fewer last-resort patients.

Nutrition and health
Over the past two years Dr M's interest has broadened to include many other aspects of nutrition. Both *Pottenger's Cats* and the writings of McCarrison (see p. 27) have influenced his conviction that many modern illnesses are directly attributable to faulty food, and are preventable.

The growing understanding of the role played by vitamins and minerals, and the damage caused by chemicals and toxic metals, also affects the way he looks at disease. He has discussed these aspects with Dr S D and Dr Patrick Kingsley (see pages 210 and 122). Among the books to have influenced him are *Your Personal Vitamin Profile* (Michael Colgan: Blond and Briggs 1982) and *Trace Elements, Hair Analysis and Nutrition* (Richard A Passwater and Elmer M Cranton, Keats Publishing Corporation, USA).

Treatment: a natural approach
Today Dr M's approach continues to be essentially a natural one, relying primarily on an overview of each patient's lifestyle and diet, on the identification and avoidance of harmful elements, and on general nutritional improvement.

He has become increasingly critical of the diets of many of the people he sees. Some rely heavily on takeaways and convenience foods; others have a monotonous diet with the same few menus repeated over and over again; most eat far too little fresh and unrefined food. 'I know it takes longer to buy and prepare a varied diet with plenty of fresh vegetables, but the improvement in general health is worth it for anyone, and for those with allergies a varied and rotated diet is absolutely essential.'

His approach varies with each individual. Children he will normally take off additives to start with, so that they eat only home-prepared foods, with no sweets, no soft drinks with colouring, and so on. If they don't respond, or if they are too ill to await the results of this slower approach, he puts them on a more restrictive five-day diet. Adults he sometimes puts on a total fast, but he acknowledges that this is not easy to cope with while working.

After two further appointments, and the reintroduction of a full range of foods, he finds that two-thirds of his patients are either clear of all previous symptoms, or have only minor problems which are usually eliminated later with some more detective work. Ten per cent will be neither better nor worse. The remaining few will still be ill; sometimes even worse. He suspects that these may well be chemically allergic, and at present he has only limited facilities for detecting and treating these.

Intradermal treatment and hair analysis
He devotes one session a week to intradermal research and treatment, mainly of chemicals and inhalants. The pharmacy makes up the solutions: fumes, gas, phenol, alcohol, formaldehyde, cigarette smoke, chlorine etc. – even newsprint for one patient. He would like to be able to expand this side of his work, and ultimately hopes to set up double-blind tests.

Dr M also uses hair analysis as a general guide. He looks for toxic levels: lead, mercury, cadmium – transients in the blood. He finds some patients are low on selenium, zinc, chromium, manganese and magnesium: he feels free to replace these.

Vitamin and mineral supplements
He also puts patients on some vitamin and mineral supplements on the *assumption* that these are needed. 'Ideally, a doctor should be able to work out the ideal programme for each individual, but until decent analyses are available inexpensively, this is probably the best that can be done.' Dr M points out that the RDA (recommended daily allowance) is not aimed at optimum nutrition; it is merely the level beneath which observable illness will be caused. There is as yet little informtion as to the ideal requirements – and in any case these are likely to vary from one person to the next.

In prescribing, he distinguishes between water-soluble vitamins

(C and all the B vitamins) and fat-soluble vitamins (A, D, E, K). It is difficult to overdose with water-soluble vitamins, while fat-soluble ones can accumulate in the body and become toxic. He may prescribe as much as 5-20 times the RDA, particularly of Vitamin C, though more often between three and six times. One problem is that yeast-allergic patients cannot take B vitamins as ordinarily manufactured. Yeast-free vitamins do exist, but they are expensive and more difficult to come by. With fat-soluble vitamins he is much more cautious, and recommends only the RDA.

Very occasionally, though not more than twice a year, he has been able to take seriously-ill patients into hospital to give intravenous feeding in order to establish a base-line on which to build. He would like to see if it is possible to get a regular improvement with each patient treated in this way, but at present the treatment is still in an experimental stage.

Patients' attitudes
With this approach he is able to give substantial relief to the majority of those who consult him. His hope is that more patients and more doctors will become alerted to what can be done, using only simple investigative techniques. 'People are too ready to put up with a succession of minor illnesses. They say "That's just the way I am," or "I'm a headachey sort of person," or "I've always been one for a spot of indigestion, ever since I was a child." They don't realize that if you're in a state of normal health you just don't have these sorts of illnesses.' Of all the long list of symptoms which alert him to the possibility of allergy, he looks initially for the five major ones: lethargy, sweating, palpitations, fluid retention, and weight fluctuation.

Diet, conception and pregnancy
Dr M is convinced that much ill health is preventable at birth and before birth. He fully supports the efforts of Foresight in this field. A good diet throughout pregnancy protects the growing infant; a poor diet equals a poor start. He quotes *Prevention of Handicap of Early Pregnancy Origin* (M Wynn and A W Wynn, Foundation for Education and Research in Child-Bearing, 1981) which showed how the bad diet of 'the hunger winter' in the Netherlands in 1944 markedly affected fertility and led to foetal abnormalities. 'The good nutrition of parents before and at conception is vital.'

The immune system in infancy

Infants continue to be vulnerable to feeding deficiencies, and hence to allergies, from the moment of birth. Their immune system then is only what is inherited; it remains vestigial for at least nine months and only gradually begins to establish itself independently over the next four to five years. The practice of giving a newborn baby a glucose feed (glucose derives from corn, a major allergen) is decidedly undesirable. Breast-feeding gives a high degree of protection. Even so, some breast-fed babies will react to substances in the mother's milk. He estimates that 60% of colic in breast-fed babies is due to cow's milk in the mother's milk; the other 40% mainly to traces of other substances, including tap water. Colic in bottle-fed babies may be due to cow's milk, tap water, or other elements in the infant's environment.

Hyperactive children

An infant with nutritional problems in its early months may well develop into a sickly toddler, and sometimes into a hyperactive child. 'Hyperactive children can destroy a family. There is no way you can control such children. They scream at all hours. They keep the rest of the family and their neighbours awake. Their parents may be suspected of cruelty. I strongly suspect that some battered babies are the hyperactive children of allergic parents.'

Dyslexia

Food problems also form part of the background to dyslexia. Writing and comprehension can change within fifteen minutes of being exposed to a particular food. 'I had one patient who, on being tested for milk, became dysphasic. Her pulse would rise from 72 to 108, and she could neither talk nor write. On a milk-free diet she is well and working full time.'

Hidden hazards

Difficulties for allergic patients are made worse by unnecessary hazards. Drugs – often those specifically prescribed for them – can contain sugar coatings, colourings or preservatives. Food labelling is still inadequate. In particular, there is no need to specify an added food, as this is considered a natural product; so some apparently innocuous foods can contain hidden dangers. Frozen peas may be sweetened with corn syrup, margarine may contain skimmed milk, unspecified 'sweeteners' may be derivatives of corn or milk.

Support Groups

In these circumstances, support groups can play a vitally important role. Individuals can alert other members to potential dangers, suggest alternatives, offer recipes and sources of pure foods. The group attached to Dr M's clinics meets once a month, usually with forty or fifty members. People come from a radius of fifty miles, with a nucleus of now-well members who continue to come to encourage others. The group invites speakers, plays appropriate tapes, and discusses relevant topics. It has also purchased water and air filters and an ionizer, which can be hired out to members to help them decide whether or not to buy one for themselves. It's an effort for some to come over considerable distances, but several never miss a meeting. The built-in support system is very helpful; and frightened patients are encouraged to ring either Dr M or his wife. Other support groups in the north are also starting up: one in Cleveland has eighty members and even raises money to send patients for treatment.

In-patient units

A major need is for in-patient facilities. The most seriously ill patients need a 'clean' environment free of all chemical pollutants, where they can be safely supervised while undergoing dieting and testing. Reactions can be severe and frightening, both to patients and their families. When they cause mental disturbances, it is very difficult for these to be handled safely outside a controlled environment. In the whole National Health Service there are at present very few beds for such patients, and those that do exist are far from ideal because their surroundings were not designed or built with such problems in mind.

Dr M hopes that eventually the need will be recognized and special units built. As he points out, the initial cost will be recouped by the numbers of previously severely-ill patients who will need no further treatment. Meanwhile, he and his wife are planning to establish a small unit based on the principles of Dr Rea and Dr Randolph in the States: purpose-built in stone, lined in ceramics, enamel steel and untreated hardwood, with marble floors and furnishings of natural fibres. Eventually they hope to be able to have two free beds, but that must depend on the clinic's financial situation. It is anticipated that the clinic will open in Spring 1985.

Meanwhile, he hopes that as patients and doctors become increasingly alerted to the reality of allergies and the importance of sound nutrition, more illnesses will be nipped in the bud and fewer people will ever need long-term treatment.

Chapter 4

The Whole Patient

'I found that wheat and corn *caused* my depression': Brenda Ferguson, age 36

I took after my father. He's had health problems all his life, which I now recognize as being allergic: bronchitis, colitis, thyroid trouble, and so on. I was always very bronchial, got tonsillitis a lot, even bronchial pneumonia. I started smoking when I was seventeen and smoked for five years. Other people's smoking affects me badly now.

I got married at nineteen. After Sara was born, in 1975, I got bronchitis in the middle of summer. Our GP was astonished.

When I was pregnant for the second time, in 1976, I began to feel really bad for no reason. I was depressed before Joanne was born, just as bad afterwards, and I stayed that way.

When I stopped feeding her at nine months, I was put on the Pill. I checked every six months with Dr Husband. He asked me lots of questions about the side-effects and so on, but I always skipped around the depression bit. I didn't want to admit to it. Then, on my third visit, there was a question about headaches. I'd been getting them for some time. I could guarantee I'd get a headache *every* time at the same day of my cycle. So I mentioned it to Dr Husband, just before Christmas 1978. He said: 'I know exactly what it is. Allergies. Come back in the spring when the children are older and go on a diet.' He took me off the Pill immediately.

I'd put on a lot of weight too after Joanne's birth – from nine stone to eleven – and I never seemed to lose it. That Christmas I put on still more. I went on a diet and got myself down to ten stone.

Then in the spring Dr Husband put me on that terrible diet. I had a colossal reaction after 24 hours. I don't remember that weekend. I went to bed. I was very sick. My mind was useless. I couldn't take pain-killers because of my diet. After five days I began to feel better.

I found I was very sensitive to eggs. When I was tested for desensitizing at the clinic I got very ill. I could hardly fill in the form about my reactions. I was shaking. My husband had never believed in any of this until he saw what was happening for himself.

Then I tested wheat and corn. It was amazing. I found it was that which caused my depression. It started gradually, then I would sink down blacker and blacker and get aggressive, and in two days I was right down. I found it extraordinary to realize that my depression was caused *only* by wheat and corn, and if I stopped eating it I wouldn't get depressed.

I've had no problems since. My weight dropped down to 9 stone 5lbs. After a few months I felt I could do without my desensitizing drops. I gave them up gradually, and finally stopped just after Christmas 1979.

If it hadn't been for the checkups, it could have gone on getting worse for years. I'd never have consulted a doctor for depression. I've always believed in positive, not negative thinking. I felt that I ought to be in control, that I shouldn't be depressed. It made me hard to live with.

I know I was lucky. Very lucky indeed. †

'Every one of my symptoms has gone': Kate, age 59

My children say I look ten years younger since I was sorted out.

I was normally healthy as a child. It wasn't until I was doing my training as a physiotherapist that I had what I called 'blackouts'. Then they went away, and didn't return until I was five months pregnant. I was under stress too because my brother had recently died.

I was thirty-seven. From then I began to go downhill quickly. Initially it was diagnosed as post-natal depression; but I never afterwards seemed to be free of illness. It all coincided with a particularly difficult period. All the parents died within two years, and for the previous five years my father was senile and had been living with us and two small children.

I simply had to soldier on. I started doing physiotherapy again twelve years ago; and because I'd always been regarded as a very dependable paramedical – capable, competent – if I mentioned the way I felt people concluded that I was neurotic or menopausal.

Eventually I made a list of all my symptoms. I still have the notebook where I jotted them down.

1. *Symptoms I can live with*   Aching joints, painful muscles, running eyes, itchy ears, urgency to urinate, constipation alternating with loose stools, swallowitis.

2. *Symptoms I can't live with*   Indigestion, migraine, aches in large joints and spine, nausea, hands when they won't move. Pains in head, flashing patches before eyes, clamping teeth (biting tongue and mouth lining). Permanent abdominal pain.

3. *Symptoms I'm frightened of*   Pain in chest, smelly urine, inability to focus eyes or understand what I'm reading or comprehend and retain a conversation, depression, inability to think. *Giddiness day and night.*

Looking at that list now I think: 'That couldn't possibly be true.' But it was at the time.

Then I began to be sent for operations. In one year I had five: a lump removed from my breast; a hysterectomy; veins stripped in my left leg; two on the bilateral carpal tunnels in my wrists.

I had migraines constantly, and terrible arthritis in my hands and spine. The pain! I couldn't even hold a kettle. This all happened at the same time. I thought the body beautiful was just falling apart.

Finally, in 1979, I got to see Dr Radcliffe. To cut a long story short, I turned out to be more chemically sensitive than food sensitive. With Dr Radcliffe's help I made an amazing improvement.

Then it turned out I had too much electricity in my body. Dr Radcliffe referred me to Dr Lester (see p. 158), who asked if I would be prepared to try an experiment, sitting with my bare feet on a copper plate wired to an earth source. I did this daily for an hour for three months, and then occasionally for another three months. It *worked*. The abdominal cramps and the pains in my legs vanished. They are brought on by sitting in plastic chairs, and now when I attend meetings and these pains occur, I go out and stand on the grass in my bare feet. It may look odd, but I know I'm not nutty. In half an hour I can breathe and think again.

I am perfectly well. Every one of that list of symptoms has gone. †

'People used to think I was my husband's mother!': Eileen Heal,* age 45

I had problems with sickness and headaches right through my

childhood. I was told they'd stop when my periods started. They didn't: I was given sleeping tablets and codeine. They said I'd be better once I was married. I wasn't. I began to be very sick and have to spend two or three days in bed. The only thing that seemed to help was toast, so I ate lots of toast.

We decided to start a family. I had three miscarriages. Then in 1965 Christopher was born – a super baby. All my pregnancy I'd been terribly sick, but I'd had almost no headaches. I think now that perhaps, because being so sick made me have no appetite, I was eating less of what made me ill.

I had three more miscarriages. They suggested I had an operation to stitch up the neck of the womb before trying to become pregnant again, which I did. I spent most of my next pregnancy in bed. I was very sick and having headaches. I had drugs to make me sleep.

Nicholas was born three weeks early. What came next was a very bad time. After wanting him so much, it was a great disappointment that I wasn't enjoying him because – as I now realize – he was allergic to milk. I was getting headaches every week: a particularly bad one the first and second days of my period. I couldn't have managed without my parents and parents-in-law.

Then my parents died. I found my mother dead in bed: a terrible shock. That started the downward spiral. I was sent to a mental home. I went there on several occasions. I was given tablets, often put to bed. I had ECT: a dreadful treatment. It did me no good. It's robbed me of my memories. Though it's probably taken away some bad memories, it's taken away good ones too.

I kept on getting headaches. I was given all the different tablets for migraine on the market, sleeping tablets, and Valium to 'calm me down'. When I was so ill, I aged so much that people thought I was my husband's mother – and he's got grey hair! If I hadn't always had strong religious beliefs I think all these things would have been unbearable.

They suggested I could have injections of ergotamine for my severest migraines. With my very first injection – joy of joys! – the migraine went completely. This was repeated every time I was specially bad; and then in 1974 I was told I could inject them myself. It frightened me. I thought: 'will I end up a drug addict?' But I told myself: 'Doctors know best.'

Then I was given Dixerit to *prevent* migraines. It was the first time anyone had tried *preventive* treatment. It did help a little.

In 1976 we decided to move to Hythe, and I became very ill

indeed – possibly because I was worried about moving, but partly also because I got hayfever for the first time. Now I was on antihistamines too.

My new GP was very supportive. He'd come out any time day or night when my migraines were at their worst. The vision in my left eye began to deteriorate. I was dragging my left foot. I got bad pains down my left side. My general health was awful.

My GP took me to hospital. All they could find wrong was a possible 'migraine in the kidneys'. I was given Warfarin – rat poison. I hated the thought. But: 'Doctors know best.'

One day in my GP's surgery I saw a notice saying that patients with migraine problems could see Dr Radcliffe. On my very first visit to him in August 1979, he tested me for phenol, and I reacted.

Three days after, with desensitizing drops, I went away on holiday. It was the first time *ever* that I'd arrived without a headache.

After we got back home, and the headaches began again, Dr Radcliffe told me he thought the cause was food. I didn't want to believe it. Then, when I got so ill I couldn't carry on with my part-time job, I very reluctantly agreed to have a go at dieting. After all, it could hardly be worse than all the pills and potions. 'Throw them away,' he said. 'You won't need them.'

I could hardly believe him, but he was right.

It took time, and several set-backs before I got myself straightened out. Once I was rushed into hospital with a suspected overdose, which was really a reaction to wheat and orange. After that, bit by bit, my health picked up. Along with my health my confidence returned. I'd grown very nervous of going out, of talking to people. Dr Radcliffe *made* me phone to report my progress; and he *made* me come and see him. I'd struggle up the hill and sit and beam at him because I'd achieved something.

Now I feel that I lead an altogether richer life. I am a totally different person. I can go out and enjoy myself. When I go to parties I use Nalcrom. I even have a small part-time job again: in no way could I possibly have anticipated this. †

Record of Eileen Heal's medical treatment

	GP visits	Maximum no. of drugs in use	Specialist visits	Reason for specialist visit	Hospital admissions
1971	9	2	Nov: Physician	Palpitations	
			Dec: Psychiatrist	Puerperal depression	ECT (1 day)
1972	12	3	Jan: Physician	Palpitations	
			Feb: Psychiatrist	Overdose	ECT (10 days)
			Mar: Psychiatrist	Depression	ECT (7 days)
			Apr: Psychiatrist	Depression	Compulsory
			May: Psychiatrist	Depression	admission for
1973	14	3	Jun: Rheumatologist	Joint pains	six weeks
			Sep: Gynaecologist	Menorrhagia	D & C
1974	12	4	Jan: Gynaecologist	Menorrhagia	
			Feb: Gynaecologist	Menorrhagia	
			Mar: Gynaecologist	Menorrhagia	Admitted for
			Jun: Gynaecologist	Menorrhagia	hysterectomy
			Jul: Gynaecologist	Menorrhagia	
			Dec: Physician	Headaches	
1975	16	5	Feb: Physician	Headaches	
1976	18	11	Apr: Physician	Headaches	Admitted for investigation
			May: Physician	Headaches	
			Jul: Physician	Headaches	
			Aug: Gynaecologist	Pelvic pain	
			Sep: Physician	Pelvic pain	
			Oct: Gynaecologist	Pelvic pain	
			Nov: Gynaecologist	Pelvic and loin pain	
1977	27	4	Feb: Gynaecologist	Pelvic pain	Laparoscopy
			Mar: General Surgeon	Pelvic pain	
			Apr: Gynaecologist	Pelvic pain	Examination under anaesthetic
			Apr: General Physician	Pelvic pain	Renal arteriogram
			Apr: Gynaecologist	Pelvic pain	
			Jun: General Physician		Assessment and treatment
			Aug: Orthopaedic Physician	Low back pain	
			Aug: Physician	Low back pain	
			Nov: Physician	Multiple symptoms	

GP visits	Maximum no. of drugs in use	Specialist visits	Reason for specialist visit	Hospital admissions
1978 17	4	Jan: Physician	Multiple symptoms	
		Mar: Physician	Loin pain	
		Mar: Physician	Loin pain	
		Mar: Physician	Loin pain	
		May: Physician	Loin pain and migraine	Renal arteriogram Loin pain
1979 15	6	Jul: ENT surgeon	Rhinitis and asthma	
		Aug: Clinical Ecologist	Multiple symptoms	
		Sep: Clinical Ecologist	" "	
		Oct: Clinical Ecologist	" "	
		Nov: Clinical Ecologist	" "	
		Dec: Clinical Ecologist	" "	
1980 3	0	Jan: Clinical Ecologist		
		Feb: Clinical Ecologist		'Overdose' (This was the diagnosis, but it was a reaction to wheat and citrus fruit)
		Mar: Clinical Ecologist	" "	
		May: Clinical Ecologist	" "	
		Jul: Clinical Ecologist	" "	
1981 1	0			
1982 1		(on GP's request)		

Dr Michael Radcliffe, MB ChB, MRCGP, Fellow of the Society for Clinical Ecology, qualified in Birmingham in 1968. After a year spent travelling round the world, 'doctoring here and there', he came back to spend the next five years on various house jobs. In 1974 he joined a partnership of four as a GP on the south coast. He has been there ever since.

Although at the time colleagues were pressing him to take an MRCP position, Dr Radcliffe made a deliberate choice to go into general practice. 'I have always been a physician doctor, never a surgeon doctor. I didn't want to find my view of medicine increasingly narrowed.' This attitude, combined with the fact that at the time his greatest interest was episodic phenomena (unexplained illnesses), made him particularly receptive to the message of Dr Mackarness's book, published two years later. 'I felt I had to see him. Either he'd made one of the most important contributions to medical thought this century, or he was mad. He came to talk to us. I met him. And he wasn't.'

The first patient he treated along clinical ecological lines, in 1977, was a 54-year-old teacher who was on the point of handing in her notice. She had been ill for a long time with multiple symptoms, and had been referred to many different hospital specialists without result. On an elimination diet, it was discovered that she was allergic only to the anti-staling agent in white bread. With this removed, she returned to excellent health.

Dr Robin Husband, MBBS, after qualifying at St Bartholomew's in 1966, did a series of house jobs there and in Portsmouth, in general surgery, orthopaedic surgery, general medicine, accident and emergency. He then went to Taplow Rheumatism Research Unit as Senior House Officer, before another year at Stoke-on-Trent as rotating Senior House Officer in Neurology, Cardiology, General Medicine, and Respiratory Diseases. After a spell in Oxford as Registrar in Rehabilitation, he went to Chipping Norton to be trained in general practice. There followed a further six-month stint at the Radcliffe before his final move to general practice in 1972. He then studied orthopaedic medicine, becoming a member of the Institute of Orthopaedic Medicine in 1977.

At Chipping Norton, Dr Husband found that there was more to general practice than was initially apparent, and that it was necessary to re-align many of the attitudes acquired in hospital medicine.

From the start he was open to different ways of helping his patients. Although his rheumatology experience proved helpful, he found that in general practice pain originating in the spine was far more common that inflammatory arthritis, and so studied orthopaedic medicine. He now does between fifteen and twenty manipulations a week.

Like Dr Radcliffe, he found that *Not All in the Mind* matched his own experience and attitudes. Already, in 1976, he had begun to be disillusioned with the pressure to send patients to hospital specialists to undergo batteries of tests. When, as was frequently the case, these proved negative, he was loth to tell them that they must learn to live with their condition. 'I learned part of this approach from one of my trainers at Chipping Norton, Dr Harry Steele. He never gave up on his patients. He was always ready to try something.'

It was largely this approach which encouraged him, also in late 1977 – to experiment with an ecological treatment. He had treated a patient in his seventies who had come to him in considerable pain, and with blood discharging from his anus. Blood tests and biopsies had all proved negative, and hospital referral was becoming mandatory. Tentatively, he asked whether the patient would be willing to experiment with a meat and water diet.

He did. One week later he was well. When foods were reintroduced, the answer was found: he was allergic to milk. The patient was delighted and remained in good health thereafter.

'I was lucky that the very first case I treated like this proved to be straightforward, and gave me a great incentive to pursue this line of inquiry. If it had proved disappointing, I might never have continued.'

Looking at the whole patient
In 1978 both Dr Radcliffe and Dr Husband went to the three-day seminar arranged by Dr Mackarness, where they met for the first time Drs Randolph, Rea and Rapp from the States, and Dr John Mansfield and Dr Patrick Kingsley (see pages 104 and 122). Dr Radcliffe wryly recalls that, although there were numerous paramedicals present, 'There were very few doctors. Most of us were almost embarrassed to be caught there. Too embarrassed even to talk to each other.'

On their return they were faced with the major problem –which still exists – that although they now were firmly convinced of the value of this approach, at once basic, logical, yet gentle, they had yet to convince both their colleagues and their patients. This they were to find surprisingly difficult.

'We find ourselves accused of a sort of heresy, of breaking away from the mainstream of medicine,' says Dr Radcliffe. 'On the contrary, I maintain that doctors like us are returning to what medicine always used to be. We look at each patient as a whole, in the context of that individual's life, diet and surroundings.

'Over the past fifty years, medicine has become over-influenced by an obsession with the different organs of the body, and by too great a reliance on tests as a measurement of illness. I have never observed illness affecting one organ alone while leaving the others untouched. And yet, when patients show a number of symptoms, the orthodox tendency is to shove them around between hospital departments, and in the end – if nothing positive comes up in tests – to stick on the label "psychiatric" and drop them in an all-purpose dustbin. We want to change the emphasis; to get doctors to look at patients as individuals, and symptoms as indications of something that has gone wrong for that particular person. As a corollary of this, we want patients to understand that what they do themselves has an effect on their health, to accept that they may be helping to create their own illness.'

Local attitudes vary between acceptance and outspoken hostility. They freely admit that at times they find it hard not to be affected by the opposition that they sense around them; from doctors who poke fun at their 'obsession with diets' to a consultant who never writes a letter without concluding: 'P.S. This wasn't an allergy.'

Patients too resist this approach. 'Among the bulk of our general practice patients there's a feeling that health and illness are something to do with the state. When they're ill they call on us to make them better, as they call on the dustbin men to remove dustbins and the postman to deliver letters. Most of them don't have the slightest idea that their health is anything to do with them. They will fight any suggestion that the sort of food they eat, or their smoking, or their drinking, could have anything to do with their symptoms. They want a magic solution and magic pills. Of course the people we treat as part of our practice are to a large extent self-selected. We see far fewer of those who do look after their health, and we don't see the ones who "don't believe in doctors". As far as our own patients go we have to move slowly.'

Patients
As a result, most of their general practice is still largely

conventional; but they are always on the lookout for patients who are prepared to accept that their illnesses could be treated ecologically and without drugs, and at any one time they will probably have five or six patients on diets.

They also treat privately a few patients from outside their area. Many come as a result of the successful treatment of friends and relatives, but they do also have direct referrals from doctors. Originally they would accept self-referred patients, but this is no longer their policy. They want at least the GP's 'willing permission'. Its absence in the past has led to difficulties with GPs, who, as they point out, are responsible for their patients' welfare; and unable to understand why these had been recommended a 'funny diet' which often temporarily left them, through withdrawal symptoms, feeling even iller than before. Drs Radcliffe and Husband realize that this means that sometimes they have to turn away patients they believe they could help, but they hope that with time, and the spread of greater understanding of clinical ecology, these cases will become less frequent.

Each patient is first given a questionnaire which is designed to disclose the connections between symptoms, circumstances, seasonal changes, and family history. This is followed by a diet tailored to the individual, possibly a complete fast, or a rotation diet, or an elimination diet. The complete fast is reserved for those with many severe problems. 'They don't actually suffer any more when they fast. They may suffer when you suggest it to them. But a fast makes life easier. They've no bother about what to eat or when, and symptoms do clear up much more quickly. However, in ordinary everyday circumstances it's only suitable for certain individuals, and it takes a supporting family.'

Treatment

They find that on a complete fast, the first symptom-free day for young patients may be the fourth or fifth, but for older patients anything from the seventh to the tenth. On exclusion diets the improvement may show early on, but may take as long as three or four weeks.

Their modified Stone Age diet relies on venison and wild rabbit (except at harvest time), fresh fish (except cod), fresh vegetables (except potato) and glass-bottled mineral water.

Of those who complete the diet, together with the slow re-introduction of foods, one third do very well, one third benefit, and one third still have as many problems as before. 'After the diet, a number of our patients never look back. They see their triggering foods very clearly. They avoid them, and we hardly ever see them again.'

Many of the rest will also be able to deal with their allergens through a combination of avoidance and a rotation diet. A proportion will opt for neutralizing drops: either because they are allergic to so many foods that those that remain cannot provide an adequate diet, or because they find that avoidance, especially for those travelling away from home, presents considerable difficulties. Dr Radcliffe estimates that at present 15-20% of patients treated ecologically use drops, but these include a high proportion of acute patients referred from elsewhere. Some can subsequently tail off the drops and even gradually reintroduce foods, provided they're taken only in moderation.

Nalcrom
Because Dr Radcliffe and Dr Husband want patients to lead as normal a life as possible, they also prescribe Nalcrom for special occasions like weddings or holidays, so that patients can eat normally without following their diets. They consider it perfectly safe as it can't be absorbed: it prevents the reactions of mast-cells to allergenic foods. However, since it's very expensive, they prescribe it only in moderation.

Some patients report that they have found Nalcrom ineffective in the past. Dr Husband believes that this is probably because the capsules were not prescribed in sufficient quantities, or the patients were not instructed in how to take them correctly. Whereas the MIMS recommended dose is two capsules four times a day before meals, he will prescribe from two to six, or even seven or eight, at a time; and he stresses that in order to protect the whole of the alimentary tract, they must not merely be swallowed but either well-chewed or the contents dissolved in water and swilled around the mouth before being swallowed.

Chemical allergies
Many of their patients are also allergic to chemicals, but they find it rare for someone to react *only* to chemicals and not to foods. The chemicals most commonly involved are gas, diesel and petrol fumes, ethanol, phenol and formaldehyde. Moulds of all kinds, animal dander, pollens and house dust can also contribute to the total overload.

Again, patients are encouraged to concentrate on avoiding allergens, but where this proves impossible they can be given neutralizing drops. 'It's a technique we never cease to wonder at. Patients are amazed when, by giving sublingual drops, we can reproduce their symptoms within minutes, and then within a few more minutes can turn them off again.'

Gas affects a surprising number of patients. At one support group Dr Husband asked how many present had problems with gas, and between one-third and one-half put up their hands. When asked when this had started, the dates mentioned appeared to coincide with the conversion to North Sea gas.

Formaldehyde seems to be a particularly potent allergen. Some patients who react to it, and who then avoid it or are desensitized to it, discover that all their other allergies subsequently improve.

Tapwater too can produce surprising effects. Patients who are being tested for this may react by having problems with writing and comprehension. Double-blind tests on some hyperactive children involving tap water and mineral water demonstrate a direct correlation between tap water and behaviour, sometimes accompained by physical symptoms. Some such children can improve on filtered water, which removes most of the chlorine, but others need to continue with mineral water.

Though children – and others – can be affected by additives in foods and drinks, in their experience this is normally accompanied by reactions to other substances as well.

Research problems
Like others in this field, Dr Husband and Dr Radcliffe would like to see far more research, but they acknowledge the difficulties when there are so many individual factors involved. Among the problems where food allergies are concerned are: the difficulties of disguising foods; selecting matchable true placebos; allowing for and standardizing the potential chemical contents of foods. Dr Radcliffe points out that, where encapsulated foods are used to disguise the contents, swallowing such capsules does not activate the normal mechanisms of the body. To reproduce normal processes, food must be first chewed in the mouth and then pass through the gullet.

Double-blind tests
In 1979 a double-blind test was carried out by Drs Radcliffe and Husband, with others, on twelve food-allergic patients, using soup as the medium. The results did not show homogeneity of response, but there was a highly statistically-significant correlation between potential allergens and symptoms. (The results are published in *The Practitioner*, Vol. 225 1651 November 1981.)

Dr Radcliffe was later invited by the editors, Dr J Brostoff and Dr S J Challacombe, to contribute a chapter on food allergy to *Clinics in Immunology and Allergy* (W B Saunders 1982). Here he discusses the difficulties of making an accurate diagnosis of food allergy, and the importance of not relying on the present tests available. He distinguishes between 'fixed food allergy' (lifelong, with immediate symptoms and a cause-and-effect relationship, with skin-prick tests and RAST usually positive), and 'non-fixed allergy', sometimes termed 'food intolerance' or 'masked allergy' (sometimes tolerable after prolonged omission, often with delayed results and skin-prick tests and RAST negative).

He goes on to discuss the principles of elimination, followed by withdrawal, challenge and avoidance. He gives tables of the foods most frequently causing reactions, and the symptoms most frequently produced (with 'mood changes' – relieved in 58% of the patients – top of the list, and 'headaches' next – relieved in 55%). Quoting also from earlier American observations, he shows how fasting and exclusion diets, followed by gradual reintroduction, can lead to detection and treatment. He also discusses in detail the reliability of currently available methods of testing.

One particularly important paper was published too late to be included, while another appeared nearly a year later. In the first, (Lancet, 20 November 1982) Dr John Hunter and others showed how 14 out of 21 patients suffering from irritable bowel syndrome were found to be reacting to specific foods. This was confirmed in six patients who were challenged double-blind.

In the second paper (Lancet, 15 October 1983), Dr John Soothill and others demonstrated that, in a double-blind controlled trial, 82 out of 88 children with severe frequent migraine recovered on an oligoantigenic (exclusion) diet. Most of the children reacted to their allergens not only with migraines, but also with behaviour disturbances. Of the foods causing allergic reactions, cow's milk headed the list, followed closely by egg, chocolate, orange and wheat. Forty-six had positive skin-prick tests to house dust, pollen, cat fur, cow's milk, and hens' eggs. Apart from milk and eggs, there was a low skin-prick test response to foods. 'Only three patients would have recovered if they had avoided only the foods to which they had positive skin-prick tests.' It is perhaps significant to note that, apart from Dr Soothill, all the authors of the study embarked on it 'believing that any favourable response, such as that claimed to substantiate the dietary hypothesis, could be explained as a placebo response.'

A gentle approach
Pending further research, Dr Radcliffe and Dr Husband are anxious to see at least a growing sympathy towards this

essentially gentle approach; particularly where the alternative is the prescribing of potentially dangerous drugs, operations, or referrals to mental hospitals.

They are concerned that even relevant research which has been published is often ignored. They give the example of a paper by Truelove and Wright* which shows an association between food and ulcerative colitis. This seems to have made little difference to the current treatment offered such patients, yet Dr Husband has relieved most of his ulcerative colitis patients with diets. (One was unwilling to try dieting.)

Rheumatism offers another example. Papers have been published connecting rheumatism and arthritis with diet, but again there has been little acceptance of this as a *possibility* by specialists. Putting patients on an experimental diet for a brief period offers few dangers, yet consultants are rarely willing to consider this approach.

If the major part played by food and chemicals in illness is accepted, the role of many specialists may change, but will remain as important as ever: perhaps even more so.

'In particular, we very much need psychologists and psychiatrists who will understand what we're doing, not only because we hardly begin to know about the interplay between mind and body, but also because in many cases, once we have vastly improved the patients' general health, problems still remain. They have adapted to a set of personal relationships which doesn't necessarily change because they have. They need to be helped to grow out of the circumstances which are no longer valid for them.'

Dr Radcliffe and Dr Husband look forward to an increased understanding and mutual trust between patients and doctors which will, they believe, lead to a deeper acceptance of what medicine can and cannot accomplish.

*S C Truelove and R Wright, 'Ulcerative colitis provoked by milk', *British Medical Journal*, 1 (1961) 154.

Chapter 5

Continuity and Change

'The alternative is dreadful': P N, age 60

In 1958 I began suffering from what they said was stress incontinence. I had vitamin injections, which did seem to partly control things, then in 1962 Dr D M started me on a gluten-free diet.

I followed that for years. I thought it was a strict diet then, but now I can see that it wasn't – I still ate things like oat-cakes. It was Coelic Society-approved, and they weren't so bothered about things like that. Or about sugar. I never ate onions though. I knew they made me ill. In 1964-5 I began to get more strict. I cut out sugars and a lot of fats. Then in 1967 I got pancreatitis and went into hospital. I told them about my diet, but it didn't make any difference. I had to eat all the wrong things – I thought it was part of the testing. I got very ill. I was *very* rude to the consultants. It was part of the reaction. You can't help it. I could hear myself saying all these dreadful things, but I just couldn't stop.

When I came out I went back on a strict diet again until 1979 – lactose-free as well as the other things – and when I went on holiday Dr D M gave me Tagomet. I found it useful just for the holidays, but I was glad to come off it when I came back.

I had a blood test at the York clinic (see page 217), and found I was still allergic to lots of things.

In 1983 I had a duodenal ulcer. It was cured in three months – partly with Tagomet syrup – and now I feel fine. I've never had time off work. Through observation, I've just gradually removed things as I realized that they had made me ill.

I overheard someone saying to Dr D M that I 'looked too well for a coeliac'. And he said 'Well – it's something you've got to work hard at.' That's true. It *is* hard work. But the alternative is dreadful. †

Dr D M, MB, BS, MRCS, LRCP, MMSA, DRCOG, MRCGP, qualified in 1936 at Guy's Hospital. After working there for eighteen months and doing locums for his father, he joined a general practice in Kingston. Apart from two years in the army, he has been there ever since.

In nearly fifty years of medicine, practised in the same area, Dr D M has inevitably seen many changes. He has also observed 'a kind of continuity', patterns of symptoms linking families together. Increasingly he found himself becoming interested in the *causes* of illness.

Like several of the doctors open to this approach, his viewpoint was transformed by his own personal experiences. As a young man he had few health problems, and 'a cast-iron stomach. In the army I could eat three Christmas dinners a week, with all the trimmings.' But in 1949 he developed a jaundice-like infection. After a further episode two years later, he began to suffer from permanent stomach troubles.

The verdict, following X-rays, was that he had a damaged gall bladder. This was removed, together with his appendix, but without any beneficial result. He continued to have problems for several years.

Then in 1958 at an Aberdeen post-graduate seminar he listened to a paper on gluten intolerance. In the description of affected patients he immediately recognized himself, and on his return cut all wheat and rye out of his diet. 'In three days I was a new man. Best course I ever went to.'

Early in the 1960s he realized that his altered diet was no longer as effective as it had been. He was becoming intolerant of other grains, such as oats, and was also reacting to beans and onions. These experiences, together with those of several of his patients whom he was now treating along similar lines, continued to shape his attitudes.

Gluten-free diets and bladder problems

'All this was very new then. I learned as I went along.' One of his first patients was a ballet teacher from South Africa. She had coughed for eight years. No one had managed to cure her, and neither could Dr D M. However, when she mentioned that she also had constant indigestion, he put her on a gluten-free diet. Her indigestion disappeared and her cough vanished (though at the time Dr D M thought this was only coincidental). At the same time stress incontinence, which she had not previously mentioned, was cured as well.

He built on this experience to help others. Another patient had for some time been distressed by incontinence problems which no specialists had been able to resolve. He prescribed a gluten-free diet for her too with the same happy effect. Since then, and following many similar successes, he has always considered deficiencies in bladder function as part of gluten intolerance.

'Many women have the urethral syndrome. That's just a name. It means a bladder problem with no infection and no pathology. A good woman bladder-wise doesn't have to spend a penny more than three times a day. A good male five. There should be no urgency. You should be able to laugh or cry or sneeze. I think most women who have trouble with their waterworks have food problems.'

Gluten intolerance covers a wide range of foods
Dr D M's definition of gluten intolerance embraces a wider range of foods than that conventionally accepted. His recommended gluten-free diet excludes all grains in all forms; all beans, dried and fresh; onions and garlic. These can be reintroduced experimentally later, and may be then be found to be safe for specific individuals. However, he finds that most gluten-affected patients cannot tolerate common bread substitutes made from soya, gram, or pea flours; and, as a useful guide, he observes that many of those who are unable to eat onions or garlic are subsequently discovered to be also affected by gluten. Occasionally patients can tolerate polished but not unpolished rice.

The prevalence of gluten
Gluten, indeed, is 'far more prevalent than generally realized. It's not a single straightforward chemical element, but a mixture of glutamine and prolamine which varies from plant to plant in the vegetable world.' It is also, he points out, related to monosodium glutamate; and, considering the omnipresence of MSG in so much restaurant, take-away and processed food, this gluten element could be the cause of many symptoms in people with an unsuspected gluten intolerance. Glutamine is also present in tea, which again could affect those who are gluten-sensitive.

Exclusion diets more effective than tests

Dr D M finds that his comprehensive gluten-exclusion diet is far more effective in identifying gluten-intolerant patients than the orthodox test for suspect coeliacs: a jejunal biopsy. For this, the patient swallows a capsule on a long piece of tubing until it reaches the small intestine. The doctor then pulls on a piece of wire in the tubing, which activates small clippers to snip off a sample of the mucous lining of the intestine. 'Not a pleasant thing to have done. I wouldn't like it myself. And a lot of those who endure these tests are children.'

The orthodox view is that if this sample does not reveal any abnormality, then the patient is not a coeliac. Dr M has found that, in practice, the results frequently do not match the evidence of an exclusion diet followed by food-testing. The observation of the remission of symptoms and their return on re-introduction of the food is, in his view, far more significant. He notes that a particularly useful diagnostic tool is a change in the patient's stools: this is objective evidence. A floating stool indicates impaired fat digestion, which is commonly due to gluten intolerance. Sinking, when on the exclusion diet, generally coincides with clinical improvement and is confirmation that the diet is correct.

'I know patients who *need* a gluten-free diet but who do not have an abnormal biopsy. To insist that it's present before you *allow* the child and that's the word, *allow* the child a gluten-free diet is absolute nonsense. The well child is what matters. The tests don't matter at all.'

As a result of his experiences, Dr M no longer does jejunal biopsies, and nor does he now use any biochemical tests. In the past he would send patients for IgE testing, but again found the results largely irrelevant. 'A lot of my patients were found to have normal IgEs, but they still had their food problems.'

Gluten intolerance and neurosis

As he began to identify more and more gluten-intolerant patients, he found to his surprise that these also turned out to be his neurotics. To his even greater surprise, when he cured their indigestion he found he had cured their neuroticism too. He has no psychiatric training, but he has been able to help many of his patients through diets. All depressed patients he keeps on a gluten-free diet. 'I personally think that *all* depression is bio-chemical in origin.'

Gluten intolerance and schizophrenia

He is also interested in the connection between food and schizophrenia. 'Dohan in the mid sixties (*World Medicine*, 16 July 1968) found that acute schizophrenic patients were susceptible to gluten-free diets. They'd get better in half the time. He did blind tests which proved the connection. Yet psychologists and psychiatrists here say it's all nonsense.'

As his experience of food-sensitive patients grew, Dr D M began to find that there were patients with symptoms which apparently pointed to gluten intolerance, but who did not improve on a gluten-free diet. At the same time he observed that others who did make progress also lost, like his ballet teacher, other apparently unconnected symptoms which previously he would never have linked with food.

Lactose intolerance

Through his patients' experiences, he became aware that lactose-intolerance might perhaps be almost as important as gluten-intolerance.

His first diagnosable milk-intolerant patient was a 'neurotic, hard-working girl – neurosis is something patients suffer from: never doctors. When she went on holiday she'd drink extra milk to build herself up; instead she'd be affected. Eventually the penny dropped. I took her off milk. She changed and became incredibly tough. Her emotional stability totally altered. She dealt with her job and her parents and her own difficulties – even with a succession of cancer operations – where before she could never have coped.'

Cautiously he began to introduce lactose-free as well as gluten-free diets, with success. Often he found that his findings matched patients' own experiences: he could show that those who had previously disliked milk might indeed be actively harmed by it. He now differentiates between two groups of milk-sensitive patients: those who dislike unflavoured milk but like cheese – they have a lactose intolerance; and those who dislike milk and also dislike cheese – they have a cow's milk protein intolerance.

A study of exclusion diets

By 1966 he felt that his observations could be of help to others. He wrote a paper on 195 of his patients who had responded to treatment with gluten-free, lactose-free, or gluten-free/lactose-free diets. In this, he explained the background, the symptoms, the treatment, and the results. In particular, he described how, among the major symptoms were *neurasthenia* (affecting 70.8%), including depression, irritability, malaise and insomnia, leading occasionally to a complete breakdown; and *bladder weaknesses* (affecting 49.7%).

He also noted how unpredictably the degree of intolerance could vary 'not only from one person to another, but also in the same individual at differing times . . . It is adversely affected by stress. The amount of gluten-containing material required to produce symptoms in a more sensitive individual is extremely small. The communion wafer contains enough gluten to cause abdominal pain in one of my patients.'

At the time, Dr D M was unable to get his paper published. 'I was told it was nonsense.' He comments that today his views and methods are fundamentally the same, except that he now knows other foods and additives can also cause problems, and he would also look for additional symptoms.

Diet and ulcerative colitis

He is still taken aback by the opposition he encounters. 'I believe that ulcerative colitis, for example, is mainly caused by diet, and often by milk. There was a paper delivered at Kingston Hospital some twenty years ago stating that milk was the cause of colitis in 10% of cases. Yet when I raised this at Kingston in the early 1970s, asking what proportion of their patients had a milk intolerance, they said that this was not taken into consideration – even though it had been one of their own doctors who had produced the paper.

'Medical orthodoxy remains very reluctant to consider food as a possible cause of trouble. Some doctors, I know, are extremely antagonistic. I think probably many of these are people who themselves can eat everything they want, and they simply don't understand that other individuals may react differently. So much depends on our own responses. We tend to judge others by ourselves.'

Symptoms potentially caused by diet

In complete contrast to accepted opinion, Dr D M has over the years assessed an increasing number of symptoms as potentially due to foods. In 1966 a South African paper on asthma, stating that 55% of asthmatics had symptoms related to food, alerted him to this possibility. Because the gut and the skin come from the same part of the embryo, skin problems too are often food-related. It has been estimated that 100% of dermatitis herpetiformis, (*British Medical Journal*, 14 December 1968), 25% of eczema and

20-25% of psoriasis is diet-related, with milk a common cause.

He believes that there is a connection between multiple sclerosis and diet, and that arthritis too is affected by diet. Research has shown, for example, that rats on a diet lacking vitamin B5 develop severe arthritis. While it should be difficult for anyone to go short of this on a normal diet, he speculates that some individuals may be unable to absorb enough of it. (He prescribes B5 for patients who have minor forms of arthritis, and finds it effective; for gluten-intolerant patients it is necessary to buy this in pure form from a chemist. The dose can be as high as 500 mgs per day if the pain is severe.) This vitamin is also effective in treating the 'restless leg' syndrome.

Proportion of food-intolerant patients

Dr D M finds it impossible to estimate what proportion of patients in an average general practice might have food-related problems. Several years ago he did a detailed analysis of patients on his list, and found that 4.5% had problems directly related to food intolerance; but, as he now observes, this was undoubtedly an over-cautious estimate, as his recognition of symptoms was then much narrower. At present 10-15% of his patients are being treated for diet-related illnesses. Again, this is unlikely to correspond with any average, as he sees such patients precisely because he is known to specialize in such illnesses.

Another indication is his experiences at a local electronics factory where he has a weekly session. Because of the recession he sees few new entrants at present; but he would normally expect to check ten new starters, of whom three would have a complaint which could be diet-related – eczema, migraine or indigestion.

The genetic side of intolerance

In his practice Dr D M finds that such complaints go back generations. He has watched children and grandchildren turn up with the same or related symptoms. The same is true of his own family. 'I'm one of eight. One sister has multiple sclerosis. One brother committed suicide from schizophrenia. The rest bar one have all recognized similar symptoms and put themselves on a gluten-free diet.'

Today most of his patients are NHS, though he sees a new private patient every two or three weeks, mainly referred by other patients or by local doctors. The two most common types of symptom are digestive and psychological, and in virtually every case the patient has previously been thoroughly investigated and no abnormality has been found. Once he too would have had little help to offer, but he can now guide them through their diets, prescribe vitamin supplements, and suggest books for them to read.

At the same time he points out that it is up to each patient whether or not they stick to their diet. 'Some people go ahead and eat what they shouldn't and say to hell with it. That's their decision. If they want to get indigestion every Friday night after their fish and chips, that's up to them. What *does* matter is that people should know what they're doing and should have the choice. If more people understood, they might be in a position to take decisions that would save them – and their families – a lot of suffering.'

Chapter 6

Allergies and the Pill

'She saved my life': Judith Mundy, age 48

I always remember what Dr Grant said when I saw her for the first time and she asked what was wrong, and I said migraines. She said: 'That's nothing. Migraines are quite easy to deal with.'

I must admit I didn't believe her. I'd suffered from migraines for seventeen years. I'd been in hospital three times for three weeks each time. I'd seen any number of specialists and I was still as ill as ever.

In fact I'd had migraines since I was a child, though I only recognize them as that with hindsight. My mother always said I was bilious, and they were described as bilious attacks.

I got them on and off throughout my twenties, and then in 1966 I got a very severe attack. I was in hospital for three weeks. They called it an ophthalmic migraine. The optic nerve virtually died through pressure; it did recover, but left me with a squint. I'd never worn glasses until then. Now I wear them to control my squint and the eye muscles.

I took ergotamine as a suppository for twelve weeks. I eventually recovered, but from then until 1973 I went on having migraine attacks. I was taking Dixerit. I was supposed to have it regularly as a preventative, but I didn't like to. I only took it when I was getting attacks.

I realized about this time that certain things would trigger migraines: mainly chocolate and cheese and wine. Gin and tonic was okay, but a glass of wine would be the kiss of death. From time to time doctors would mention that cheese and so on were bad for migraine, but no one ever asked me about my diet in detail, and I never thought about it.

In 1973 I went back to hospital. I had one test after another, including brain scans under anaesthetic after fluid had been injected into my veins. The only diagnosis was migraine.

In 1980 I was an in-patient again: more tests and more injections. And more drugs. I felt I was going crazy. My mind was wandering outside my body. I didn't tell them, but I washed some of the drugs down the toilet.

When I came out my GP kept on with the injections. The migraines subsided but I was *very* weak. I hadn't even the strength to bath myself. Then a friend came to see me. She said that while she was at the Health Food Bar in Harrods she'd got talking to an American, who'd had operation after operation in the States for stomach problems. Nobody had ever found anything wrong until she'd seen a Dr Ellen Grant over here, who'd discovered she was allergic to grasses and dairy products. Now she was fine.

I rang up Charing Cross, where I already had an appointment, asked if they knew of her, and went to see her in June 1980.

She saved my life.

She sat me down. She talked to me. She took my medical history. And she put me on the lamb and pear diet. I started on Thursday. On the Monday I got a rash all over my hands and I felt awful. When I rang Dr Grant, she said I might be reacting to the lamb, and to switch to fish. But it wasn't the lamb or the fish. It was the drugs I'd been taking coming out. It felt as though I was putting my hands in stinging nettles.

Then, when I started adding foods, what I was most allergic to was flour and wheat. That was a great shock! I loved cakes and pastry and buns. I'm allergic to corn too. I found that when I put corn oil on fish instead of simply grilling it, I had the most awful headaches.

I lost weight and felt marvellous. I hadn't felt well for years. There are still odd days when I'm naughty and I eat the things I shouldn't and then I *do* get a headache. But I know what's causing it. That's quite different from how it used to be. It was so frightening, knowing you might get one any moment and never understanding why. I did feel there was some connection with my periods; shortly before they started was often the time I'd get one, and I got fewer after I'd had a hysterectomy. Doctors said there was no connection, but I'm sure there was.

Dr Ellen Grant is the only one who's ever listened to what I had to say. Other doctors didn't. They just looked in their little books and gave me another little pill. It's awful when doctors look at you in hospital and say there's nothing wrong with you, and you have this awful pain. There was one day in 1980 when I felt there was nothing to go on for. I'd seen all the top specialists and there was nothing they could do. I felt I was at the end of the road.

Now I am in the pink. I never take anything, and I only get a headache when I over-indulge in my allergic foods. †

'My terrifying migraines were all chocolate and citrus fruits!': Doris Hasler, age 58

My migraines started shortly before I was forty. I'd never had them before. It was partly menstrual, I think, since I often got one two days before my period, but then I did get them other times as well.

I was given ergotamine, Dixerit and suppositories. They helped a lot to start with. Then I began to get migraines four or five times a month, and each one would last four days. Until you've had migraine you don't know what it's like. It's not like a headache-but-worse; it's something *different*. I'd get this pain on one side of my head, a foul taste in my mouth, sometimes sickness. I had to lie down on the migraine side. If I didn't, I felt as though my eye and the migraine part of my head was suspended and hanging in space. I can't explain it.

Towards the end I felt as though I was never free of headaches. As soon as one was over another one would start. They became really terrifying.

I was referred by my GP to Dr Grant in 1978. After I'd had tests done, I went on the five-day diet. When I began to reintroduce foods I found that all that caused my migraines was chocolate and citrus fruits!

I used to have grapefruit for breakfast, but certainly not every day. And I'd eat chocolate – my husband would bring in a box or the odd bar – maybe every week, but again certainly not every day.

Once I'd cut these out I didn't get migraines again. Well, only very very occasionally. But I never get them the way I used to. Grapefruit and chocolates! I'd never have thought of it myself. †

Dr Ellen C G Grant, MB, ChB, DObs, RCOG, graduated in 1958 from St Andrew's with a commended degree, a merit in Obstetrics and Gynaecology, and a medal in Pharmacology and Therapeutics. After two research jobs in Dundee (in Therapeutics and Obstetrics), she moved – following her marriage in 1959 – to London, where she took another research post at University College Hospital. In 1961 she was employed as Medical Officer with consultancy

status by the Council for the Investigation of Fertility Control,
where she helped the Family Planning Association with trials into
the contraceptive pill. She left in 1968 to go to Australia with her
husband and family, and on her return worked again for the FPA
until she resigned in 1971.

In 1972 she was sponsored by the Migraine Trust to join a
Migraine Clinic in Guildford; in 1974 she moved to the Migraine
Clinic in Charing Cross Hospital, where she stayed until 1980.
Since then she has divided her time between research, private
practice, lecturing, writing for medical journals, and working on a
book based on her 25 years' research and experience on the
background and effects of oral contraception.

Over the past quarter of a century Dr Grant has become
increasingly concerned with examining the delicate balance of
health and the interrelationship between mind and body. Her
interest in allergy forms only a part of her much wider enquiries,
but in recent years it has come to assume an ever greater
importance. Her experiences with many hundreds of patients,
together with her recognition of her own allergic problems (she
now knows that she reacts to petrol fumes, gas, some chemicals,
and certain foods and drinks) has led her to see allergy as a
rapidly growing problem: while her years of investigation and
research have led her to the conclusion that one of its major
causes is the damage which may be done to the immune system
by the oral contraceptive.

Initial research on the Pill

When she began her research work on the Pill in the early 60s,
Dr Grant was, as she says, 'still full of enthusiasm for everything.
I used to go round giving lectures promoting the Pill. I saw it as a
great leap forward.' Soon, though, she began to do endometrial
biopsies – analysing samples of womb linings – obtained from
healthy volunteers every six months while they continued
taking the Pill.

'I was given a microscope and specimens to study to discover
exactly what the Pill was doing to the tissues and the blood
vessels. As a result I was one of the very few people in the world
who could see directly what big changes the Pill was producing.
By noting and analysing the changes in the tissues and blood
vessels it was possible to relate the *psychological* symptoms the
patient was reporting to *physical* changes in the womb. Some
women were complaining of migraines, depressive mood
changes, aggression; it was possible to relate these mental states

to actual enzyme changes. Before the trials, the incidence of headaches in women was 17%; during them, depending on the different contraceptives used, the incidence varied between 8 and 60%. The severity of their headaches, and also their weight gain, led to several women abandoning the trials in the first few months.

'By the time the results of all the tests were published in 1968-1969* it was clear that there was no dose of the Pill suitable for most women to take for any length of time, and I believe this is still true. Most women stop within three years, from actual physical and *not* from psychological side-effects. The ones who have few or no symptoms and still seem all right after this time have minimal vascular changes; the others show marked differences.'

On her return from Australia, she began to hold FPA clinics in Surbiton and Kingston, and was shocked to find what was to her an unacceptably high level of illness in patients. 'I remember one holiday clinic I took. The patients – thirty or forty per session – were all meant to be all right; just coming in for a quick word and another prescription. I was finding that half of them either had high blood pressure or were on anti-depressants.'

Migraines, the Pill, and smoking
Dr Grant's paper on the causal relationship between the Pill and headaches led to her sponsorship by the Migraine Trust. After a brief interval at the City Clinic she went to Guildford, where she continued taking biopsies and measuring immune processes and enzymes.

She began to be asked what – if the main cause of migraines in women was the Pill – could be the trigger for men. Over the next few years Dr Grant worked out that it was *smoking*. She first became interested in this as a possibility when she realized that the serious vascular complications caused by smoking were the same as those caused by the Pill, suggesting similar underlying mechanisms. When the acute patients at Charing Cross, the hospital where she went next, were grouped according to their habits, a pattern began to emerge.

There, the Migraine Clinic saw both chronic referred patients from other hospitals throughout the country, and acute self-referred patients, those living and working locally whose

*'Relationship between headaches from oral contraceptives and the development of endometrial arterioles', and 'Enzyme changes', *British Medical Journal*, 3, 1968; 'Venous effects', *British Medical Journal*, 4, 1969.

migraines had brought them into the clinic for emergency treatment. There were differences between the two sets of patients: and in analyzing these Dr Grant discovered statistically significant relationships.

Percentage of different migraine patients given acute treatment

	Male	Female
Nonsmokers (M) and non-Pill-users and non-smokers (F)	15	10
Smokers	35	33
Pill-users		49
Pill-users and smokers		57
Pill-users and smokers and ergotamine-takers		78

It was clear not only that smoking on its own could precipitate headaches, but that the Pill on its own was more dangerous.

Treatment of migraines
In 1967 Dr Edda Hannington, at the Middlesex Migraine Clinic, began to pursue another line of inquiry. She asked patients whether they thought foods might be contributing to their headaches. Some thought not, but others had indeed noticed a connection and, moreover, had found that foods were more likely to affect them at period times or when they were on the Pill. They named in particular cheese, chocolate, alcohol and citrus fruits.

Dr Grant began to take this approach too into consideration. She found that many of her patients were completely cured merely by stopping the Pill, smoking and medication. Half of the smokers and a third of the former Pill-takers had no further migraines at all, even though these included many who had suffered from migraines most of their lives. Others were either much improved or somewhat improved.* Those who still continued to get headaches were put on Dr Hannington's basic elimination diet, and a further proportion improved. Most of these patients had previously been prescribed a large variety of painkillers and tranquillizers, and had found that they were useless, caused unpleasant side-effects, or became addictive.

Following the publication of *Not All in the Mind*, Dr Grant

*See 'Smoking and Migraine', by Ellen C Grant and F Clifford Rose, Chapter Five of *Smoking and Arterial Disease*, Pitman Medical, 1981; 'Oral Contraceptives, Smoking and Ergotamine in Migraine', by Ellen C Grant et al, in *Current Concepts in Migraine Research*, Raven Press, 1978.

began to use full elimination and rotation diets for those patients who were continuing to get migraines despite having left off smoking, medication and the Pill. At the International Conference of the Migraine Trust in London in 1978 she gave a preliminary paper on the highly encouraging results, and was greeted with much outspoken opposition. 'Many there just could not believe that helping patients could be so simple.'

Food allergies and migraines

A full report, 'Food allergies and migraines', was published on 9 May the following year (*Lancet*, 1, 1979). It described how sixty migraine patients (52 female and 8 male) had been put onto a five-day withdrawal diet followed by elimination diets. Apart from migraine, most also had many 'non-specific symptoms', including lethargy, depression, anxiety, flushing, dizziness, abdominal pain, constipation, diarrhoea, dysmenorrhoea, menorrhagia, and rashes; signs such as obesity, high blood pressure or breast lumps; a history of recurrent infections, especially cystitis; and rheumatism.

These patients had recorded 624 reactions, ranging from one to thirty foods per patient. The commonest foods causing symptoms and/or pulse changes were:
- wheat: 47 (78%)
- orange: 38 (65%)
- eggs: 27 (45%)
- tea and coffee: each 24 (40%)
- chocolate and milk: 22 (37%)
- beef: 21 (35%)
- corn, cane sugar and yeast: each 20 (33%)
- mushrooms: 18 (30%)
- peas: 17 (28%)

When they henceforth avoided their own identified danger foods, *all* patients improved, with a dramatic fall in the number of days each month when they had headaches or migraines. Only nine (15%) continued to have headaches or occasional migraine attacks. Before the diet, an average of 115 tablets per patient per month had been taken: after it, only 0.5 tablets per month.

Dr Grant observed that both immunological and non-immunological mechanisms could cause food intolerance; and concluded that: 'It is clearly preferable, if possible, to prevent the development of food intolerance, for a severely restricted diet is not desirable.'

The Pill and abnormal protein levels

To prevent allergies from developing it was clearly essential to know what provoked them. In her speculations as to possible causes, Dr Grant had begun to ask whether the Pill might not be contributory here too.

Several years previously one of her patients had reacted very severely to the Pill. After only two tablets she had collapsed, lost consciousness, and had had continuous head pains and depressions for two years. She was known to have almost no immunoglobulin A, like her son. As he had had constant respiratory infections he had been tested at Westminster Hospital Immunology Unit and found to have a complete absence of IgA. Dr Grant wondered whether similar mechanisms might not be involved: whether the Pill had continued to attack this woman's immune system for two years because of this hereditary defect.

Previously, IgE levels had been used, and indeed still are, to test for suspect allergic tendencies. Now Dr Grant began to wonder whether migraines could be associated with other, equally valid, immune abnormalities. She asked for her patients' immunoglobulin levels to be measured. At the Guildford clinic, it was found that most had values within the normal range, though some were too high or too low. At Charing Cross she discovered, with the help of Dr Bruce Muller, that after patients stopped the Pill, avoided smoking, stopped ergotamine, or changed their diet, their abnormal protein levels (IgA, IgM, IgG) returned to normal levels.

Damaging effects of steroids

Dr Theron Randolph in the States had for many years been warning of the 'harm being caused by the widespread use of the new steroid wonder drugs'. He had shown how both cortisone and prednisone had serious long-term effects, including *permanent damage to the immune system*. Most oral contraceptives contain two steroids.

The Pill, blood antibodies and white blood cells

Several independent studies had also shown potentially significant changes in women on the Pill. In 1971 Dr J M Joshi and others had found the formation of blood antibodies was inhibited in some women on the Pill. The following year Dr C Hagen and Dr A Froland at the Royal Liverpool Hospital showed that white cells from Pill-takers had a depressed response to testing to PHA (phytohaemaglutinin).

The Pill and conventionally-recognized allergic symptoms

In 1974, in their report of a study of 23,500 Pill-users begun in 1968, the Royal College of General Practitioners found that traditional allergic conditions were significantly increased. Ear, nose and throat surgeons had noticed in the 60s an increase in hayfever in Pill-users, and ophthalmic surgeons reported that Pill-users had more trouble with contact lenses than others. A French allergist, Dr C J Falliers, wrote to the *Lancet* (2, 1974) to report several cases of severe Pill-induced allergies which disappeared when the Pill was discontinued. In 1979 Dr J L Beaumont, also French, discovered that one in three women on the Pill had antibodies to ethinyl oestradiol, a constituent of all combined pills. Women who had developed thrombosis and phlebitis had the highest anti-EO levels. These antibodies were found two months after the Pill had been started, and for years after it had been discontinued. Dr Beaumont said that these persisted as 'an immunological scar'.

The Pill and other allergic mechanisms

The Pill hormones also change plasma cortisol levels, and alter the ratio of free to bound cortisol. This affects both allergic mechanisms and the biochemical pathways which control blood vessels (causing headaches and thrombosis), and mental effects such as depression and anxiety. In 1982 Dr Hannington and others reported that patients who experienced migraine attacks only after starting the Pill also had a significant increase in sticky platelets. Four to six months after stopping it, there was a decrease in symptoms accompanied by a reduction in the extent and rate of platelet aggregation. All these changes increased the likelihood of abnormal immune and biochemical reactions to foods and chemicals.

Liver function and allergies

Dr Grant went on to examine alterations in liver function. When she asked for the antipyrine clearance rates of her migraine patients to be measured by Dr Ifor Capel and his team at the Marie Curie Memorial Laboratories, Oxted, they were found to be most abnormal in patients with reactions to the largest numbers of different foods.

Zinc/copper ratios

The zinc/copper ratios in the body are also affected. Copper levels become higher in Pill usage even than in pregnancy, while the zinc level is lowered. As Dr Grant puts it: 'The liver is just a bag of enzymes. It needs the right levels of copper and zinc to work properly, otherwise it works too slowly or too fast.'

Overweight and anorexia nervosa
She also found that the pills which caused the biggest vascular and mood changes also had the greatest effect on weight gain or loss. Some Pill-takers gain weight rapidly, others more slowly, while yet others get thinner and may suffer from anorexia nervosa. Here the Pill works by blocking the normal controlling mechanisms in the brain, the hypothalamus and pituitary gland. (See 'Allergies, smoking and the contraceptive pill', in *Biological Aspects of Schizophrenia and Addiction*, edited by G Hemmings, John Wiley, 1982.)

Chemicals, moulds and lead
The Pill, of course, is by no means the only substance which can damage the immune system. Among her own patients, Dr Grant has found several affected by other drugs; natural gas; exposure to chemicals at work; and to petrol, diesel or aviation fuel. Fungi also cause severe reactions; thrush (candida) affects many; vitamin B tablets, which contain yeast, can be a cause of headaches. Mycotoxins can damage the immune system. In Russia during the Second World War 100,000 people are believed to have died of mycotoxic-induced disease as a result of eating bread made from mouldy grain. The increasing exposure to lead, according to several specialists including Professor Bryce-Smith at Reading University, is also an important cause of food allergy.

Continued research
In 1976 Dr Grant was in touch with Dr Mackarness to discuss with him her ideas on the possible connections between the Pill and food allergies. She found him interested and helpful, and in 1978 went to attend the Clinical Ecology Group Meeting in Miami. On her return she was asked to undertake research on the connection between oral contraception and malignancy, and to write a paper on allergies and the Pill for *Nutrition and Health*, the McCarrison Society's journal, and for the *Dyslexia Review*.

Current practice
Pressure of work means that Dr Grant now has less time than she would like to treat patients, and at present manages to see only about two new ones a week. Because of her past connections

with the migraine clinics, she still sees a high proportion with migraines, but she also helps others with a wide range of symptoms, including children with hyperactivity and learning problems. She prefers to have a GP referral.

'My attitude is to find out all I can, to do as little invasive treatment as possible, and to give as much support as possible, including prescribing vitamin and mineral supplements according to the results of laboratory analysis.

'The battle remains to tackle the basic causes. Water, air, everything affects us. Other pollutants *are* important but, I believe, less important than the Pill. The Pill contains steroids which have a direct effect on the body's regulating mechanisms, and on a woman's ability to deal with everyday stress, with pollution, smoking, alcohol and other environmental hazards. Why things go wrong is all the same basic reason. Allergy is simply part of a biochemical reaction.

'What I want above all is to get this point across, and to prevent further damage done both to ourselves and to our children.'

Dr Ellen Grant's *The Bitter Pill* was published by Elm Tree Books in April, 1985.

Chapter 7

Neutralization and Beyond

'I was yellow, wasted, always in pain, and completely crippled': Joe Ekers, age 27

From the time I was seven I'd periodically wake up unable to move my left leg. I'd have body-scans and so on, but the doctors never found out why. Each time I'd have to rest for months until it cleared.

Then at fourteen I got what I thought were fallen arches. My feet hurt. The doctors said it was my heel-knobs, and they took off part of the heel. That only made things worse. My feet got so painful I could barely walk. I went back to hospitals and specialists, and finally they diagnosed ankylosing spondylitis.

By this time, I was being affected all over my body. My ribs were fusing together, and so were my jaws. They gave me drugs to try to kill the pain. The best one, they found, was indomethacin – Indocid.

I began getting the blackest depressions. Hallucinations. All kinds of psychiatric disorders. I was seventeen by this time and at art college, trying to get a portfolio together to apply for a degree course. I began to lose the power to concentrate, or to draw. The doctors said all this was the result of the disease – that it was normal for people with ankylosing spondylitis to be depressed.

They sent me to a psychiatrist, who blamed it on over-possessive parents. I got worse and worse. On one occasion I tried to cut my arm off. I smashed it through a panel of double-glazing and sawed it round and round. I was put together with microsurgery, and while I was in hospital the psychiatrist came to see me and said he didn't feel he could do any more.

I thought it might help if I actually got into degree college. I got in on my own ability – I'd had to leave my art college – then when I started in autumn 1977 I got so bad within the first three weeks – with both the rheumatism and the psychiatric problems – that I couldn't cope. My parents had to come and take me home.

Back at the hospital the rheumatologist suggested that I saw another psychiatrist. I went to see him with my parents. He asked what drugs I was on, and when he heard about the Indocid he looked very serious and said had it been cleared that it was suitable for me. My Mum said yes, because the first psychiatrist was supposed to have checked my drugs. So the psychiatrist said I should be sent to a mental hospital. I was a danger to myself.

At the hospital they weren't keen on my parents coming or even telephoning. They thought they were hassling me. They even turned me against them – the very people who had looked after me right through my illness. Meanwhile my parents had picked up the tone of the psychiatrist's voice, and they set out to check up on the drug. Luckily one of our relatives is a chemist, and through her we managed to get the manufacturers' leaflet. The senior chemist, when he heard about me, was horrified. He said that only recently he'd heard about two other cases like mine who had both been on Indocid: one man who'd thrown himself off a building, and another who'd suddenly taken to petty crime and ended up in prison.

When my parents read the leaflet they saw that it specifically warned that there might be allergic reactions, and it listed psychiatric symptoms. I'd had virtually every one. The manufacturers said that a patient should be taken off the drug at the first sign of any one side-effect, and I'd been on it for three years. What's more, I'd been put on twice the recommended maximum dose.

My parents were very angry. They came to my hospital at once, but they weren't allowed to see me. So they asked the doctors whether they'd seen this leaflet. They said they didn't have the time to read all the leaflets that came in. When my parents showed it them, they said the best thing was to ask me how I felt about it and ask if I wanted to come off it.

When the doctors came, they just asked if I was happy with the drug – nothing about the mental side. I said 'Yes.' As far as I knew, the drug was keeping the pain at bay, although now, when I look back, the physical side had waned already before I went into the hospital.

My parents then *insisted* on seeing me and showing me the

leaflet. As soon as I read about the psychological reactions it all made sense. I was livid. I went to the hospital chief and said I was discharging myself. I took myself off the drugs – Indocid wasn't the only one – and after three days of permanent withdrawal symptoms all my psychological problems went.

With the help of my parents I picked myself up. I had hardly any rheumatic problems – just occasionally. I'd get twinges or pains that would start in my feet and work their way up my legs. I took any sort of job, barrow boy, shifting crates of beer. Anything.

After several months of this I began to draw again. I decided to go round Europe, drawing and watching artists. I came back with a portfolio of really good drawings, and on the strength of these I was taken into Richard Williams, the leading film animators: only as a tea-boy at first, but waiting for the chance to get into animation. Within four months I began to have problems with my feet – at first just on and off, but then they began to get bad.

Later that summer – this was 1980 – I got my break at last as an assistant animator. At the same time something went horribly wrong. One week I was walking around. In pain, but walking. Two weeks later all my joints were swollen. My knees were like melons: no exaggeration. I lost a whole stone. I was totally bedridden. I couldn't stand the pain. It was burning through my body. I was back on drugs. I'd have taken anything. In two months I went down from 11 to 7½ stone. My Mum thought I was dying.

I was given steroids to get the swelling down. If it didn't come down, they said, I'd be left very badly crippled. They warned me that I'd be crippled anyway, but these would help. I improved gradually until I could walk a little with crutches. The doctors suggested that what was needed now was radical drug therapy.

It was about this time that I saw a TV programme about an actor who'd had rheumatoid arthritis and had totally recovered after going to the States for allergy testing. That made me think. We had actually wondered about allergies. My Dad had read *Not All in the Mind*, and we'd tried leaving out foods but without any result. Not surprisingly, as I found out later. Anyway, my parents offered to send me to America. Then they heard about AAA, and through them they heard about Dr Mansfield.

So we told the doctors no, I wasn't going to have this radical therapy, I was going to his clinic instead. They hit the roof. They said the treatment had never been proved, that all these doctors were quacks, and I'd come crawling back six months later on my hands and knees. They tried to put pressure on Mum when I was out of the room. She was worried out of her mind. She rang Dad. He said 'Let's try. After all, it'll only take a week.'

It was the middle of the bad winter of 1980/81, and snowing. They wrapped me up in blankets with hot-water bottles and drove me there. They had to carry me in. Agony. Agony. I couldn't walk any more. I was yellow and wasted. I was in such pain I couldn't sleep. Only five or ten minutes at a time.

As soon as Dr Mansfield saw me he said I was a classic case. He said that four out of five rheumatoid arthritis cases they could cure and with my history of an allergic reaction to drugs and so on I was definitely curable. My treatment would start as soon as possible. 'Within two months you'll start having your Joe back again.'

I was too far gone to believe him, but it was true.

First I went on the elimination diet. The pain got bearable but wasn't gone. Dr Mansfield said that because of my state I would need titration. My parents booked into a hotel nearby so I could go in every day. I was found to be allergic to everything. There was no way I could eat without desensitization. Dr Mansfield gave me drops to build up a sound diet of 35 different foods. I kept to it with religious strictness. I ate only the foods I was protected against. At the same time I was also treated for inhalants, gas and so on.

In two months my condition had started correcting itself. My joints were moving. The pain was going. I still had a ravaged body. It's not easy to see yourself changed from a good-looking young man into a hunched, skinny, shrivelled person with protruding joints.

I went for physiotherapy. By slow degrees I continued to make progress.

By December 1981 – a year after I'd first seen Dr Mansfield – I was well enough to think of going back to work. Richard Williams had kept the job open for me – this had made a fantastic difference. *And* they'd continued paying me for seven months. Tremendous again.

When I first went back to work I was on crutches. Within a week I was using a stick. In two months I was back to normal.

Everyone at work understood and was marvellous. They could see the change for themselves. They'd seen me at my worst, and how I was now. I was a different Joe altogether. It wasn't only that I was better physically. My head was much clearer. My whole personality had brightened up.

Before I'd been back at work seven months I was making it as an animator. Now it's getting better and better all the time. The allergic treatment I received gave my body the opportunity to recover for the first time in my life. After a period of this, I gradually came off the desensitizing injections. Now I need nothing. I eat normally as long as I'm careful. I have never felt better in my life.

Now I'd like to do all I can to make this approach more widely understood. My Mum writes to everyone she thinks will be interested. I've talked to radio and TV reporters. I just wish doctors would change their approach *quickly*. We wrote a letter to the ones who had warned us against going to see Dr Mansfield, saying we appreciated their concern, and we were grateful for all they'd tried to do for me, but that I *had* gone, I'd made this progress, and now I was well. We never got an answer, not even a courtesy one.

Not that it's their fault – the doctors'. They've never been told about all this. I had the best treatment possible for years, at dreadful cost. Thousands of pounds of skin tissue testing and drugs and so on. I would have gone on needing this for the rest of my life. Yet my desensitizing treatment only went on for two years. Many people don't even need that. All they have to do, if it's a few foods that are bad for them, is just avoid them. No expense at all. If only doctors would go to these clinics and see for themselves, I don't see how they could *not* be impressed. Shortly after I started at Dr Mansfield's I saw an appeal on TV – all these little children with splints and twisted limbs – and they asked for money for *drugs*. I was so angry. When you think that probably all they need is not to eat eggs, or milk . . .

'It wasn't the dog at all': Malcolm Himat, age 50

I was always perfectly healthy as a child. None of my family ever had any health problems.

I was about 33 before I got my first attack. I'd been to the pub, and when I got back I felt ill and shivery and I found I had lumps on my scalp. I thought at the time it must be something to do with a dog I'd made a fuss of while I was out, but I know now it wasn't that at all.

Then I was quite well again for two or three years. The next episode was when I went to Spain on holiday. I got welts all over my head and body and couldn't stop itching. That lasted two days. Afterwards I was fine for several years, until gradually the attacks started again. This time they lasted longer – for as much as a week at a time.

I saw my GP, who said it was an allergic reaction. I was given various anti-allergic drugs, fed on tranquillizers and given ointments: calomine at first, but then hydrocortisone.

The attacks would stop, but they'd always come back again. I was referred to a hospital for allergy tests – skin-prick tests – but I had no reactions. Then I was sent to St John's Hospital for Diseases of the Skin in Leicester Square. It was a relief to learn that I hadn't got one, but otherwise I was no wiser.

Then, four years ago, I got a very bad attack indeed which went on for six weeks. I had lumps all over the place, a temperature of 103, and vomiting.

Some while after this I heard about Dr Mansfield's work through my wife. I went to see him in 1980. I was put on the lamb and pears diet and then brought the foods back one by one. We finally narrowed it down to Chinese takeaways, and then to monosodium glutamate. I must have been building up my reactions to it over the years and finally reached an overflow point. The vomiting was an attempt to get rid of it; it was acting like a poison.

I'm in the wine business, and I do a certain amount of entertaining. It's difficult to be sure of avoiding MSG when you're eating out, so Dr Mansfield made a distillate and prescribed me the correct strength. I started taking the drops under the tongue, and I used them for about a year. Then I tried without. I'd sometimes get signs of itching, but it would only last for two or three hours.

Now I'm perfectly all right. My wife is careful about what she buys and cooks the rest of the time, and I find I can cope with a Chinese takeaway perhaps once a week.

Dr John Mansfield, MRCS, LRCP, DRCOG, MSE, after qualifying from Guy's Hospital in 1960, spent two years in various hospitals here and in the States before entering general practice. In 1968 he went to Banstead, where he has remained ever since. He was introduced to clinical ecology in 1976 by Dr Mackarness. Over the next few years this interest grew into his major preoccupation, and in 1982 he moved into private practice in order to specialize in this field.

Looking back now, Dr Mansfield considers that he was, from the start, 'fertile soil for clinical ecology'. Aspects of his medical training disappointed him, with too much emphasis given to the rare and complex, and too little to the commonplace and preventable. He wanted people to have relevant information about health issues and to take responsibility for their own well-being. In 1969 he wrote *Avoidable Death* (Cassell, 1970) to try to make such concepts generally understandable.

Some years later, when he was himself training GPs and looking for research projects along similar lines, he heard about Dr Mackarness. He read *Not All in the Mind*, took along his trainees to meet him, spent several days in Basingstoke, and returned alerted to the possibility of allergic patients in his own practice.

Diets in general practice
His very first clinical ecology case he remembers clearly. He had been looking after her for five years, seeing her every few weeks. She was grossly overweight and suffering from palpitations and severe depression. On the sixth day of her fast 'She turned up and kissed me – the only patient who ever has! Her eyes were shining. She was totally different.' She proved to be allergic to only three foods which, as a schoolmistress, she had been eating almost every day: potatoes, tomatoes and carrots. Once she avoided these her weight dropped in three months from 13 stone to 8½.

His initial reaction was total amazement. Surely if a response like this could really be so simple, it would have been discovered and put into practice years ago. However, thrilled with this result, he ventured to treat another four patients. 'They were unbelievably successful. Best I've ever had!'

Over the next five years he went on to treat between three and four hundred NHS patients, most of whom responded well. Feeling that Mackarness's total fast was too much to contemplate for most of them, he suggested instead five days on those foods right at the bottom of the list of potential allergens. Initially, the combination he most frequently recommended was lamb and pears (later used by other doctors and referred to as Dr Mansfield's diet), but if patients normally ate these frequently, he would suggest instead fish and another fruit or vegetable.

He recommended this course only to those he felt would respond well; those who positively preferred not to take pills. He would first explain the theory, and only when this was accepted as a possibility would he proceed with the elimination and restoration of foods.

Desensitization therapy
In October 1977 he went to San Francisco for the Advanced Seminar on Clinical Ecology. Here for the first time he saw the

Miller technique of intradermal testing for foods, followed by desensitizing injections or sublingual drops, demonstrated by Dr Phyllis Saifer, and afterwards spent several days sitting in on her clinics.

On his return he began using this technique for both diagnosis and treatment, with the help of Dr Joseph Miller's *Food Allergy Provocative Testing and Injection Therapy* (Charles C Thomas). 'At that time I had many patients making valiant attempts to cope with multiple allergies, and therefore on difficult and often limited diets. With the drops or injections to assist them, their life became far more tolerable.'

As he began to treat more patients, and to look for connections between an ever-wider range of symptoms, his experience gradually built up. His successful patients told others. More and more people became aware of Mackarness's book. He was invited to lecture throughout the country. Soon patients from outside his own practice wished to consult him, which could only be done privately; while the desensitization therapy could not be carried out on the NHS. The additional income was shared with his three partners, who helped to shoulder the extra burden. Over the years he eased out of general practice, until he finally left in May 1982.

'It was primarily the excitement of working in a new field which motivated me. I'd spend hours on the phone in the evenings talking to the other doctors – very few of them – who by now had also started to treat patients in this way, and we'd swop our experiences. It was amazing to watch people responding, often after years of failed treatments.'

Patients

By now Dr Mansfield has treated at least four thousand patients in this way. A large proportion come from the home counties, but he also sees people from right across the country, particularly from areas where there is no resident clinical ecologist. He is consulted by at least two new patients a day; about five hundred a year. He likes patients to be referred by their GP, or at least to have a letter of approval. However, he will see patients without referral, particularly if they come from abroad. Dr Mansfield will always, unless the patient specifically opposes this, write a follow-up letter to the patient's own doctor.

Today he still starts by putting most of his patients on to a diet, particularly those whose histories indicate that the case is likely to be simple. Where the diet successfully identifies the problem, and where the patient both can and will avoid the harmful foods, then treatment stops there.

Simple/complex cases

Where he suspects that the patient's case is complex, with a vast range of symptoms going back over many years, then he omits the diet phase. 'The chances are that by now they have multiple allergies, and putting them through the diet can be a very traumatic procedure. When you start bringing back their foods they find themselves going in and out of reactions all the time. They will end up – not always, but in most cases – with skin titration, so they might as well do it from the start.'

At the same time, he is aware that this provisional division into simple and complex can be 'very, very wrong. It's only a rule of thumb. Some supposedly complex cases can turn out to be simple, and vice versa.' At present Dr Mansfield eliminates the diet stage for about 25% of his patients: those cases he suspects are complex; those on a range of drugs which they are frightened to abandon for the length of the diet; and those – especially from abroad – who can spare only limited time.

Intensive courses

In normal circumstances he tests patients over a period; for certain selected cases he adopts the short intensive course used by Dr Miller in the States. This involves two sessions per day, each testing four or five foods. At the end of the day, the patient leaves with suitable drops for any foods which have produced reactions. The same procedure is repeated each day for a week until the patient has a possible diet of 32 foods, and the probability of no adverse symptoms at all.

Treatment

Following testing, the patient is assessed for suitable treatment. For some (approximately 2/3) he prescribes injections; for the other 1/3, sub-lingual drops. For most, it is a question of convenience or attitude rather than effectiveness; but for some, approximately three per week, injections work where the drops fail.

In practice he finds that the majority of patients opt for some desensitization. Even those who rely primarily on avoidance like to have neutralizing drops to use on the odd occasion, such as eating in a friend's house. Others are virtually forced by their circumstances to take them. Some use the treatment daily, others only two or three times a week. Most can gradually lessen the frequency until they find they no longer need them.

In Dr Mansfield's opinion, desensitization is not simply a convenience. Avoidance, for severely allergic people, can lead to increased allergies to foods eaten as replacements.

Points changing

The biggest single drawback to food desensitization is 'points changing': gradual changes in the body's responses which involve a parallel change in the solution of the drops to neutralize the allergens. Patients with only four or five allergens rarely experience these; problems arise mainly with multiple sensitivities. At the same time, patients can do a lot to help themselves by scrupulously following a rotation diet.

'Points changing' is also affected by chemical allergies, which affect a high proportion of food allergics. Dr Mansfield finds natural gas a particular problem. Although drops can protect against occasional exposure, the only effective solution is the removal from the interior of the house of the gas appliance. (Central heating boilers may be safe placed outside the main area, in a garage or outhouse.) Chemical allergies are becoming an ever-increasing problem, and for severely-affected individuals special in-patient units are badly needed.

Candida

For the past two years Dr Mansfield has also been treating selected patients for suspected candidiasis, as a result of papers presented by Dr C Orion Truss at a meeting of the US Society for Clinical Ecology ('Tissue Injury Induced by Candida Albicans' *Orthomolecular Psychiatry*, 1978, 'Restoration of Immunological Competence to Candida Albicans', *Orthomolecular Psychiatry*, 1980). Although candida albicans is a yeast which is frequently present and normally harmless, in some cases – when the internal balance is upset by antibiotics, the Pill, or drugs such as cortisone – the yeast infection spreads and can affect the whole immune system. Treatment usually consists of increasingly high doses of Nystatin powder, combined with a sugar-free, yeast-free diet. Neutralizing doses of candida can be helpful in some patients.

Rheumatoid arthritis and multiple sclerosis

His particular interest is in patients with rheumatoid arthritis. Over the past six years he has treated some four hundred patients, and his experiences have convinced him that this is environmentally caused. A pilot study carried out with Dr Gail Darlington at Epsom Hospital in 1982 showed that 80% of rheumatoid arthritis patients put on an elimination diet and reintroduction of foods had their symptoms completely or considerably alleviated. Those who did not respond had previously been on long-term cortisone and penicillamine. He observes that rheumatoid arthritis is particularly satisfying to study since, unlike some other allergically-caused diseases, it produces many objective criteria for assessment, and therefore improvement can also be objectively measured. A follow-up study involving seventy patients is now in process.

Multiple sclerosis, too, he is convinced is environmentally caused, although very difficult to sort out and clear up. He has treated some patients successfully, but others have not responded.

Clinical ecology in the UK and the US

Dr Mansfield believes that the time is ripe here for a major breakthrough in attitudes to environmental allergies. It has been suggested to him several times in America that, although there has been far more relevant research carried out in the States, and although clinical ecologists there have been treating patients for far longer, general acceptance may advance more rapidly in the UK.

The prime reason for this belief is that there is not such 'an enormous money-making opposition'. The biggest difference between the two countries is seen at general practice level. Here all GPs get the same fee per patient per year regardless of whether that individual attends every week or once a year: 10% of the average GP's patients constitute 70% of their work. The result is that, though most clinical ecologists are now in private practice, there is no reason for this to create a clash of interests. When a patient returns to a GP completely or substantially improved, a time-consuming burden will have been removed or lightened. The more extensive the symptoms, the truer this is.

In the States the contrary is true. Provided a patient can pay, one with many symptoms – each, according to orthodox medicine, presenting a separate problem – is a lucrative source of income. A doctor who suggests tackling the cause at source is too often seen not as a colleague but as a rival.

At consultancy level, however, British practitioners may be almost as resistant to change as their American counterparts: not primarily because of any financial considerations, but because it is difficult for someone who has spent years specializing in a particular branch of medicine to accept that much of their treatment is superfluous, and that in some patients the illness itself would disappear if the cause were correctly identified. In Dr Mansfield's experience, rheumatologists have so far shown themselves most open to this approach, psychiatrists most rigidly opposed.

'I remember one patient referred by a GP. The soles of her feet were so tender that she could only walk a short distance. When she got out of their car her husband had to walk backwards in front of her with squares of carpet that he kept shifting. She'd been having psychotherapy for a year,and arrived with a twenty page report saying that she had sexual fantasies involving feet. We discovered her problem was grains. No grains, no sore feet.

'I owe a lot to my first patients. I was fortunate that they were so simple. I would like to encourage fellow-doctors who wish to try this approach to start with cases which are potentially straightforward. The temptation is to try to solve the real hard nuts – the very ones which would prove difficult to solve even with years of experience – and then, when they prove obstinate, to conclude that it's the theory itself which is at fault. Initial success is very heartening, and the more doctors adopt this approach, the more patients can be helped, and the more our common pool of experience will spread.'

Dr Mansfield has contributed 'Food Allergies: Clinical Aspects and Natural Allergens' to *Toxic Hazards in Food*, edited by D M Conning and A B G Lansdown; Croom Helm, 1983.

'The guilt was devastating': Kate Bailey, age 34, talks about her son Tom, age 4

A hyperactive child is *not* simply an unusually active child, one whose problems could easily be sorted out with better management techniques. I know now that for a long time Tom's behaviour was not normal at all.

He was born when I was thirty. Both his father and I were solicitors – perfectly ordinary sort of people. He's our first child: our only child. I couldn't face having another one after him.

It was a normal birth. He was breast-fed, and an easy baby for the first six months. *Very* easy. I used to meet other mothers in the street and wonder what they complained about. He began to change when I introduced mixed feeding. I started with fruit purees – home-made ones; and sometimes, when I felt I hadn't enough milk, I gave him supplementary feeds. He became tetchy, difficult.

At eight months I stopped breast-feeding altogether, and the trouble really started. He stopped sleeping properly. We might get him to bed by 11 pm. He'd be up three or four times a night, and awake again at 6 am. My husband and I worked out a shift system. Fridays and Saturdays I'd sleep in the spare room, and my husband would see to him. The rest of the week Tom was my concern.

At 9½ months he got up and *ran*. From then on my life was just to follow him two steps behind. The accidents started. He fell from his high chair. Ran into doors. Dropped a lamp on his feet. In the next two years I had ten trips to the hospital – he needed stitches nearly every time.

'We're seeing you rather often, Mrs Bailey,' they said. I told them: 'You only see him the times I *don't* catch him. Nine out of ten I do.'

I ran around after him all day long. He became very aggressive. Violent. Kicking. Punching. He couldn't control himself. He'd get very hot, and was always thirsty. He'd drink four or five glasses of water in the night. Because of this his nappies were always soaked, and he had a permanent nappy rash. He had terrible eczema as well – sometimes his clothes would stick to him.

When he was fourteen months old we tried to have a holiday in Spain. We had to come back early. It was impossible. We never slept, and we were desperately tired. He ran shrieking down corridors. He threw all the glass ashtrays off the tables and tipped them over. One day, by the swimming-pool, he forced up the manhole cover and threw it 10 feet down in the deep end.

We had to put him into a bed before he was a year and a half – he just threw himself out of his cot. He'd show obsessive kinds of behaviour as well. He'd get string and tie the kitchen chairs together, and go into wild rages if you touched anything. We just had to live with it.

Of course there was no question of going back to work, or of leaving him with anyone else. They couldn't cope. He'd throw things. He'd hurl himself around. He had no control at all.

I don't know what would have happened if it had gone on much longer. We were both absolutely at the end of our tether. Sometimes I'd sit down and cross my arms and hold very tight onto myself, and then ring my husband and say 'Come back right away or I'll hit him.'

We got virtually no help. My GP never mentioned anything about diet, just referred us to a skin specialist for the eczema. He only offered cortisone creams, and I didn't like using those. The hospital used to send a district visitor round after each accident, but she gave no help either. No one ever suggested that he might be the way he was because something had *caused* it.

When the problems started I thought it had to be my fault. My mother said 'What that child needs is a good slap.' Other people made it clear that was the way they felt as well. I was on the point of seeking the help of a child guidance clinic when everything changed.

Shortly after Tom was three, a friend's father in the north who's a GP with a particular interest in allergies heard about us. He recognized *at once* that his problems were due to allergies. It was through him that we eventually came to consult Dr Monro.

We found that he's allergic to a whole list of foods – and to preservatives, colourings and additives. He reacts to cats, washing-up liquids, cotton, and phenol and turpene.

From the moment we started using his desensitizing drops the change was amazing. He's had regular nights of sleep ever since then, from 8 or 9 at night until 7 in the morning. His character has changed. He sings! He can play with other children. His temper tantrums are down 90%. He'll sit and listen to a story, or watch a television programme from beginning to end, and then tell me what it's about. On good days he's quiet and composed and peaceful.

He's now started, a year early, at a small school where the teachers are aware of his problems. He's learning to concentrate. He knows his letters. He's beginning to read.

I think that the worst thing was that I *knew* something was very wrong, but no one could tell me what it was. The guilt was devastating. I thought that either he'd inherited this temperament from us, or else that I had mismanaged him appallingly. At times I felt threatened – I believed he hated me. The difference this knowledge and help has made is incredible. †

Dr Jean Monro,MB, BP, LRCP, MRCS, MSc, qualified from the London Hospital in 1960. She went on to take house jobs there before moving to Hemel Hempstead in 1961 to work in Paediatrics, General Medicine and Surgery; and in 1962 in Geriatric Medicine. In 1963 she was appointed Registrar in Geriatric Medicine, and remained associated with the West Hertfordshire Group of Hospitals until 1979. In 1975 she became Honorary Clinical Assistant at the National Hospital for Nervous Diseases, where she held research appointments with Dr K J Zilkha for the next eight years. From 1979 to 1982 she was Medical Assistant in the Department of Geriatric Medicine of Edgware General Hospital. She now divides her time between a research appointment at the Hospital for Nervous Diseases and her clinical ecology work, carried out partly in a central London private hospital and partly in her own clinic.

Dr Jean Monro has for long had a personal reason to be interested in nutrition and its effects: her husband and her son are all coeliacs. Since, in addition to grains, they are unable to tolerate preservatives, additives or colourings, she has always fed her family on pure foods. She wrote one of her first papers for the DHSS on hospital diets, and in 1971 began to help Cherry Hills with her books on food. She too was married to a coeliac, Lawrence Hills of the Henry Doubleday Research Association (see page 249), so Dr Monro was doubly interested: both in the experiences of the wife of another coeliac and in the promotion of wholefoods.

Dr Monro co-operated with Cherry Hills on three books, *Good Food Gluten-free* (Roberts Publications, 1976) *Good Food to Fight Migraine* (Roberts Publications, 1979) and *Good Food: Grain-free, Milk-free* (Roberts Publications,1977). She also began writing nutrition articles under her own name and under pseudonyms for the medical press, and in 1974 she wrote a booklet for doctors on the nutritional management of disease, *Some Dietary Approaches to Disease Management.*

Different Diets
Her personal experiences with the dietary treatment of illness led her in 1968 to adopt this approach to help patients: eliminating foods, and then reintroducing them at the rate of one per week. In 1971 the Schizophrenia Association of Great Britain began to send her patients; and in 1973 others were referred to her by Sanity (see page 248). The following year, with Dr Zilkha, she began using diets on migraine patients in the Hospital for Nervous Diseases.

In 1975 she started doing research; and as her family grew older she was able to become more intensely involved. Action for Research into Multiple Sclerosis funded research into the effect of fatty acids on metabolism, and special diets – mainly eliminating animal fats – were given to patients. They were not tailored to individuals, and were discovered to be helpful to some but not to others.

Clinical ecology
Dr Monro took an active part in the developments following the publication of Dr Mackarness's book, and was one of the founder members of the Clinical Ecology Group. In 1979 she began to use intradermal testing and neutralizing drops, and in 1980 went for the first time to the States to meet Dr J Miller and to study the background and progress of clinical ecology there.

Since then she has been back twice every year by invitation, and has recently chaired sessions and presented papers at the First and Second International Conferences on Man and his Environment in Dallas, Texas.

Reliability of tests

She has treated over three thousand patients, both NHS and private, with clinical ecological methods. Virtually all have first been put on diets, with titration used on difficult patients and those who are left with very few safe foods.

Dr Monro finds that intradermal testing gives an accurate estimate of the sensitivity of the patient. It depends on the careful observation of weal and flare (see page 22), and the precise observation of symptoms by both patient and doctor. She points out that other more conventional tests also depend on how they are used and interpreted.

To begin with, tests depend on good laboratories staffed by good technicians. The RAS test (see page 22) uses radioactive isotopes, which decay: their accuracy therefore relies on a technician who recognizes this and makes allowances for it. Even so, the RAS test can give false negatives if the patient has not recently been eating the suspect foods. It can also be misleading in that the scale for foods is much lower than that for inhaled allergens; it is important that a low reading should be recognized as significant.

Other tests are not necessarily meaningful. The mere presence of IgG antibodies may not always indicate allergy. Six per cent of the population have IgG antibodies after a meal, and everyone has a few. It may not be the mere fact of their presence so much as their rate of clearance that is important. All that matters is that some people will have symptoms from them. Even where an imbalance of mast cells is revealed, this might result less from the over-production of histamine cells themselves than from the inadequate response of other cells supposed to repress them ('Food allergy in migraine: study of dietary exclusion and RAST', *Lancet*, 2, 1980).

Finally, as Dr Monro points out, the best test is useless if it is not in the hands of someone who can use it to guide the patient to the correct management of the illness.

Chemicals and metals

Both testing and the correlation of symptoms and exposure indicate that a high proportion of Dr Monro's patients react to chemicals or metals. Several have major problems with tap water. 'There are 150 chemicals in ordinary tap water, and even the purest spring and distilled waters will have minute proportions of chemicals or metals. For a handful of patients, finding a water they can tolerate is perhaps *the* major problem.

'At present, we haven't the right surroundings to test people for chemicals. Without a pure environment, it's difficult to prove that, for example, it's the chemicals in water that are producing reactions, rather than pollen from nearby fields.

'Among the metals, nickel is proving a particularly powerful allergen. After I suggested to certain patients that they should wear stainless steel SOS bracelets, I found that some actually got worse. They were reacting to the minute nickel content: not a local skin reaction, but a systemic reaction. One patient's heartbeat reached 180.'

Trace chemicals in foods also affect some people. A proportion of patients will react to grains grown organically, but not chemically; some will react to one apple, but not to another from a different source.

Pesticides

From case histories, it is clear that pesticides are a problem. One patient was exposed to Pentachlorophenol and Lindane: illness started two days later. Another, who had suffered from years of illness, with asthma, eczema and colitis, had been treated and made a good recovery. 'This summer while driving in East Anglia she was sprayed from an aeroplane. She became ill. It was diagnosed as flu; she was given antibiotics and became seriously ill. Treatment can get people better, but they always remain vulnerable.' Often, as the developing illness takes over, the initial trigger is overlooked; it is only after close questioning that it can be recalled and recognized.

Dr Monro hopes that conditions in her new clinic will be of particular help to these chemically-sensitive patients. At present she sees about five hundred new patients a year, but she hopes that eventually, as her facilities expand, she will be able – with the help of her staff – to treat many more.

Patients

Her patients come from all over the country and from abroad, usually through recommendations from friends or colleagues. Some are sponsored by their governments: Australia, Israel and Canada have all sent patients. Others have come from as far afield as Czechoslovakia, Saudi Arabia, Norway, France, Germany and Peru. There is no government help at present for UK citizens, with the exception of those working abroad for the Foreign Office.

Most overseas patients have to be taught to manage their condition completely on their own, because once they return there is no ecologist locally who can help them. With care, it is perfectly possible to do this. She instances one Australian woman who arrived from Perth weighing 4 stone: she had been ill for years and bedridden for twelve months. When admitted, she was found to react to every food. She was placed in a room with filtered air and swathed with cotton. She was put immediately on stodge plus the appropriate drops; potatoes, bananas, venison. In three weeks she was discharged to stay with Dr Monro's housekeeper. After visiting a friend she became exposed to fungi and had to be readmitted, but learned to test herself and inject herself. Before returning to Australia she was walking ten miles a day.

Of all her patients environmentally treated, 80% are very much improved. The other 20% need perseverance: 'The maze can be difficult to thread.' Of these, perhaps half will continue to present problems: they will acquire new symptoms or fresh sensitivities. She believes that there is no one she has completely failed to help; but there are some who, at the present state of knowledge, cannot be helped adequately.

Electrical sensitivity
Over the past two years, Dr Monro and her colleague, Dr Raymond Choy, have become increasingly interested in the close connection between allergically and electrically sensitive people.

Preliminary experiments have shown that patients have a receptive sensitivity to some frequencies. (They may also emit their own frequencies, but this has yet to be demonstrated.) Such patients may react adversely even to infinitesimally narrow frequencies. 'It sounds weird, but we *know* it is so. We have studied patients in a room constructed along the lines of a Faraday Cage, screened magnetically, and they no longer react.'

Some patients are very vulnerable to pylons and electrical equipment; even to other people. Reacting patients were initially taught to get rid of their reactions by standing or lying on the grass, and thus earthing themselves. However, since this method proved inconvenient for people living or working on top-floor flats or offices, these were shown how to earth themselves by placing a one-pin plug in an earth socket (a method emphatically *not* to be copied unsupervised).

The effectiveness of this was demonstrated by a patient who was highly sensitive to nickel. When she held her hand over a nickel plate it would shake. When the plate was earthed, her hand no longer shook. When blind-tested (i.e. when the plate unknown to her was unearthed/earthed) her responses (hand shaking/steady) were still completely accurate.

The experimenters then placed other substances between the unearthed nickel plate and the patient. Some of these obstructed the frequencies; some – glass among them – did not. Following these observations, they also found that certain patients would react to allergens held near them in a glass container.

The discovery of individual reactions to electrical equipment throws new light on other aspects of illness. For example some patients, when withdrawn from their habitual allergens, will suddenly collapse. Dr Monro and Dr Choy now know that this is an electrical phenomenon. They can reproduce the occurrence using electrical equipment, and control it using the correct frequencies.

Two centres are currently studying aspects of this manifestation: the Department of Zoology at Manchester University under Dr Robin Baker, and the Department of Electrical Engineering at Salford University under Dr Cyril Smith.

During the Second International Symposium on Man and His Environment in February 1984, Dr Monro and Dr Choy showed how the effects of neutralization techniques could be mediated electromagnetically. They believe that such demonstrations point to an important new area for investigation.

Research projects

While most of Dr Monro's time is spent on treating affected patients, she sees much of the way forward lying in research work. She is currently analysing, with a grant from the Migraine Association, the computerized data of her three thousand patients. With a grant from the Myalgic Encephalomyelitis Association, she is involved with others in research into T-lymphocyte surface markers, and with Dr C Smith is conducting research into electromagnetic phenomena. She is also in the process of carrying out a five-year study, with Dr I Barlow at the University of Aston, into preconceptual nutritional deficiencies, with the help of a DHSS grant.

'We have to convince those who are not yet convinced of the credibility of different methods of testing, and of different – often complementary – methods of treatment. At the same time, we mustn't stay locked in to studying only these. There are many other avenues of approach and, of them all, I believe that the whole field of electromagnetism and changes of electrical response will prove the most rewarding.'

Among Dr Monro's published papers are:
'Pantothenic acid in coeliac disease', *British Medical Journal*, 14 Oct 1972;
'Pantothenic acid in schizophrenia', *Lancet*, 1, 1973;
'Migraine', *Progress on Migraine Research 1*, Pitman, 1981;
'Food allergy in migraine', *Proc. Nut. Soc.*, 42, 1983.

Chapter 8

Chemical Hazards

'I worked out it was the gas that was causing my problems':
Evelyn Gray, age 76

When I went last year to see my doctor he told me to go away: he had real patients to see to with real illnesses. If I hadn't had my daughter with me I don't know what I'd have done. I came away really upset. I felt it all the more because I've always looked after myself. There've been years when I've never seen a doctor. I've always been healthy – an outdoor person. I love gardening.

My trouble started in 1979. My husband had a stroke. My daughter was worried about all the work I had with our coal fires, and suggested we install gas central heating. It was put in at the end of 1978. One day in February I was just sitting there when I got what felt like the most terrible heartburn. I felt I was burning right down inside in my gullet and down to my tummy. I felt as though there was poison inside me.

I waited for it to go away, but it never did. I felt as though I couldn't breathe. And I'd get very depressed. I'd go out and stand in the garden in the middle of the night just to get some air into me. I'd spend hours walking and walking – never mind if it was in the middle of blizzards. If I was out long enough I'd be all right. I'd feel clear again. Then when I got back it would start all over again. My mouth would be burning. My lips would be bitter and swollen.

I began to work things out.

Years ago I'd had a gas cooker. Once a fortnight, maybe once a month, I'd go ashen white and icy cold. My husband would take me upstairs and pack me into bed with a hot water bottle. After twelve hours I'd be wet through with perspiration. It would be two days before the attack was over.

In 1960 we were told that the gas pipes were rotting outside; we'd need to replace them all. We decided instead to switch to electricity. From the time we changed I'd never had another attack.

Then I remembered another occasion. I'd gone to London to visit a friend and see *Lock up Your Daughters*. I found I simply couldn't breathe in her flat. We went out for the day, and I was fine; but as soon as I got back I felt dreadful again. I had to leave early and come home. I said to my husband at the time: 'I don't think we should ever have central heating.' But I'm not one to fuss, and I forgot all about it.

I began to remember all this, and I worked out that it was the gas that was causing my problems. I went to my GP and told him what I thought, but he said 'Nonsense!' Then I saw another doctor who told me all my problems were only what were to be expected at my age.

Finally I was told about Dr Kingsley. I phoned him, and went to see him – I've seen him three times altogether. I'd already moved to an all-electric bungalow and was feeling better, but I still wasn't well. I discovered that I was being bothered by chocolate and milk – and possibly butter. I've cut them all out. I'm sensitive to highly chlorinated water too, so now I use filtered water.

It's difficult. All my friends have gas, so it makes visiting almost impossible. I can smell it the moment I go through the door. Some understand, but I've also had some very unkind remarks. My daughter is very good and very helpful, but I still miss my husband very much. Nobody has heard of anyone else like me, so it's hard not to feel peculiar. I feel isolated and lonely.

'I sobbed more than ever before in all my life': Shirley Nyland, age 48

I've always been positive. Optimistic. A doer. Yet for the past twenty years I've been suffering from bouts of extreme exhaustion. I felt as though I was always pushing against myself – forcing myself to keep going.

I was on the Pill from 1964 to 1965. I didn't feel well on it. I had bad headaches at times, and only half-day periods. My exhaustion started then. I came off it after a short while.

At first I thought it would pass. Then, when it didn't, I saw my GP. I was prescribed tranquillizers. I got worse, and was told I was depressive. In 1972 I saw a consultant psychiatrist, and went voluntarily into a psychiatric hospital. I had six courses of ECT and was put on drugs.

When I came out again I felt better for a while, and even started a part-time job in a boutique. I enjoyed it; my husband was very supportive and my two children were both at school, yet I still felt exhausted. Some people might say it's because I'm too fussy, too particular – but I don't think so. I like to do a job well, and I really didn't think I was tackling anything beyond me. Yet I found I was completely flaked out all the time. I had what I called a 'faraway feeling'. Very detached: as though I wasn't really there. I was on the outside looking in.

When I went back again to my GP, I was prescribed more anti-depressants. I don't like taking tablets, and I could not accept that from now on this was going to be my way of conducting my life. I didn't see *why* I should feel like I did. I'd had one or two difficult times, like everybody else, but they were way back, and I simply didn't see how they could affect me long-term.

I tried homoeopathy for twelve months, without any real benefit. From them on I struggled on my own. For three whole years I never slept for more than an hour a night, and I was petrified every moment of the day. I felt permanently threatened and panicky. I was chasing my own tail.

Then a little over a year ago I saw Dr Kingsley's name mentioned in a newspaper article on orthomolecular treatment. I went to see him for the first time in May 1983.

He took hair samples, did blood tests, gave me a diet sheet and did glucose tolerance tests. On August 16th – I remember the date well! – I started a five-day fast on Malvern water. I stopped smoking and stopped the sleeping tablets I'd been taking.

Dr Kingsley was immensely supportive at the end of the phone. Without him I could not have coped. My husband was fantastic, and so was the consultant psychiatrist I was seeing. I had terrible withdrawal symptoms for eight weeks. I wouldn't ever want to go through that again. I was disoriented, frightened, completely detached. I couldn't sleep for five weeks. In the first five days I lost 10lbs. It emphasized that I must be reacting to something specific.

Yet when I started reintroducing the foods I found that I rarely produced symptoms, though sometimes my pulse tests showed dramatic changes – when I tried milk, for example, my pulse rate shot up twenty points – but except that butter gave me a headache I experienced no other problems. Dr Kingsley prescribed me thyroxine and the Foresight vitamins. My symptoms still seemed much the same, so he asked me to go for testing with injections.

The first four things he tried didn't produce any result. Then, with the fifth, I started trembling, and I burst into an uncontrollable fit of crying. I felt so silly afterwards. I sobbed more than ever before in all my life. Dr Kingsley didn't tell me what had caused this reaction until I'd had a couple more tests, then he told me that it had been house dust.

I went home with drops for the dust. At first they didn't seem to work: then on the tenth day I suddenly felt very much better. The faraway feeling had gone. It hasn't ever returned.

I'm still not completely better, but I'm sure it will come. I'm still going back to Dr Kingsley, and he's been trying different things to see if we can't get rid of everything: Nystatin, then increased thyroxine, and most recently different blood tests. The worst reaction to an injection I've has so far – apart from the dust – was to ethanol, which you find in all sorts of things around the house: sprays and so on. I got a sudden surge in my chest. My heart thudded so hard it felt as though it would burst open; then I got weepy and tremulous. I have drops to treat that too.

It's frustrating, because I've got so far forward, but I still can't crack it. I'm still tired. If you fight it, you make it worse. If you accept it, you feel miserable about it. It's very stubborn: but with Dr Kingsley's help I'm sure we shall beat it in the end. I feel very strongly that it's something physical which is bringing about my mental state, and not the other way around.

Dr Patrick Kingsley, MB, BS, MRCS, LRCP, FSCE, DA, DObst, RCOG, qualified from St Bartholomew's in 1965. After a year in Barbados – 'packing five years' experience into one' – he returned for a spell in Anaesthetics and Obstetrics in Kettering General Hospital before joining Fison's Pharmaceuticals. He remained there for eight years, first as medical adviser and then as clinical pharmacologist, while also working in an honorary capacity for half a day a week at Nottingham City Hospital Allergy Clinic. Early in 1977 he resigned to enter general practice and to start carrying out ecological investigations. In 1981 he left the NHS in order to be able to specialize in this area.

Throughout the early 1970s Dr Kingsley became increasingly interested in the less common aspects of allergy, and in particular in unusual combinations of symptoms. In the Nottingham Allergy Clinic he observed that a number of patients with hayfever also suffered from mouth ulcers. Reasoning that since sodium cromoglycate (Intal) was known to prevent allergic reactions in the lungs, it could perhaps also prevent reactions to substances put in the mouth, he added it to toothpaste. The mouth ulcers disappeared.

He gradually began to recognize that relationships existed between foods and apparently disparate symptoms in a way that was not acknowledged by orthodox medicine. In 1974 he treated a patient's intestinal problems with SCG (now known as Nalcrom) with excellent results. Double-blind tests were a total success. The paper subsequently published in the *Lancet* (10 November 1974) was the first to describe this method, which is still recommended by Fison's as the standard treatment for food allergies.

Illness and allergy
Having looked for published work on related subjects, and finding very little apart from some studies by Dr Mackarness, Dr Kingsley went to visit him to discuss the possibility of setting up double-blind studies. On attending his Basingstoke clinic he found that the work Dr Mackarness was carrying out was totally unsuited to this; but meeting and talking to him 'opened my eyes. My whole perception of illness and allergy changed. What I'd been semi-conscious of for some while was now finally brought out in the open.'

On his return to Nottingham he fasted his very first patient in the City Hospital in 1975 ('to great consternation'), carried out sublingual testing with the help of local dieticians, and found his patient considerably improved after she avoided her incriminated foods.

General practice and clinical ecology
These experiences confirmed a growing desire to return to full-time clinical medicine, and eighteen months later he took over a general practice near his home in Leicestershire. In the next four years and four months, while carrying on a normal practice, he also did ecological investigations on as many patients as possible.

At the end of this period he went through all his papers and found that he had had a panel of 2335 patients. Of these, 21% he had never seen at all, 50% he had seen between one and fifteen times; 36% between fifteen and fifty times; 3% more than fifty times – i.e. over ten times a year.

Out of all these patients, he was forced from sheer lack of time to select only a proportion of those he felt might benefit from

Mackarness's approach: his criteria being the willingness of the patient to accept it, previous lack of progress, and the general failure of conventional treatment. He graded his patients according to the severity and extent of their problems, and adjusted his approach to suit their circumstances.

In all, he treated 213 patients with non-classical allergies: i.e. 12% of those patients he had seen at least once.

With 98, he had a general discussion of possible causes for their symptoms. Often this alone had eased the problem. Where for example the patient was drinking a great deal of coffee or tea, and this was then cut down or out, the patient's symptoms were generally alleviated.

Sixty-two, put on a full fast followed by the reintroduction of foods, found that only one or two foods were implicated, and by avoidance were either completely cured or very much improved.

Thirty-four, also on full fasts followed by reintroduction, found that they were sensitive to so many foods that total avoidance was difficult, but made an excellent recovery with the help of desensitization.

The remaining nineteen, including twelve very difficult cases, were still left with many problems after fasting and reintroducing foods, mainly because they were also severely affected by environmental factors. They accounted for sixty hours of treatment each over the four years. (This contrasts, as Dr Kingsley points out, with the average 2½ minutes per patient per consultation in some practices.)

The patients selected presented a wide range of symptoms: many with migraines (very successfully treated); all kinds of aches and pains and general fatigue; many with an assortment of vague multiple symptoms; and several cases of cervical spondylitis. Some had epilepsy (he remembers particularly one girl who had previously kept falling into the fire, suffering severe burns, who 'responded beautifully', although still not completely cured); and there were several cases of Crohn's disease (one patient who was very severely affected was 'a fantastic success' on SCG in tablet form).

He would have liked to have been able to treat many more patients in the same way, but was hampered by sheer lack of time. He found himself going to bed at eleven and getting up at five. At the same time he was often disheartened by the lack of willingness of some patients to adopt his ideas. 'They'd keep turning up with a whole variety of symptoms, but the moment I tried to talk to them about diet they'd show no interest at all. Their eyes would glaze over.'

Private practice
During his years as a GP he had also begun to treat private patients arriving from all over the country, partly through word of mouth recommendation from successfully treated patients, and partly referred by Dr Mackarness or through AAA.

Eventually there came a time when Dr Kingsley felt he had to choose between general practice and clinical ecology, since time spent on one was inevitably time taken from the other. Finally he decided that it would be more sensible to make full use of the specialist knowledge he had acquired, so in August 1981 he went over entirely to private practice. He still has very mixed feelings. As a GP, he was able to help many patients by detecting their problems at an early stage. Now he sees a high proportion of very difficult cases: the failures who have already gone the rounds. If their basic problem had been diagnosed earlier, many of these would never have become ill; just as others today, if picked up right at the start by their GP, would never progress to such a complex stage.

Dr Kingsley prefers to have a referral from a GP; he encourages patients to tell their GP and asks their permission to write and keep their GP in touch. However, he feels that an individual patient has the right to advice and treatment, and he will therefore treat a patient whether or not the GP concurs. (As a matter of politeness he will see no one living in his immediate area without a GP referral.)

In fact there are very rarely problems. Most patients have already discussed the matter with their doctors, even if they come without a formal referral, and most agree quite happily that their doctor should be advised. He sees no difficulties in this approach as long as what he is doing does not conflict with the GP's own treatment; but where innate contradictions would arise, such as taking a schizophrenic off GP-prescribed drugs, then he will refuse to interfere and will not treat the patient without the agreement of the GP and the local hospital concerned.

Causes and symptoms
At present he sees three or four new cases each week. Though they come from all parts of the country and from abroad, the majority are probably from the Birmingham conurbation.

Dr Kingsley estimates that 75% of his patients are reasonably easy. Even though treatment may be prolonged, the causes for the various symptoms can be found, are found, and treated. Many patients are already aware that something is wrong; they may even have noticed a pattern of reactions, but fail to put the information together. He instances a young woman who worked in a department store, and who suffered from extreme fatigue, aches, tingling limbs, nausea, clumsiness and confusion. She was worse in summer. At week-ends she was well, except when she went to church, where she always became ill. She immediately became worse when she went back to the shop each Monday, and was better again by Friday (adaptation). On St. Valentine's Day, surrounded by a special promotion of roses, she became very ill indeed. She had most of the necessary information, but had not been able to identify her main trigger – which was flowers, and roses in particular.

The other 25% have problems which are much more difficult to diagnose. Of these, most will ultimately be significantly improved, some will be left with minor difficulties, and about 5% will still have major problems.

Reactions to chemicals

With many patients, and in particular these more difficult ones, it is obvious from the start that food is not the main cause of their illness. When patients fall asleep by gas fires, or habitually get migraines in a car, or a bloated abdomen when visiting large department stores, then their history alone will suggest that reactions to chemicals are, for them, more important.

Dr Kingsley observes that the medical profession is not yet attuned to taking such reactions into consideration. Instead, the orthodox attitude is to look for psychological causes: the patient who falls asleep by the fire is replaying experiences from in the womb, the patient who has problems in the department store suffers from claustrophobia. These might be possible explanations, but they cannot be generally true.

In his experience, reactions to chemicals are an increasingly common cause of illness. By 'chemicals', Dr Kingsley means anything environmental which is not put into the mouth: perfumes, after-shaves, formalin, North Sea gas, butane and propane, diesel and petrol funes, toilet-fresheners, floor and furniture polishes, detergents, man made fibres, outgassing from plastics, wood and coal smoke, paint fumes, pine extracts, sawdust and chlorine. Chlorine in tap water causes many problems, and the presence of chemicals in food is often a major cause of symptoms. It is far easier to avoid unwanted mono-sodium glutamate than the unsignalled and unsuspected traces of fertilizers and pesticides.

Intradermal testing is particularly valuable where chemicals are concerned, not least because patients are not used to the idea that these can be harmful. Once it is demonstrated to them that they do in fact react to perfumes, polishes, plastics and so on, it is much easier for them to accept that these can and do make them ill. Dr Kingsley makes all his own chemical extracts, in a base of saline which he then deep-freezes. 'You can make an extract of anything. In Canada I made an extract of Kleenex.'

When testing for chemicals, he starts with those which seem most likely: if the patient lives in an all-electric house, for example, gas can be left until later. He generally starts with phenol and ethanol, and then goes on to perfumes, formalin, car and diesel fumes, man-made fibres and PVC. These are basics, because most people are exposed to them most of the time. Then there are other individual irritants, depending on the different case histories: tobacco smoke, xylene and tolene (the ingredients of fresh paint), and aerosols. He almost always also tests for inhalants.

Some reactions to chemicals are astonishingly rapid. 'One patient reacts strongly to diesel fumes – unluckily her husband's in the haulage business. When tested with the appropriate solution, the unfortunate woman's stomach bloated up within five minutes. It took considerably longer to go down again.'

Whether testing for chemicals or foods, he never tells the patient what is being tried. If the patient produces a list of suspect substances, he will select from these for testing, but not in any known order. This is always, therefore, single-blind testing.

Food testing
Where foods as well as chemicals are implicated from the case history, Dr Kingsley prefers to start with a dietary approach. Overweight patients are usually fasted, slim patients put on a rotation or limited diet. During the period of a diet, he always ensures that he is accessible to the patient at all times.

After this, he normally proceeds to provocative testing, as he finds it useful not only to detect unsuspected allergens, but also confirm what the patient has discovered or suspected. For food intradermal testing, when making extracts himself presents practical problems, he uses the stronger Bencard solution which is actually designed for skin-prick tests. The weaker solution (100th or 1000th of the skin-prick solution), designed for intradermal testing is, he finds, unsatisfactory: this can often be the turn-off point for the individual patient, and so produce no symptoms at all.

The interpretation of tests

He observes that there is a difference between atopic and non-atopic patients. Atopic patients will react to skin-prick tests, but these results, without symptoms, may mean nothing. Non-atopic patients may not react at all, as the dilutions are too low to affect their skin, yet the same solutions used intradermally will produce reactions. What matters, in every case, is the interpretation of the tests.

While Dr Kingsley welcomes any research into all kinds of testing, he points out the difficulties. 'I was actively concerned for many years in setting up similar tests, and I know the problems involved. When you're dealing with people, there are so many variables; so many complications over what is a true control group; and over what is a true placebo – if such a thing exists.'

Hair analysis

He also prefers each patient to have a hair analysis at the very beginning so that he can identify any toxic elements present, particularly heavy metals. Lead is probably the main problem. 'If we assume that prehistoric people had a level of one unit of lead in their bodies, then today in comparison we have five hundred units. The toxic level is set at two thousand units, therefore the five hundred unit level *must* do some damage.' Dr Kingsley treats high lead levels homoeopathically: the treatment may take several months, but it is possible to remove the lead completely.

Candida

Along with the hair analysis he also tests for candida. He decides on further treatment depending on past history and the degree of skin reactions. For women the significant symptoms are gynaecological and period problems, hysterectomies, the Pill, steroids, vaginal discharge (not necessarily diagnosed as 'thrush') and 'cystitis'. For men the symptoms are prostatic problems and any condition requiring antibiotics, especially sore throats and acne, particularly if Tetracycline has been used. If the skin reaction to candida is severe, Dr Kingsley begins by treating it homoeopathically, though if it is only moderate he may start straight away with Nystatin.

Drops and injections

Dr Kingsley prescribes both drops and injections. Though both are equally good in protecting patients from symptoms, the injections are 'infinitely better' in actually desensitizing. However, they are not suitable for everyone, and there are problems, such as sterilization. With either drops or injections, it is possible for patients to cut down on their frequency over a period and finally stop using them altogether.

Most patients need five or six consultations, including testing. Some will continue to return even when there is no real medical reason to do so. 'I used to try to discharge these, but it's not always possible. The psychological side is very important. Many patients have lost so much confidence that they *need* support. I'm often the first doctor who's believed what they say; sometimes the first who's even bothered to *listen* to what they say.' He emphasizes though that this support is secondary to the work he does. His patients get better not simply because he cares for them, but because he can find out what is wrong and thus point out the way to regain their health.

Dr Kingsley is always looking to the future, and in interesting more people in this approach. He is Treasurer of the newly formed British Society for Nutritional Medicine; chief medical adviser to Foresight; and recently, as a committee member of the British Society for Clinical Ecology, helped to organize the highly successful 1984 international meeting.

His aim is always to help patients to lead as normal a life as possible. Some years ago a patient of his whose migraines had completely disappeared – following detection and avoidance of her food allergies – went back to her consultant. In due course, Dr Kingsley received from him a letter which contained the words: 'I have reassured her that the migraines may return, and that when they do I shall be ready to see her again.' His hope is that as the clinical ecological approach spreads he will receive fewer such messages.

Chapter 9

Enzyme Potentiated Desensitization

'I don't think I can save the little one':
Eunice Rose, age 49, talks about herself and her family

I was never well as a child. I had very bad urticaria, and what they called bilious attacks which would last about five days. When I got married and left home I became quite well. They said I'd grown out of it. Of course I realize now that I was eating differently, and I'd simply left a whole lot of allergens back in my parents' house.

In 1954 our first child was born. Andy was a 10½lb baby, and he nearly died at birth. It had been a long labour, and I was very ill too. They took him away and put him in intensive care, where of course he was bottle fed. In two days his weight had dropped to 5½lbs. He projectile-vomited after every feed.

I didn't even see him for a month. He was allowed home at six weeks, and from then until he was eight he had two major operations and several minor ones. Altogether he spent four years in hospital.

When he was 8½ we went to live on a dairy farm. Andy's vomiting attacks got worse. Our new GP checked up, and found that his hospital notes showed a glandular disturbance. He suspected a milk allergy. I just couldn't believe it. Andy had always drunk so much milk.

But I tried cutting milk out. After just one month Andy was 100% different. He could write properly where before he'd done mirror writing. From then on he was fine, except for one time when a doctor – a new one – pooh-poohed the idea of milk allergies. Andy began drinking milk without telling me. He didn't get stomach troubles, but his ankles packed up. One became very swollen and wouldn't support him. Finally the doctor said to him: 'If you come back again with ankles like that I'm going to put you in plaster up to your thighs.'

Andy confessed to me that he'd been drinking milk. He stopped then and there, and he's never had any more trouble at all. He's one of the lucky ones.

Michelle wasn't. She was born in 1963. She had eczema and nappy rash. She was a difficult feeder. She screamed and screamed and wouldn't sleep. She was so different in temperament from Andy that we never realized the connection. And nor did our GP.

She began losing weight. There was projectile vomiting. On her first Christmas Day I took her to our doctor – a different one again – because she was passing blood. Her tummy was rock-hard, but he said not to worry, she was probably constipated. She was a miserable, ill-tempered child. She never ever smiled. I couldn't cuddle her. She didn't want to be touched. I suppose now it just hurt her too much.

Our doctor told us I was worrying too much about her, and I should do something else to take my mind off her. We were in the middle of the country, without much money and with my husband away in the Merchant Navy, so I started to foster. Our first foster-child had sickle-cell anaemia – though I didn't know it then – so she was very sickly too. I felt it must be all my fault.

A new doctor, an Australian locum, came to visit her. When she arrived Michelle had just vomited. The doctor sent her to hospital for tests. Finally they found that she had a hiatus hernia and lesions in her intestines. She was too small to be operated on, so they said she would have to wait until she was five, and then she'd have to be operated on again at intervals. They told me to build her up with milk, eggs and fruit.

Then Mandy was born in 1967. It was fantastic. She slept well from when she was born until she was ten months old. That was when we moved to Hinckley. She wasn't eating solid food – I couldn't get her to swallow – so she was only on a bottle. I gave her exactly the same national dried milk, but the moment we moved she *changed*. She cried and cried all night long, and got terrible diarrhoea. Our GP – a new GP, of course – said: 'It's probably the change of water. She's got to get used to it.' He was more right than he knew. She was allergic to the water. She never did get used to it.

Our marriage broke up at this time. My husband had always been in perfect health himself. He couldn't accept that his children weren't perfect. It was a terrible time. Mandy's diarrhoea went on and on. She just dripped. She was hyperactive. She screamed all night and all day. If I got two hours' sleep I was lucky. Our neighbours complained. They went and asked for reduced rates.

The Medical Health Officer came and was very supportive, but he had no idea either what was wrong. I never thought to mention to anyone that Andy was on a milk-free diet. With hindsight it seems extraordinary.

Mandy still couldn't sit, but at twenty months she managed to walk. We couldn't get her to eat food. She was still on a bottle; I'd put rusks in but it was no good trying her on solid foods. Her tongue was so swollen she couldn't get the food past. She never spoke a word until the Christmas just before her fourth birthday, and then it was a whole sentence: 'No, it's my birthday present.'

Two months later she began to get ill. She was underweight and getting worse. By then she was eating little bits of food, but never a proper meal.

At 4¼ she woke up very ill indeed. From then on she got steadily worse. I brought her down stairs and put her on the sofa, and she lay curled up in a ball under the blankets. She wouldn't eat or drink. The GP said it was a virus infection. She lay there for over four weeks. She ate nothing, and drank only well water from friends. We didn't *know* that our tap water was bad for her; it was just that she liked it, and they kept bringing it for her.

At the end of five weeks she suddenly said: 'I'm better.' She got up. Then she began to eat, and began falling ill again. She started school, and our GP said she must eat school dinners, or she'd be taken away from home and put into care. He thought I was being an absurdly over-protective mother.

So Mandy stayed. There was a battle royal over dinners, which she won. The doctor began to think perhaps it was the child and not the mother who was at fault. There wasn't much wrong with the way Mandy got on in class, but he decided she was maladjusted, and the label stuck.

Meanwhile Michelle had been just about coping. They'd decided to postpone operating because she still wasn't strong enough. Then at six she began to go deaf. It happened very quickly. When she had an ear test at school they found her hearing was very, very poor.

She went to hospital to have her adenoids and tonsils removed. She was there for a fortnight, but her throat was still bleeding when she came home. She seemed to have a cold all the time. Our GP – another new one – said it was hayfever; it was November. She had to start wearing glasses, because apparently one of her optic nerves had been damaged in the operation.

By the time she was eight she was a mess. A sad straggly-haired girl with huge sunken eyes who was always ill.

When Mandy reached six and a half she was very very poorly. Vomiting, very underweight, with thin, dead hair. Our GP still had no idea what was wrong with her. She was sent to three hospitals – they both were. Nobody ever could give us any idea whatever about what was wrong.

She started getting nosebleeds; dreadful nosebleeds. Our GP wouldn't believe me. She was pot-bellied and her ribs stuck out. One time when I saw him I insisted that he weighed her. She was two stone. When he swung her up to sit her on the desk she bled all over him. It was a haemorrhage. Off to hospital again. *Still* they found nothing wrong.

Two months later her weight was down further. She was on drugs. She wasn't going to school any more. She had a cracked skull. She was a *mess*. One night I put them to bed and lay down on the sofa. I thought: we're not going to make it with Mandy. Then the TV came on.

A doctor said something about 'milk allergy'. It was about Dr L M treating milk allergy in a milkman. I sat up. I saw his treatment and I listened to his talk. It was like a switch being put on.

Next day I went to our GP. He said he didn't know anything about L M. It took one and a half days on the phone to track him down. Then I went to the surgery to get a referral letter. The doctor said he wouldn't write one. I took off my coat. He said: 'What are you doing?'. I said: 'Having a sit-in.' He said: 'You can't. I've got patients waiting.' I said: 'I've got sick children waiting.' I sat there for three quarters of an hour, and he wrote the letter.

Two days later we met in the street. We looked at each other and we both laughed. He apologized. He said he'd been up for two nights seeing patients. I said: 'I've not had a night's sleep in six years.'

I had to wait another three months before I finally saw Dr L M in September 1974. I liked him straight away. He spoke *to* you, not *at* you. He asked questions, and he *listened* to the answers. Although he usually didn't do skin tests, he did them anyway on Michelle and Mandy, and the results were dynamite. They were highly allergic.

'I don't think I can do anything for the little one,' he said. He christened her The Mouse. But he agreed that we'd try. Both of them started to have treatment that day. They were too ill to go on a diet, and by this time even a drink of water made Mandy vomit.

To start with it didn't seem to make much difference. But very slowly things improved. Michelle began eating properly. And Mandy, after two years, suddenly began to get really well.

Then we had a fantastic three years, going up every six weeks for the treatment. In the winter term Michelle and Mandy were the only children who hadn't had time off for colds or flu.

Then, just before Christmas 1979, we went to St Mary's for the next treatment, and it was like walking into fog. We knew something was wrong. Dr L M called all the patients who were waiting and said: 'I don't know how to put it, so I'll just say it straight. There is no more treatment.'

We couldn't take it in. It was like a death sentence.

Over the next months, with other patients, I set up an action group. We met Dr L M, we set up a committee, we contacted the Health Authority, we did everything we could.

The children both started to get poorly again. Mandy went downhill very quickly. She began vomiting blood and was admitted to hospital immediately. Finally the diagnosis was that she had cyclical neutropenia: her white blood cells were destroying each other. Eventually the paediatrician concluded that allergy was implicated, and wanted to give Mandy tests. He explained that they had to be double-blind tests with the food disguised. He settled on testing milk first. She had to drink concentrated milk protein.

The morning she tried this out she said it was horrible, but she drank it. I had to leave her to meet the action group, and just before I returned they gave her a second lot. When I came into the room where she was, I found her on top of one of the nurses painting her instead of the murals she was supposed to be doing. Mandy was absolutely uncontrollable. It was very frightening. She was drunk. She had the DTs. This went on until 1 am, and then they called a doctor. He couldn't do anything either. We didn't know what was happening. It was the first time that Mandy had been like this. I realized later that the milk had been coloured with tartrazine, and a lot of it. She'd never been chemically affected before, except for the tap water.

We were up all night coping with her. It took all of us to hold her down on to a bed. We couldn't put a covering over her. She pinched all the skin off her body where she thought cockroaches were coming out of her.

I took her home again the following weekend in a terrible state. She had foot-rot. All the skin was falling off between her toes, on top of her feet, and off the soles.

Three weeks after that the rash came. It started on Saturday. By Monday, her body was smothered. Our GP said it was eczema. She was given a powerful anti-histamine which put her to sleep for fourteen days, but removed the eczema absolutely.

All this time our action group was trying to work out a way of making Dr L M's treatment available. We asked the hospital if we could borrow him for half a day a week. We had agreement, and spent £6000 setting up a clinic. Then, 10 days before our first appointments, we were told the hospital had changed its mind.

Meanwhile Dr K E had decided to start using Dr L M's treatment. We went to his clinic the week before Easter, 1981. It was the first treatment they'd had for eighteen months.

It was fantastic. After one more treatment Michelle was okay. She hasn't needed another for 2½ years.

Mandy began by reacting badly. Then in July Dr L M left the hospital, and in August she had a further treatment from him. In between that and the next time she was dreadful. It's a wonder I didn't strangle her – it's a wonder no one else did. What I didn't realize was that she was getting through almost a bottle of orange squash a day. She was hooked on tartrazine.

Dr L M spotted it, and luckily Mandy was so ill by that time that she wanted to come off it. She suffered terribly from withdrawal symptoms. It took her two weeks to get over it. Now she goes back every three months for treatment, and she's fine. To look at her now you'd never know that she'd had any problems.

Our group has developed into the National Society for Research into Allergy. We badly want to get more trials done into treatment, for all the Mandys who don't know that they're affected, and all the other Mandys who are about to be born. We want doctors to understand, and for children to be taught about it. The earlier it's picked up, the more can be done. †

Dr L M, MA, BM, BCh, qualified in 1959. Following a 'three year rat run', he became Registrar in Allergy at St Mary's, Paddington. In 1964 he was appointed Lecturer in Applied Pharmacology, so that he could both keep his clinics and carry out research. He remained there, working on his enzyme potentiated vaccine, treating patients and studying results, until he took early retirement. Since 1981 he has been continuing and developing the same work in a private capacity.

Dr L M has devoted the last twenty years of his life to his

investigative and practical work on a vaccine which, developed initially to help relieve hayfever patients, can be also used to treat food-allergic sufferers.

The impetus for his research came from his early experiences in the hayfever clinic at St Mary's, where three thousand sufferers were attending each year. This meant that there was an enormous number of patients who could be studied, tested, and asked to take part in trials.

Bacterial vaccine
Right through the first half of this century, allergy was considered to be due to bacteria, and patients were treated with a bacterial vaccine. A swab was taken usually from the patient's nose, together with a sample of blood. The swab was cultured in the blood, and if the bacteria overgrew this was considered to be the cause of the allergy. The culture was then made into a vaccine and injected. This process remained the basis of all allergic treatments until 1948.

It was then that Dr A W Frankland – a leading figure in allergy – joined St Mary's as Registrar. Realizing that this approach had never been adequately tested, he set up double-blind trials. Fifty-eight per cent of patients with the active vaccine improved, but so too did 55% on a saline placebo. His results were published in the *British Medical Journal*, and the use of bacterial vaccine was discontinued.

Potential non-bacterial causes
However, when Dr L M joined Dr Frankland's team at the Wright-Fleming Institute of Microbiology in 1962, he was still inheriting patients who had previously been vaccinated in this way. He found that some had in fact been very well on this treatment, which suggested that bacteria had for them been the prime cause, while others had become ill after their first injection. Among these was a group of patients who reported that whenever they were on a course of antibiotics, their nasal polyps (small growths which can follow prolonged and severe hayfever) would shrink and disappear, but would then return after three weeks. Another group reported that when they took Enterovioform, their symptoms were alleviated. Neither of these findings matched with a bacterial allergy theory.

Since at that time Enterovioform was prescribed for dysentery and stomach upsets, the response in the last group of patients suggested that there could be a connection between the effects of food in the system and allergy. This possibility was confirmed by the observations of individual patients who were telling him that they knew they could be upset by different foods – usually after a delay of hours or even days.

Experimental dieting

By the middle of 1964 he was beginning to select patients with asthma and rhinitis who conformed to the criteria for 'intrinsic' airways allergy as described much earlier by Dr Rackemann (see also p. 142) in the States and placing them on an experimental diet. A pattern emerged which indicated that people could have bacterial allergies, or food allergies, or both.

It was obviously important at this stage to have a trial of the effects of an exclusion diet, and to publish the results. Forty-seven patients were selected, none of whom was known to be food allergic. Twelve dropped out at various stages. Of the 35 who went on to complete the first two diets, 21 had rhinitis, 5 asthma, and the rest eczema.

All these kept to their exclusion diet for three weeks. They omitted all milk except Carnation (allowed because its heat treatment had destroyed the protein responsible for many allergic reactions), eggs, custard, salad cream, chicken, all fruits and vegetables and all foods containing nuts or pips, yeast products, pork products and liver, fish, cheese, onions, alcohol, shellfish, honey and chewing gum. All patients were also prescribed 250mg of Enterovioform three times a day. Patients who failed to respond to this diet then went on to follow a stricter diet for a further week, omitting all milk, fruit and wheat.

At this point – after one month – only five patients showed no sign of improvement: they withdrew for alternative treatment. The other thirty went on to eat their suspect foods for a week and to observe any symptoms thus provoked. From two months from the start of the trial, the patients then returned to a normal diet apart from those foods they had identified as harmful. There followed a further month without Enterovioform, and then assessment by an independent observer.

Results

Out of the 35 patients who completed their diets 30 showed improvement: 5 had lost all their symptoms, 18 were 75% better, and 7 were 50% better. All the patients but one had proved allergic to two or more groups of foods. The group affecting the largest number of patients was 'pips and nuts': a very sizeable one, including tomatoes, berries, citrus fruits and their products, chocolate, coffee, melons, cucumber, marrow, peas and beans, spices, peanuts and olive oil. Eleven of the patients adversely affected by foods particularly liked and ate unusually large amounts of those most harmful to them.

Three of the improved patients subsequently proved to require the Enterovioform alone; seven needed both that and the regime.

Eight patients also found that certain foods caused additional symptoms (vomiting, diarrhoea, abdominal pains) to those for which they were being treated. It seemed clear that food could affect patients, even though the mechanisms were, so far, unknown.*

While avoidance of harmful foods was the obvious answer for his food-sensitive patients, this was not always possible. In these early diets Dr L M had not attempted to identify all forms of food sensitivity; his prime aim was to establish a diet which was both simple and inexpensive. Some foods might not be accurately pin-pointed, and some patients found it difficult to follow a strict diet. Dr L M began to work on an alternative method of protection.

Dr Popper's research into hyaluronidase

The course he was to pursue was based on the preliminary researches of Dr Popper, an Ear, Nose and Throat surgeon who had been a refugee from Hitler's Prague. On his arrival in London, Dr Popper had eventually found part-time work in a Hackney hospital, combining it with a small private practice.

In Hackney he found that many of his patients were suffering from nasal polyps, a growth containing hyaluronic acid, a jelly-like substance. Dr Popper speculated that it might be possible to break down this acid by injections of an enzyme called hyaluronidase. In 1958 he began using this treatment on his patients. The polyps remained unchanged, but his patients stopped sneezing. The following year he tried the treatment on his hayfever patients with the same results. A significant number of his patients benefited, and the treatment appeared to last.

After another year's successful treatments, he approached a prominent drug company, who financed him and provided him with supplies of hyaluronidase. Two years of frustration followed, in which some patients improved while others did not. Eventually, he realized that the differences were not in the patients but in the different batches of hyaluronidase.

*Although the trial was completed in 1967, the results were not finally published until 1970: *Annals of Allergy*, Vol. 28, June.

Dr Popper turned to another drug company, which promised to produce pure hyaluronidase. At the same time he joined St Mary's as a clinical assistant, and Dr L M began to be involved in his work. He was asked to assess the value of hyaluronidase.

Initially Dr Popper tested this on six patients. He gave all six of them pollen: then to four he gave injections of hyaluronidase, and to two, saline placebos. After three weeks, they returned to be given more pollen: four were unaffected, while two became very ill.

The drug company then invested a considerable amount of money in further trials, with the unfortunate result that the patients appeared to do better on the placebos. The company withdrew their support, and Dr Popper died shortly afterwards of a coronary.

Dr L M's continuation of this research

Convinced by Dr Popper's work, Dr L M was sure that hyaluronidase could and did work; for it to work only sometimes could only mean that there must be something else significant besides the hyaluronidase itself: something which was sometimes present and sometimes not. Moreover, the injections could only work provided that the patients had been first exposed to pollen – yet it had not been possible for Dr Popper to *control* the amount of pollen given.

He arrived at a potential solution to the second problem first. He calculated that it should prove possible, by scraping a small patch on the patient's arm, and applying a mixture of the allergen and the hyaluronidase in a small cup strapped over the area, to allow a controlled amount of both to percolate gradually through the layers of the skin.

His first patient in January 1966 was a complete success, with results that confirmed what Dr Popper had found. He went on to use the same method on others. By the autumn, he had used five lots of hyaluronidase: one was wholly successful, two partially, and one not at all. Knowing that it was virtually impossible to obtain absolutely pure hyaluronidase, Dr L M obtained a list of the known contaminants. Among these was a list of enzymes.

He bought these in pure form from chemical companies, and began to dose the non-working hyaluronidase with these, testing one at a time. The fourth cured twelve patients. He had discovered the answer: beta glucoronidase. He then proceeded to lace each batch of hyaluronidase with beta glucoronidase. The results showed that the combination did indeed work, but the method was both less scientific and less reliable than he would have liked. He wanted to refine it, make it patentable, usable by everyone to treat sufferers everywhere.

The National Research and Development Council contributed towards further research, and paid for an assistant. He began carrying out tests on guinea pigs and rats: first making them allergic, and then applying the hyposensitization.

There were (mostly practical) difficulties over the experiments, and after a year, with problems still unsolved, the grant – and the the help of an assistant – came to an end.

Dr L M began to use mice instead, so that the tests, with the results, could be put through within weeks instead of months. He was funded for three years by the Asthma Research Council; and he was able to demonstrate a connection between this work and a double-blind trial with hayfever sufferers.*

Treatment and patients
During this period he went on treating patients, for hayfever to start with and later for mixed symptoms.

This treatment is *specific*: i.e., it only works for an antigen which is put in the cup in the right dose. Initially he began by treating single allergies absolutely specifically. After five years of such treatments, he was beginning to observe a pattern in his patients: they were recruiting approximately one new allergy every three years. Dr M speculated that it might be possible to prevent this development by adding mixed allergens (carefully calculated to include all the groups of foods commonly eaten) to the vaccine. He began to adopt this procedure in 1971, and after eight years' experience there was considerable evidence that it was working. Patients did not appear to be recruiting fresh allergies.

Dr L M realized that, in order to test the validity of this assumption, it would be necessary to take all patients off the vaccine (thus causing them to relapse), and then to wait to ascertain whether new allergies would develop which had not been present before treatment started.

Clearly this experiment would not be ethical, as it would involve cutting off treatment which had been shown to be beneficial; but unexpectedly the circumstances changed. In 1979 St Mary's decided that it would no longer be possible for Dr L M to continue preparing his vaccines in the hospital's laboratories, or to carry out further research there; shortly afterwards he resigned. Since patients could now no longer

Annals of Allergy, Vol. 31, November 1973.

have their regular doses of vaccine, it would prove possible to determine what long-term benefits – if any – this process had in fact conferred.

At this time, 1000 patients were currently using his vaccine and awaiting a further dose: 400 with hayfever and 600 with mixed symptoms. His successor, Dr K E, subsequently wrote to the patients with mixed symptoms to offer them further vaccine if they wished, although it would now have to be given privately. Of these, one-third wrote back to say no more was needed as they remained perfectly well, one-third reported slight symptoms but not sufficient to warrant their returning, and one-third wanted another dose.

By 1983, between Dr L M and Dr E, all patients needing further treatment had been seen. Of all these, only twelve reported developing a new allergy; thus there was a strong indication that mixed-antigen vaccine gave protection against the development of further food allergies.

Benefits of EPD

Over the past three years EPD has been used to treat at least another thousand patients both here and abroad.

Dr L M believes that this method of hyposensitization is both effective and harmless in a wide range of cases. It is both simple and safe. Because the cup can be removed instantly if adverse effects are felt, any possible ill effects are stopped immediately.

'It's scientific. It's been tested. It can be taught to other doctors. What I like about it is that patients just sit there and get better. All they need is a few doses a year initially, depending on the allergen. Then these can gradually be decreased, and often, after an interval, stopped completely.'

At present this method cannot be used for certain other non-food allergies, of which the most important are chemicals added to foods; though Dr L M feels that with further experiments and research there is no reason why this too should not be possible. It can however handle specific pollens, dusts, mould spores or bacteria.

He has now successfully used this method on patients with a wide range of symptoms. A very recent development has been that he can now prove, through a series of X-rays, that there may be actual regeneration of the bones in patients with rheumatoid arthritis who are treated in this way. While he considers that rheumatoid arthritis 'is an entitity on its own', he believes there is evidence for a link with diet in at least a proportion of cases. A trial with 22 patients (15 sero-positive) on allergen-exclusive diets showed that 20 subsequently noticed an improvement, and 19 reported that certain foods would repeatedly exacerbate their symptoms. The greatest delay before improvement was 18 days. There was considerable variation in the interval between provocation and reaction (from 2 hours to 2 weeks), and an average of 2½ sensitivities per patient. The largest single allergen was grains, which affected 14.*

He estimates that his treatment has a success rate of approximately 75-80%. He finds that where EPD fails, conventional desensitization by the injection of larger and larger doses often succeeds: and where this fails, his treatment succeeds.

Two groups of patients
This may well reflect a basic difference between two groups of patients. Dr L M points out that as long ago as 1928 Dr Rackemann in the States observed that there were two types of asthma sufferers.

Group 1 contains patients with a raised IgE reading: most are under forty; males outnumber females by two to one; conventional prick-tests are sometimes positive; response to the allergen tends to be rapid. These are the patients with conventionally recognizable 'allergic' symptoms and are seen by classical allergists.

Group 2 tend to be older (though a sizeable group, mostly female, start to show symptoms in their teens); women outnumber men by four to one; the IgE level is normal or low; conventional skin-prick tests are usually negative; and reactions to the allergen are usually delayed. Most of the second group never go to conventional allergy clinics, as their symptoms are not diagnosed as due to allergy.

Patients in both groups may suffer from food allergies, and there are some patients who fall between the two categories, but Dr M feels that the distinction is helpful in obliging doctors to look more closely at sufferers and their problems.

PIMS patients
Another group of patients in whom Dr L M is interested suffer from what he terms 'PIMS': Psychological/Irritable bowels/ Migraine Syndrome (Syndrome – a collection of symptoms). It seems that a high proportion of these sufferers are also allergic to foods. Such patients will suffer from all these symptoms either simultaneously or at different times, and all 'behave like

*Clinical Allergy 10: 463-7, 1980.

opium addicts to the things they're allergic to.'

He distinguishes between four different stages, analogous in each case to the developing pattern of opium addiction.

In *stage 1*, the patient gets more than normal pleasure from food. There is a disturbed reaction in the polypeptide hormones in the gut: these are also present in the brain and in the nervous control system, and there is a close reaction between the two.

In *stage 2*, there are signs of withdrawal symptoms when the food is not consumed.

In *stage 3*, the opium-like reaction to taking the allergen becomes stronger. The patient gets sedated; finds difficulty in remembering things; is sometimes confused; becomes very sleepy after lunch and finds it difficult to cope in the afternoon. As one expressed it: 'It's as though a roller-blind comes down between me and the world.' If they miss out on their allergens, they have flu-like symptoms.

In *stage 4*, the patient becomes over-excited, and has rapid mood changes (this compares more closely with opium-*like* drugs, rather than with opium). They may become wild and act bizarrely, or they may go into a state resembling a coma.

Stage 5 leads to a general breakdown, in which the patient may leave both work and family.

Dr M looked at fifty patients who suffered from all three symptoms: i.e., psychological problems, irritable bowels, and migraine. Of these fifty patients, eight were male (mean age 38, age range 24-66); forty-two female (mean age 38.2, age range 17-63). Twenty-two could not ascribe the onset of their symptoms to any particular event. Out of the remaining twenty-eight, seven had observed the same symptoms since childhood; six had begun to notice them after childbirth; four after an anaesthetic; five after a viral infection; two after starting on the Pill; and one each after the menopause, possible exposure to insecticides, a diagnosis of anorexia nervosa, and the effects of a five-day diet.

Dr M observes that if GPs pick up patients as soon as they show signs of PIMS (i.e. with the concurrence of these three symptoms), so that they are correctly diagnosed and treated, the symptoms will stop and patients will return to normal health. If, however, these signals are mis-read, patients will proceed to develop further and still further symptoms.

Hyperventilation

Forty per cent of PIMS patients also hyperventilate: breathe so deeply and intensely that the excess of oxygen to the brain can produce still more bizarre symptoms. These can distract the investigator from the core of the disease – the allergic reaction – but it is essential that it be noted and dealt with.

In the last two years there has been a change of attitude towards hyperventilation: it is now recognized that it takes both allergists and experts in hyperventilation to deal successfully with this problem. It is important to recognize that sufferers hyperventilate unknowingly, often in their sleep. They have – unconsciously – discovered that hyperventilation can give an opium-like boost, and the associated effects can give rise to a whole range of symptoms.

Current work
Dr L M spends the greater part of his time working in his own laboratory – designed and constructed entirely by himself – preparing his vaccines and carrying out further research. He devotes two days a week to patients who come from all over the UK and from abroad. Most of those he sees are referred by doctors who understand what he does and accept that it works, but he does also accept patients from doctors who may still be dubious but are nonetheless willing actively to co-operate.

He is currently writing *Allergy From Scratch*, a comprehensive work studying background mechanisms, and is also increasingly called upon to lecture on his unique approach.

Among other relevant papers by Dr M and others are:
Enzyme potentiated hyposensitization I: *Int. Arch All*. 42: 152, 1972;
Enzyme potentiated hyposensitization II: *Ann. All*. 31: 79, 1973;
Enzyme potentiated hyposensitization IV: *Ann. All*. 34: 290, 1975.

'The most unexpected aspect was the liberation of my true personality': Peter Milner, age 38

By 1981 I was thinking of jacking in my job: I'm a lecturer in mechanical engineering. I couldn't add two and two together. I was in pain from my arthritis. I was suffering from a long list of symptoms. I was anxious and depressed. I couldn't cope with the work. I couldn't teach.

Right from childhood days I'd had recurrent health problems: bloat, digestive disturbance, bladder pains, poor physical fitness, palpitations, blocked nose, minor arthritic flare-ups, mouth ulcers and bleeding gums. Of course, now I know that these symptoms can all point to allergy, but no one suspected it then.

Many of them went on to become more frequent during my mid-twenties, but without being severe or persistent enough to cause me any real concern. Then, in late 1975, I acquired some strange, never-diagnosed infection – with persistent sore throats, severe bowel disturbances, sudden bouts of sweating, and exhaustion – which lasted intermittently for over two years. I know it *was* an infection because it responded temporarily to antibiotics in 1976 and 1977, and because several colleagues and friends fell ill in much the same way, though to varying degrees. Of these, four discovered independently that our frequent attacks of creasing abdominal pain and diarrhoea – which developed after several months of illness – were due to milk. Two then recovered steadily after cutting out milk, but the other two (myself included) went on to develop many more food allergies; although it was a long time before either of us realized the true cause.

Over the next two years my condition deteriorated. I rarely felt well, and was often too exhausted to get out of bed and go to work. I suffered from depression, anxiety, headaches, sprue-like symptoms, meaty-smelling urine, generally deteriorating digestion with nausea and passing blood, and all sorts of aches and pains. Despite a battery of medical tests, no diagnosis except 'psychosomatic' was made.

Eventually, in 1979, I was referred to Northwick Park Hospital Clinical Research Centre for a series of tests for various auto-immune disorders. All these were negative, except for a series of skin tests which showed a slight reaction to mixed flour.

The specialist (so I eventually discovered) reported to my GP that I should be looked at for further food allergies, and treated for chronic anxiety and depression. However, my GP chose to ignore the allergy aspect. In fact, he told me I couldn't possibly be allergic to milk, even though I offered to give a very dramatic demonstration of its effect on me!

He put me on an anti-depressant. Next day, I was *totally suicidal*. I managed to get back to him, and I was referred first to a psychiatrist and then to a clinical psychologist – after being told to continue with the anti-depressant.

It was about this time that I read two books on food allergy. It became very obvious that I was highly allergic, but I was now so ill both physically and mentally that I couldn't make much sense of what was going on. The trouble is, you make every possible effort to cope with the outside world, against increasing difficulty as time goes on, and yet there are no dramatically obvious physical symptoms. All that the rest of the world sees is evidence of mental deterioration. They simply see you gradually going nuts.

However, I felt relaxed with my psychologist. Here at last was someone who was prepared to listen and to help. At first, she didn't believe I was food-allergic; at the same time, she was puzzled by my wide range of moods and mental ability. Eventually we sorted out a dietary regime which enabled me to discover that grains in general, and wheat and vinegar in particular, were at the root of many of my symptoms. I was addicted to both: getting through a loaf a day and emptying a bottle of vinegar without even tasting it.

Over the following months I eliminated more foods as it became clear that they caused trouble. Most fruits, for example, would now provoke an arthritic flare-up in my wrists, knees and hips. Some, including damsons and strawberries, also gave me a profound mental fogginess lasting about two days.

I kept on trying new foods, but eventually I became allergic to these too. By September 1980 I was ill despite a very restricted diet. (I suspect now that I'm also allergic to my own gut flora.)

I couldn't think rationally. I was permanently exhausted and in severe difficulty coping with even the routine parts of my job. I suffered from acute insomnia at night, partly due to anxiety, and partly due to an incredibly uncomfortable sensation in my limbs (like a severe ache 50 miles away!); while during the day I found it increasingly hard to stay awake. I became intolerant of noise, light – indeed of the whole world.

By this time I didn't know where to turn. Then I heard about Dr E's treatment, and felt that for the first time there was a ray of hope. I went for my first desensitization in April 1981.

Two days later I felt magnificent, both physically and mentally. I found I could now eat several foods which had previously caused trouble; others I still couldn't – or at least not without some symptoms.

A year later, after several more treatments, I could eat most foods in normal quantities. Milk came right about then, and I've never reacted to it since.

Now, after three years of treatment, there are many fewer rogue foods left. I recently stopped smoking, and feel better than ever. I can cope well with my job, except when I need my next desensitizing; and my batting average at cricket (which in one season had declined to 1.67: I couldn't even see the ball) is now back well into double figures.

The most unexpected aspect of the treatment was the liberation of my true underlying personality, which had been latent for half a lifetime. It was very difficult at first to harness effectively this more vital and less submissive personality, particularly when the old one would return whenever I needed desensitizing again, or ate a food which was still wrong!

It was well worth enduring the early problems: the quality of my life is now better than it has ever been. Rather than being a passive recipient, as I had been right from childhood, I am now an active participant.

Dr K E, LRCP, and SE, LRFPSG, had 'a perfectly conventional background until this interest in allergies'. After qualifying in 1961 from Edinburgh and going on to various house jobs, he became a Registrar in Ear, Nose and Throat. Feeling that this was too narrow a speciality, in 1967 he became a GP. During the next few years he met Dr L M, attended courses and meetings on allergy, and in 1975 began holding part-time hospital clinics. From 1980 he has divided his time between an NHS allergy clinic at the Royal Berkshire Hospital, private practice, his own laboratory, advising two commercial companies on allergic illnesses, and writing.

From his early years as a GP, Dr E began to recognize 'allergy' as a basic cause of illness in a proportion of his patients. He found there was no one to send them to, and no one to train him how to treat them. Accordingly, he embarked on a programme of self-education. At the same time, his wife-to-be introduced him to the potentiality of enzyme-potentiated vaccination: allergic herself, she had been attending Dr L M's clinics for her asthma, which had subsequently proved to be caused by allergies to foods.

After meeting Dr L M in 1968, Dr E was impressed by the possibilities his vaccine opened for treatment. He set out to acquire as much expertise as he could, from reading, lectures, and the experience of others.

'It's certainly not an ideal way to learn – you have to be very determined to find out anything at all. It's difficult to get any sort of teaching in allergy. It doesn't feature as a job option for doctors. As long as it doesn't there's no training needed, and therefore no specialists to give the training. The UK hasn't even one junior lecturer in allergy, therefore they can't train anyone in allergy. All those students go out knowing very little about it, and so in their turn can't teach it either. Most allergists and immunologists are consultants in something else.

'There are very few doctors in the whole country earning

money from full-time work in allergy – probably no more than you could count on your fingers and toes. People in medicine in the UK don't care about the status of allergy. We are a more endangered species than the Siberian tiger.'

Gradually, working and studying in his spare time, Dr E's knowledge and experience increased. Reluctant though he was to abandon general practice, he began to feel that he would be of more use to the community if he used his understanding of allergies full-time. After 'taking a deep breath and taking the plunge' in 1980, he has been encouraged in his decision by the rapidly increasing interest in and understanding of allergies, as doctors and patients alike begin to appreciate the sheer size of the problem.

Incidence of allergy in one general practice

In 1974 and again in 1979 Dr E analysed the allergy incidence of the entire population of a New Town general practice ('The incidence of allergy – has it changed?', *Clinical Allergy*, 12, 1982). After the five-year interval he found a rise in the incidence of allergic complaints for both sexes: for males (particularly prone to hayfever and asthma) from nearly 20 to 27%; for females (more prone to drug and miscellaneous allergies) from 25 to 32%. Significantly, just under *a third of the whole practice* was affected by *known* allergically-caused illnesses.

Dr E believes that these statistics, for a number of reasons, underestimate the part played by foods. He himself estimates that the proportion of the population affected by food is at least the same as that affected by hayfever: around 5%. In other words, at least 2¾ million people in the UK suffer in this way.

Patients

Because of his current situation, he feels that he sees as wide a cross-section of allergic patients as anyone else in the country. Through his hospital clinics he treats about a thousand new patients each year, most of whom are referred for conventionally recognized allergies and are therefore treated with classical immunological therapy. He finds that many patients, particularly those with inhaled allergens, respond well to this. If the diagnosis is carefully made the results are good; the therapy is convenient, the costs are low, and are met by the NHS.

At the same time he also treats between five and seven hundred new private patients a year. Most are local, but a sizeable minority come from all parts of the country and abroad. He insists that all private patients are referred by doctors. These

cases are far less straightforward, as they are mainly patients
who have either failed to progress through conventional methods
or who have not previously suspected allergy at all.

Ingestant allergens

Many of these are subsequently found to be sensitive to
'ingestant allergens' (Dr E prefers this term to 'food allergens'
since, as he points out, some of the substances causing reactions
are additives rather than the foods themselves). As a starting
point, he asks all these suspect cases to go on elimination diets.
He was already using these on patients in general practice as far
back as 1968, and has found them highly effective in tracking
down ingestant allergens – far more so than any laboratory tests.
'RAS tests are of little use – they measure the wrong thing, while
the accuracy of skin-prick testing for foods varies between 40%
and 60%. That means that the reliability of the result for any
given food is simply hit and miss.'

He suspects that all such tests are fallible not because they are
wrong in principle, but because they involve extracts of foods
and other ingestants in their raw state, and not as they actually
affect the body. Many foods are cooked; they are then altered
first by the saliva and then by the digestive juices. 'You've only
got to watch a baby being sick. What comes up – even after only a
couple of minutes – isn't what went down.' He considers that all
such tests will continue to be unsatisfactory until it is possible to
use substances which have undergone a suitable metabolic
change.

Chemicals

Like Dr L M he also considers that reaction-causing chemicals
such as fumes from plastics or petrol are not allergens. They are
more usefully thought of as 'non-specific irritability'. However,
he adds that at present – lacking adequate methods of testing –
this must remain a somewhat academic distinction, and in
practice the treatment remains the same: avoidance wherever
possible.

Rheumatoid arthritis

He feels there may also be an essential distinction between
different forms of illnesses masked by being grouped together
under the same label. For example, he has had several patients
with joint pains who have come to him with the previous
diagnosis of rheumatoid arthritis, and who have responded well
to an elimination diet. 'When you look back into their tests, you

find that these hadn't originally produced classical results. They were termed rheumatoid arthritics and treated according to this diagnosis, but they might never have had rheumatoid arthritis at all.'

Schizophrenia
In the same way, Dr E thinks that there may exist both schizophrenia – or what is now termed schizophrenia – and another schizophrenia-like illness which responds to dietary changes. If a 'schizophrenic' successfully treats him/herself – which is by definition impossible – then the diagnosis must have been incomplete.

Treatment
Dr E is a firm believer in the avoidance of allergens and the modification of life-style as sole treatment, as long as this is possible. Thirty per cent of his patients cope very well on this regime. They come off all drugs, and, provided they keep to their new way of life, they remain free of symptoms. This straightforward approach can be highly satisfying. One patient who had been receiving five different drugs for asthma was found to be allergic to yeast: she had been taking daily tablets for ten years, following the advice of a friend. After cutting out yeast her asthma disappeared, and she no longer needed drugs.

In planning his patients' revised diets, he has the help of the hospital nutritionists. He also finds inspiration in the *Manual of Nutrition* (by David Buss and Jean Robertson, Ministry of Agriculture, HMSO), which not only examines the different roles played by different foods, but also suggests viable alternatives: for example, someone who is milk-allergic can receive added calcium from watercress.

For patients for whom conventional therapy is unsuitable and for whom adequate avoidance would mean an inadequate diet, his approach depends on whether they are NHS or private patients. He is unable to offer EPD at the hospital, since the NHS at present does not recognize this and will therefore not fund it. Understandably, Dr E is not happy about this, and is looking for other ways to help his patients. His current efforts are directed to correcting mineral and vitamin imbalances due to poor diet, and to the use of pancreatic enzymes and drugs to induce tolerance to trigger foods. Privately he uses EPD, finding it successful long-term in all but a handful of cases.

Clinical ecology and orthodox medicine

Dr E believes that the diagnosis and treatment of food and chemical allergies is a branch of orthodox medicine, and is increasingly being recognized as such. 'I'm now having patients referred by GPs who I think a few years ago wouldn't have done so.' He welcomes both this wider view of medicine and the work and opinions of clinical ecologists, because it encourages 'looking at medical problems with an open and curious mind.' He mentions a recent example: a patient complained of a rash on his lips, round his mouth and on his fingers. Instead of handing out a cream, the clinical ecologist managed to establish the cause. His patient frequently played bowls; the green had been treated with Paraquat, and every time he spat on his fingers before bowling he helped to distribute the poison on his skin.

'I think most doctors before clinical ecology, and many still today, wouldn't have asked the questions and so wouldn't have got the answers. We have a lot to learn from the work they're doing.'

He would like validation for the treatments currently being offered for food and chemical allergies, but recognizes that this may be a long time coming.

Research difficulties

Research involves a search for repeatable facts. It aims at codification. Research into allergies is into symptoms that do not easily classify. Most allied studies are at present being carried out by immunologists, who concentrate for months on minute details: eighteen months' work can be devoted to ten blood samples. Although this is important, it has little direct relevance to patients or their symptoms.

Most research today is 'registrar research'. A registrar must publish two papers. It takes six months to set up a project, six months to do it, six months to get it published, 'and then six months to hawk it around'. When registrars become consultants they need never touch research again.

Some branches of research are particularly difficult and even dangerous. Projects looking at stomach illness might take ten or even twenty years, and some of the techniques involved could be harmful to the patients concerned.

As for independent research, it is extremely difficult to raise the funds to carry this out. Any one project might cost £250,000. To research into the effects of natural gas would cost three or four years' salary for a researcher, laboratory costs during that time, technicians' salaries, and the payment of all kinds of backup services.

The current lack of laboratory-based research leaves Dr E with a problem. While he wants to be as scientific as possible in his analysis and urgently wants validation for what is being done, 'there is more to life than any single mode of treatment, and what matters is to help the patient'.

Problems with double-blind tests

He is unhappy about an insistence on double-blind trials. Not only is it difficult in practice to do such testing, as disguising food in quantity is always a problem, but it would be unethical to do repeated challenges with foods which had already been found to cause reactions. 'Understandably, patients don't want to do this either. Anyone who has already suffered a bad reaction will not willingly court another. There's also the possibility that severe reactions could be actively dangerous, even resulting in death through anaphylaxis.'

Meanwhile, he feels that it would not be right to deny an effective treatment because it is not yet known *how* this does what it does.

Current projects

Like Dr L M, Dr E spends a large part of his time in his own laboratory preparing his own vaccines. He is currently working on several research projects, both for himself and the two companies he advises: on epidemiology, skin-test reactivity, late reactions on skin and nasal tests, and storage mites. He has also been working for a considerable time on the problems of producing starchfree drugs, which are difficult to find. Many patients are also fruit-sensitive and so find it difficult to get an adequate amount of Vitamin C. He is considering the possibility of extracting it from scurvy grass.

Because he feels that GPs are put off learning about allergy by immense 'door-stop volumes', he has written one small guide, covering mainly inhalants (*Pocket Guide to Allergies*, Arlington Books, 1982), and participated in another, *Allergy Therapeutics* (with A T Adams and J Duberly, Balliere-Tindall, 1982).

Thanks to his particular situation, with both NHS and private patients, and with the help of a wife who is both an allergic herself and an excellent cook, Dr E feels that he never loses sight of the patient's point of view, and that he can offer both support and practical help.

Chapter 10

Allergy and Electricity

'The police told me: "This boy needs help" ':
Mary Johnson* talks about her son Stephen,* age 19

Stephen is nineteen now. He's had health problems all his life, almost since birth. Oddly enough, his twin brother has always thrived. The only thing that's wrong with him is short sight, while Stephen's sight is fine.

Anyway, by the time he was fourteen months old he was wasting away with constant sickness and diarrhoea. His brother was really bonny. People in the street used to say: 'You can tell which one's your favourite!' Daft things like that. Even the doctor said I must be treating them differently, but that just wasn't so. When he got offensive motions, my GP said it was a sign of malnutrition. I didn't understand it. I was feeding him all the good things, and yet at fourteen months he only weighed 13lbs.

When he was fifteen, he was seen by a consultant and he was taken into hospital for four months. They discovered he was a coeliac. We had to follow a special diet, and with the help of the hospital doctor I worked things out. It wasn't just no wheat or no rye. Barley was dreadful, and oats. It went straight through him. As for soya, when I tried it it nearly killed him. That was in 1979: I got special soya bread on prescription, and though it's not nice to say it, there was water just pouring out of his bottom. He lost 1½ stone in two weeks. The only thing he'd had different was the soya bread. I cut it out and he put the weight back on again.

Then his marvellous hospital doctor died, and Stephen began to get worse. Last May, in the space of a month, everything went wrong. He was made redundant. He lost his wallet with all his money. He had accidents on his motor bike. He got concussion and a broken nose.

Then one day he went to call on someone, found they were out, and broke into their house. He left his motor bike outside and his helmet on the doorstep. He sat down and helped himself to a drink and he was sitting there smoking when the phone rang. He came to and had no idea what he was doing there. He came back home, and the police came round.

We were sick with worry. We'd never had anything like that before. The children had had their ups and downs, but we'd never had any sort of trouble. The police were very kind. They said there was something odd about it, breaking into somewhere and leaving your bike and helmet right outside.

Then he went into hospital with appendicitis. A week after he got back I dropped him off at a shop, and a little while after I came in the police rang. He'd broken into another house and set fire to it.

My husband said he wanted nothing more to do with him. The police said 'Hang on. Don't cast him off. It doesn't make sense.' Some time before – just like an Enid Blyton story really – he and his mates had found a box of jewellery in a wood. They'd rung up the police and returned it and everything – it turned out to have been dropped after a burglary. So the police said that the way he was behaving was out of character.

The next thing was my mother was rushed into hospital with cancer. Stephen was away in prison for a week. It was a dreadful time. Then almost as soon as he was back we got *another* call from the police. This time it was to say he'd smashed three windows. I told them: 'I wash my hands of him!'

The police were still puzzled. They said: 'This boy needs help.'

Then, by sheer chance, Stephen's solicitor heard Dr Lester talking on the Jimmy Young Show about diet and violence and so on, and he rang me and said that it sounded to him as though this could be what was the matter with Stephen. I didn't believe it. I said: 'Stephen's just gone to the bad.'

But the solicitor persuaded me to take Stephen to see Dr Lester. That was in October. He was put onto the Stone Age diet right away, and in only two weeks the improvement was fantastic. It was though someone had lifted a heavy weight off him. He was more awake, more alert. He began sleeping better. As soon as he cut out coffee he lost his irritability. He was back to being our son again.

He has drops now to help him with things he can't avoid, and to help him cope with foods when he's eating out.

He understands very well what's happening. The testing at Dr

Lester's was interesting. With soya he got very irritable. Rude, yawning, wanting to stop and go home, and nasty with it. I was shocked, but Dr Lester said not to worry, that was just the effects of the soya. I wouldn't have believed it, but now it makes so much sense.

Dr Lester gave evidence in court, and Stephen was put on probation for two years. Now he has a full-time job. He gets himself up and off to work. He's polite. He's a much nicer person! He says himself that he feels much better – he knows where he's going.

Without Dr Lester I don't know where we'd have been. There was no hospital or clinic that could help. Nowhere to go at all. I think the family could have broken up. We've all benefited directly too. We're eating more sensibly. Our 23-year-old daughter had bad eczema, which got much better on the Stone Age diet. Good food at home *works*.

When you read things and you hear people talking about the trouble they're having with their children, I wonder whether it might be the food that gets at them. I've had interesting conversations with other mums.

It was a very frightening experience. Imagine – having the police round three times in one month! I used to dread waiting for him to come back again whenever he went out, and every time the phone rang I was wondering whether it was going to be the police again. I'll never forget it.

'For fifteen years I've been abnormally tired': Anne Masson*, age 48

I've been in good health all my life – except that for the past fifteen years I've been abnormally tired; the sort of fatigue ordinary medicine can't do anything about.

When I work I'm committed; I get a boost of adrenalin and it sees me through. Back home though it was another story. I couldn't seem to get on with anything. I'd no physical energy either – I just knew I wasn't as energetic as most of the people I meet.

My GP thought it was a psychosomatic illness: I was too tired to do what I didn't want to do. Well, I can understand that's what it looked like, but I felt there was more to it than that.

Eight years ago I had skin problems, and was treated with low dose antibiotics. They were effective, but it meant that I had to keep on with them. I wasn't happy about it, so I went to a homoeopath. His treatment worked, up to a point. My skin got better and I felt generally better. He also happened to be an osteopath; when he retired he recommended Dr Lester.

Initially I went to see him about occasional back troubles I had. Then I began to mention a few other things – like my fatigue – and we discussed the problems of modern life. He did a hair test, and found that I was low to very low on minerals. He started me on these, and at the same time he started to talk about the possibility of allergies. It was completely new thought to me. At the same time it made sense. I used to get very rapid increases of weight, and then if I went on a vegetarian diet I'd lose it again just as quickly. It wasn't difficult to accept that certain foods might be harmful to me.

Dr Lester wanted me to go on the Stone Age diet and then reintroduce foods, but I knew I couldn't follow it faithfully. My life and my work are too irregular for me to be able to cope. So instead I went to his clinic for tests. In my first two sessions he found I was allergic to coffee (I was drinking a pint a day) and to tea (about the same); also to wheat, rice, yeast, milk, cheese, oats, corn, and cat's fur. Later, he found I also reacted to some other foods.

Now I avoid what I can, and I have protective drops to help me when I can't. They seem to work well provided I don't eat anything too frequently. I used to want at least eight hours sleep – ten was better. I'd sleep like that day after day. Now I just don't need the same amount of sleep at all. As long as I'm careful about what I eat, I feel much better and much less tired.

Dr John Lester, MB, ChB(Edin), MA(Oxon), FLCO, after qualifying in 1944, worked in hospitals for five years, and then entered general practice. He qualified as an osteopath in 1954, and finally ceased being a GP in 1955. Since then he has specialized in osteopathy and other aspects of complementary medicine, with a particular interest in the effects of electricity on the body.

Dr Lester's concern over what he sees as the misdirection of modern medicine dates back forty years. Very early in his career he became disillusioned with modern synthetic drugs. His first doubts arose when he learned of the consequences of M&B treatments on servicemen in Italy towards the end of the war. When soldiers were found to have VD they were penalized by losing pay. They soon discovered that they could use half the prescribed dose to apparently clear the symptoms, and sell the other half illicitly to a mate in trouble. The consequence was two people incorrectly treated, and the consequent creation of resistant strains of gonorrhoea. Further experiences led him to conclude that antibiotics were a strong weapon – but a double-edged sword. One of the side-effects was to sterilize the gut, killing helpful elements as well as harmful.

Alternative rather than drug-based medicine

He stopped using any but the simplest of drugs – probably not more than six – and used antibiotics only to save life. Initially he encountered a lot of resitance. It took time and effort to explain what he was doing, but he found patients willing to listen and accept.

As he became increasingly concerned about the implications of 'toximolecular' medicine, he turned to osteopathy, vitamins and minerals. He found his osteopathic practice built up almost entirely through references from other patients rather than through doctors. 'I believe that then I only converted one GP a year. Most were either indifferent or openly hostile to my approach.'

Sexual problems and electricity

It was in these very early years, too, that he began to speculate about the effects of electricity on the body. In 1953 he read *Sex Perfection* by Rudolph von Eben (Rider, 1952), a psychiatrist who, concerned about the rising divorce rate and the dissatisfactions of divorcing couples, had concluded that a major cause was the emphasis (usually by the male) on quantity rather than quality: on the frequency of intercourse rather than on the pleasure and satisfaction deriving from it. Finding an Arab couple who could see each other's auras while making love, he asked them to experiment with different approaches. Ultimately he evolved a technique which left them both happy and satisfied even though their love-making took place only once in five days.

In his general practice Dr Lester also had to advise married couples with sexual problems. Each would accuse the other of various faults, and intelligent people would squabble over pointlessly silly things. Following von Eben, he began to wonder whether sexual problems might not also be electrical problems. Human beings are collections of protons and neutrons, taking in electricity from many different sources. He hypothesized that sexual attraction might be at least partly an electrical phenomenon, and a good sexual encounter a way for both partners to neutralize each other.

Having successfully recommended von Eben's approach to

several couples in difficulty, Dr Lester began to consider how far other health problems might also be affected by electricity. He points out that humans are the only animals not continually earthed. In developed countries, and particularly cities, virtually everyone is habitually exposed to electrical induction effects from wires and cables in and around the house. They are also affected by carpets, furnishings and clothes made of man-made fibres; while even ordinary domestic equipment – hair-dryers, televisions, cookers – creates an electro-magnetic environment. Moreover, most are unable to discharge their own electrical production, which should be earthed, because of the insulating effect of bitumen and synthetic soles.

Effects of electrical fields
Moreover, a certain proportion of the population is routinely exposed to high magnetic fields, such as those working with powerful electrical equipment, or living beneath powerlines. (In 1981, Stephen Perry and other demonstrated that significantly more suicides occured at locations of high magnetic field strength.)*

Over the years, Dr Lester has come to conclude that we are all affected by the electrical fields which we encounter. In many – perhaps most – cases, the effects are minimal, but where the exposure is high, or the individual for whatever reason particularly sensitive, then both physical and mental health may be affected.

He has been trying to find a method of assessing patients' electrical sensitivity, though so far without entirely satisfactory results. He also believes that certain individuals may also affect electrical equipment. He remembers one instance when, as he manipulated a patient's leg, an electric fire beside them altered the tone of its low hum in exact rhythm with the flexing and unflexing.

Although he cannot yet rely on any kind of accurate testing, Dr Lester has been encouraged by a number of successes to screen his patients for the possibility of electrical involvement. In nine out of ten cases this is without result, but in the tenth it proves highly successful – often where other approaches have failed.

Patients affected by electricity
He particularly recalls three of his many cases. The first was a man who complained of tired, aching feet, and said that he could now only play nine holes of golf at the weekend. He had seen

*Health Physic, Vol. 41, 267-277.

specialists at a London teaching hospital and been given arteriograms and other tests, but without result. Initially, Dr Lester could find no reason for this problem. However, observing that he was wearing nylon socks, he suggested a change to cotton socks and leather-soled shoes, which resulted in 36-hole games on both days of the weekend. The second was a nine-year-old girl who suffered from terrible nightmares. On switching from nylon nightdresses to cotton, she slept soundly. The third was a woman who used to cause electric sparks whenever she touched her husband in bed. On changing from an electric blanket to three woollen underblankets, the sparks disappeared and 'matrimonial bliss was instantly restored'.

Through his osteopathy, 'earthing' techniques, and treatment with vitamin and mineral supplements, Dr Lester was able to help many of the patients who came to him. Increasingly, though, he became concerned about those who were arriving in ever greater numbers with symptoms which orthodox medicine could not diagnose, and whom he too was failing to treat satisfactorily.

Personal experience of allergy

The clue to a cause for at least a proportion of such patients' ailments emerged through his own illness. In 1979 Dr Lester began to suffer from both physical and mental symptoms. His orthodox colleagues were unable to help other than by offering surgery and tranquillizers. The surgery, he thought, was pointless; a proposal to 'strengthen' his ankles when both his knees and hips were suffering too; and the tranquillizers he rejected.

It never occurred to him that 'allergies' might be the cause of his symptoms, and it was by sheer chance that he shortly afterwards met Dr Mackarness. He agreed to give a talk on osteopathy organized by the Wrekin Trust, and, learning he would be sharing the platform with a doctor who was a complete stranger, he set out to read his books.

Mackarness and individual susceptibility

'My eyes came out on stalks. Here was this chap answering all the questions I wanted to ask.' The idea of 'allergies' or individual susceptibilities he found immediately acceptable. It was a logical extension of the hyperinsulin diet he had used for over twenty years; on minimum carbohydrates, and no tea or coffee, two out of five of his migraine patients had been cured.

In the next few months not only did he largely sort out his own problems through dieting and with the advice of Dr

Mackarness and Dr Mansfield, but he travelled once a fortnight to Basingstoke to sit beside Mackarness in his clinic, and watch how he and his patients worked together.

'I was completely bitten. I knew he was on to something important.' What impressed him particularly was the *instant* and demonstrable reaction of patients to a substance which was adversely affecting them, such as the woman exposed to North Sea gas who fell sound asleep within minutes.

It was while sitting in on a patient consultation with Dr Mackarness that Dr Lester wondered whether one particularly obstinate case might be the result of sensitivity not only to foods but also to electricity. Mrs M was an intelligent woman who had made a 30% recovery through Dr Mackarness's help, but who was deeply frustrated because she seemed unable to make any further progress. She was threatening suicide.

'Earthing' a sensitive patient
'Parts of her story reminded me strongly of my ideas on the damaging effects of electricity in the body. I decided to get her earthed. I prescribed her to sit in a chair or walk with bare feet on the lawn for an hour a day. She was a changed woman overnight, and made a complete recovery. For 2½ years now she has been perfectly okay. She's a good wife and mother and working again as a nurse – a good nurse. Although the hospital where she is knew her before, and although she had a file of notes an inch thick, and although they can see she is well, they still think these ideas about electricity are absolutely stupid.

'Yet I could demonstrate that she is electrically sensitive. When television reporters came to interview her she got angineurotic oedoema – her face and body swelled up and her skin became pink as though she was covered in nettle rash. She thought it might be heat from the lighting, but it was the electricity from the high-voltage cables. I told her to take her tights off and stand on the grass, and it all disappeared in five minutes.'

Patients and treatment
After Dr Mackarness retired to Australia, Dr Lester took over the running of his clinic (now only part-time) at Basingstoke, and also began to use his approach in his own practice. He estimates that over the past three to four years he has seen over five hundred allergic patients: at present he examines between four and five new ones each week. Almost all of these are desperate – patients who have already done the rounds elsewhere.

His treatment varies depending on the symptoms and the individual history. He may use the Stone Age or other alternative diets; he may use intradermal testing, though he now aims to use this for diagnosis as little as possible; and he may also use blood or sweat tests or hair analyses. His goal is to get his patients healthy by whatever method seems the most suitable.

Though he recommends avoidance of known allergens wherever possible, he gives sublingual drops where he feels these will make life liveable for the individual patient.

'There are some things people find it difficult to avoid entirely unless they're going to lead lives like hermits. Moulds are another serious problem. I've had several patients who were made extremely ill by moulds in their house. They moved, and regained their health. I think this is the right solution – not just to give them drops to enable them to stay and still be bombarded by what makes them ill – but it depends on people's finances and their situation. And I get some desperate people who can't eat and so can't live. For them, drops are a crutch: a good method of support.'

Ideal and less ideal foods

Dr Lester divides his patients' foods into four categories:

1. Foods they must never eat at all.

2. Foods that they can eat once every four days, or less frequently, protected by drops if necessary.

3. Foods they can eat occasionally (when out for a meal, for example); again protected by drops if essential.

4. Foods it is quite unnecessary for them to ever eat at all.

He emphasizes the importance of rotation, and the avoidance of repeating favourite foods. He also gives what he calls his shopping list:

1. Good foods grown naturally in a pollution-free environment.

2. Good foods grown organically and polluted only by rain-water and air.

3. Foods grown with chemicals, but otherwise untampered with.

4. Foods tarted up and preserved: waxed apples, painted and smoked fish, tinned foods, coloured foods, packaged foods.

5. Non-foods, which are pure chemical substances: mono-sodium glutamate, saccharine, etc.

Shopping for foods only above line 3 is ideal; for some
people, essential. Others must restrict themselves even more
severely, and are unable to venture beneath line 2 without risk
of severe illness.

Extreme reactions to minute allergens
'Some individuals can't tolerate even a minute dose of something
that's bad for them – whether it's a food or a preservative or a
colouring. I remember one patient being tested with .05ml of
altenaria – a mould – who became absolutely unmanageable.
She tried to bite my arm, she called me all the names under the
sun, and it took three of us to keep her from breaking the place
up.

'She'd been treated by a psychiatrist for fifteen years as a
schizoid. She was heading for divorce. She was violent. She'd
hit her husband over the head. When she was bad her eyes
would cross as though she were drugged. She'd ring me up and
accuse me of running off with all her money.

'She reacted dramatically to all her positive tests. On phenol
she was on the floor in thirty seconds. On milk she reverted to a
five-year-old. Animal dander was one of the worst.

'Interestingly, she had been perfectly normal until she'd
married; she was a farmer's wife. The animal dander and the
mould proved the principal triggers. She was a nurse: she could
drink tea safely at work, but back home in her mouldy house the
tea would have a strong effect.

'They both moved away from their old house, and she's now
absolutely cured.'

Case histories
Dr Lester is certain that many physical and mental symptoms
would disappear if only doctors were trained to recognize the
clues to the causes. He instances two very different cases.

The first is a 3½-year-old boy who had been seeing a
paediatrician for a year. He had been having from 5 to 20 stools a
day, had been constantly ill and on antibiotics for a whole year,
and had failed to gain any weight at all. After ten days on the
Stone Age diet plus Nystatin he had put on a pound in weight,
was down to one or two stools a day, and had become 'a
delightful little child. His mother was enthralled. Before, she
hadn't known where to turn.'

The second was a young man of 29. After fourteen days on the
Stone Age diet neither his father nor his hospital could
recognize him – his father reported that he had had his first

intelligent conversation with him for months. His previous diet had included at least thirty cups of tea with two teaspoons of sugar per cup, plus plenty of sweets and Coca-Cola. 'Unfortunately he went straight back on to the Coke again and went sky-high. Now he's in a straight-jacket. I don't know how to handle him. He needs to be in an understanding hospital environment for three months on a strict diet. Then he'd see the results for himself, and would have the motivation to persevere. As it is, he's likely to be dependent on the state for ever.'

Effects on criminal behaviour

He estimates that possibly 30% of inmates of detention centres and prisons are there as the result of the diets they have followed in the past, and of the institution food they are then given. He points out that the cost of keeping them rises all the time, and yet no one seems prepared to authorize wholesome diets, even experimentally. The practical and investigative work in the States of criminologists such as Alexander Schauss (*Diet, Crime and Delinquency*: Parker House, 1981) demonstrates what can be done, through the consideration and application of the principles of sound nutrition, to reduce certain types of violent and motiveless crime.

Causes of allergies

Dr Lester is very much concerned with speculations about the possible causes of allergies. He sees as two possible causes the deficiency of essential fatty acids and the presence of thrush. If the deficiency is made good or the thrush cured – neither of which is easy – then the allergies often melt away.

'Essential fatty acids are the essence of the membranes of every single cell in the body. If we eat second-rate fats – hydrogenated fats – which we encounter all the time in cakes and biscuits, then the cells themselves can be damaged. If there is eczema of the cell membranes, it's hardly surprising if there's also eczema of the stomach or the skin.'

Attacks on the immune system

He has no idea of the causes of mould yeast in the body, but he feels it may be an indication that 'we are already one rung down the ladder.

'The immune system is being attacked all the time by chemicals, additives, junk food. A Rolls Royce is a Dinky toy compared to the intricacy of the human body, and unlike feeding a car with petrol and oil, feeding the body affects and can alter its very structure. If we're not built of the right materials, we get the wrong format of energy.'

Dr Lester believes that for some – possibly many – people today the basic functioning of the body is changing: either because their immune system has totally broken down and cannot cope, or because the yeast infection is turning the intestine into a colander rather than a sieve, and is therefore letting through into the blood stream and lymphatics large, undigested molecules of foods and chemicals. Normally, with good digestion, proteins are broken down into small blocks from which the body can rebuild its own proteins; with bad digestion, or an impaired intestine, these undigested larger molecules may instead be absorbed into the body. They are foreign to it, and are treated as such, thus causing allergic or intolerant reactions.

He considers that the use of sublingual drops or injections is preventive rather than corrective; the immune system is warned of what's ahead and gathers its forces to cope. What actually takes place is only speculation.

If, for example, a patient is known to react to wheat, is it to the wheat itself or to the chemicals in the wheat? If the body subsequently reacts to organically grown wheat, is it because it is still carrying traces of chemicals, or because the body is used to recognizing a molecule of wheat + chemicals, and then continues to react in the same way to a pattern of wheat only, since it is unable to distinguish between the two?

'At present this is simply idle curiosity, since it's virtually impossible to find wheat which is purely organically grown. It will take years to get rid of traces of chemicals in the earth. The question itself, however, is important.'

Resistance to medical innovations

Dr Lester feels that in general the medical profession is firmly closing its eyes to the work that he and his colleagues are doing. He resents the attitude and the opposition that he encounters.

'If the orthodox medical profession is so good, why haven't they already cured the patients who come to us? Even if what they think we have is only a magic wand, why aren't they in there waving it too?

'They can't see the wood for the trees. They sit in the back seat and talk about double-blind tests. Has anyone ever done double-blind tests on tartrazine? They produce opinions and we produce results, yet they *still* refuse to consider what we're doing.

'I produced a set of ten slides demonstrating medical stubborness, and another ten non-medical ones. There's Lind and his work on oranges and limes and prevention of scurvy: even after the Royal Navy finally took it up it was another ten years before the Merchant Navy followed their example. There was Brown and his long struggle to get anaesthetics accepted. Mesmer faced hell over his proposals on hypnosis: now it's used and taught. Sauerbruch's work on surgery on the thorax had to wait thirty years before it was adopted. One of the saddest cases is Semmelweis. When he insisted in the lying-in ward at the Vienna General Hospital in the 1840s that doctors coming from dissecting corpses should wash their hands before attending his patients, he cut down puerperal fever deaths from 20%-30% to 1%. His reward was to be driven out of the hospital and out of the country. He saw his ideas resisted for twenty years, and finally died in an insane asylum.

'I have no doubt that this approach too will be adopted in the end. It is just a tragedy that so many people will continue to suffer in the interim, and often be accused of being "neurotic" or looking for attention, told that their illness doesn't exist at all or that it's purely psychosomatic. No one has *ever* yet demonstrated a psychosomatic illness.

'I was going to include Rachel Carson in my list, but I recently heard that the States are going to produce a commemorative stamp for her. It shows that things can change and do change – even today.'

Dr Lester was awarded the first prize at the 2nd Clinical Ecology competition, in 1982, for his paper on 'Are allergic patients safe going all-electric?'

Chapter 11

Techniques of Measurement

'I was told I had MS. I thought I would never recover':
Pat Hobson, age 49

(First interview)
My father, my sister and my daughter all have a background of
allergies. My sister and my daughter were both very difficult
feeders as babies. My sister could only take carrot juice for the
first six months.

MS first manifested itself in 1968, and then again in 1973.
Between 1976 and 1979 I had several periods in hospital. My
sight was affected, and also my balance. Walking became
difficult.

I found it very difficult to obtain any information from the
medical profession. I really couldn't afford to be ill or out of
action, so I decided to find out about recent research into MS,
and see what I could do to get myself well again. I'm a biology
teacher, and my scientific background certainly helped me.

I started by going with my daughter to Newcastle to see
Professor E J Field who has a diagnostic test for MS. He
confirmed that I had MS, but my daughter hadn't. He prescribed
Naudicelle capsules: evening primrose oil, containing linoleic
acid, gamma-linolenic acid and two other fatty acids. He
explained that, while this was not a cure, it would give me longer
between attacks, and they would be less severe. This is exactly
what happened. (MS attacks the myelin sheath surrounding
part of our nervous system, and Naudicelle helps by supplying
the correct fatty acids to make myelin. I still take six Naudicelle
capsules a day.)

I also heard of and joined ARMS – the Action for Research
into Multiple Sclerosis (page 248) – which proved a great help. I

learned that diet seemed to be involved, and I tried the one they recommended. When I cut out fatty foods, ate green vegetables and fruit, more fish and liver and less red meat, I felt a lot better.

At the same time, I read that some people benefited by cutting out gluten, and I also discovered that there was such a thing as individual food sensitivity. After I read Dr Mackarness's book I wrote to him, but he could only treat patients in the Basingstoke area. I needed to find a doctor in the north-west who could treat for food sensitivity. I certainly didn't see any point in giving up my favourite foods unless I had evidence that they were actually harming me.

Then one day, by chance, someone called on me who'd been to Dr Kenyon, and I discovered that he had evolved his own food sensitivity test. I first went to see him in April 1981. He found that I was sensitive to wheat, corn, cow's milk and dairy produce. With great difficulty I eliminated all these from my diet. I actually got withdrawal symptoms when I gave up milk – which was very odd!

When I first saw Dr Kenyon I had already improved, but I was still ill. I could only walk for short distances. I had no energy at all. Within weeks of my first visit I was feeling completely well. I was able to walk with ease. By Whit I was able to decorate and – to my delight – could even climb a ladder and paint a ceiling. I also lost 1½ stone in weight.

(Two years later)
I have remained absolutely well ever since. Recently, I've been under a lot of strain and stress – I've been made deputy head of a large Liverpool comprehensive – but I've had no recurrence of MS. As long as I take the Naudicelle, and keep off fatty foods, wheat, corn, cow's milk and cheese, I'm very well. The symptoms (numbness, tingling in the legs etc.) will return if I have a period when I eat the wrong foods. For example, I was away at Easter and it was all vegetarian cooking – really delicious, but all things I can't eat, such as wheat and cheese, and I didn't want to make a fuss, so I ate it. I wasn't very well for two or three weeks afterwards.

In 1983, a consultant at the Royal Liverpool Hospital said that he could find no evidence of MS at that time. Except for having to be careful, I have no problems at all.

'It's costing me a lot of money! I have to have all new clothes!':
Thomas Bolton, age 47

(First interview)
When I first went to see Dr Kenyon, I'd had asthma or bronchitis – the GP was never sure which – for ten years. I'd had prick tests years before, but they didn't find anything. I never for one moment thought of allergies. To my mind, it had all started when I broke my nose three times playing rugby. The asthma began then. I'd never had anything before.

It got worse and worse. All my GP ever gave me was painkillers. I'm a self-employed builder, and as time went by I was taking twelve weeks each year off work. I was 16st 7lbs, and I was on drugs five or six times a day. By last Christmas I'd thrown in the towel. I'd given up all hope. The doctors could do nothing. They never said anything about food. In fact they weren't interested at all at the finish. I'd tried everything you could get from the chemist, but nothing made any difference.

Then the relative of a friend of mine said to see Dr Kenyon. I knew nothing about this kind of treatment, but I knew the relative had had a lot more ease, and I thought: 'Let him have a go.'

He found I was allergic to milk, beef, pork, diesel fumes, wheat, citrus fruits, dust, dust mites and cigarette smoke. Seven days later I got drops through the post for five different things. I took them for a full week and then went back. I got a second lot of drops sent. Now I've come in for the last lot.

After a full week I gradually took less and less of the drugs. After a fortnight I wasn't taking any at all. It was the first time I'd been clear of asthma in ten years.

In the nine weeks since I first came I've lost two stone. I feel a lot better for it. It's costing me a lot of money! I have to have all new clothes! Food – I've always liked food, but I've stuck to it. It's been a hard slog, but well worth it.

(Two years later)
I'm 300% better than when I first went to see Dr Kenyon. I've never had asthma since. I've never needed to use the breathers again – and I was using them five or six times a day before I saw him. Just a little bit of a something when the pollen count's high. I go to Dr Kenyon's successor, for a check-up twice a year, but there's nothing wrong with me at all. A little bit of raised blood pressure at the moment because I've put on weight again, and I'm going to have to see to that. Apart from that, I'm fine. †

Dr Julian N Kenyon, MD, MB, ChB, graduated from Liverpool Medical School in 1970. After two surgical house jobs he went on to do conventional surgery, and then taught anatomy for a year before gaining his primary FRCS at Edinburgh. After his MD, he returned to Liverpool to the Department of Child Health. In 1974 he decided to leave surgery and enter general practice. At the same time he began to study acupuncture, and in 1976 he resigned in order to travel and to study alternative medicine in depth. On his return from Europe and China he re-entered general practice while also offering specialist clinical ecology treatment privately. In 1982 he left the NHS to set up, with a colleague, a centre to teach, research into, and treat patients with alternative therapies.

When he first qualified, Dr Kenyon was drawn by 'the interest and glamour' of surgery; but before long he found himself questioning the rationale for some of the procedures he was helping to carry out. In particular, much of the open-heart and lung cancer surgery horrified him. In some cases he wondered whether the operations were of any benefit to the patients at all.

Conventional and alternative medicine
In 1975 Ivan Illich's *Medical Nemesis* appeared (republished as *Limits to Medicine*, Penguin, 1976). This book, with its account of the damaging side-effects of drug-based medicine, had a considerable influence on him. His subsequent move to general practice was, he felt, a step in the right direction, yet he remained depressed at 'how little positive good mainstream medicine was accomplishing. I was impressed by the success of alternative approaches; also by their innocuousness, at a time when patients never seemed to do as well as promised by the drug advertising I was reading. This was particularly the case with those on anti-depressants.'

His early forays into acupuncture both stimulated and frustrated him. In his experiments with chronic pain patients, those whom conventional medicine found it difficult to help, he 'was pleased and surprised' that he could actually improve their condition. On the other hand, he found it difficult at that time to get clear and accurate descriptions of acupuncture and its effects.

He began to see illness and health from a different point of view from that instilled by his training. Conventional medicine, he concluded, was interested primarily in big changes in the body; in alternative medicine, a minute alteration could be significant. He was later to feel that this was particularly true of the early symptoms of allergy, which often begin as small shifts in the pattern of the body's functioning: a warning that a change is taking place and damage is being done. It is when the warning is not heeded and the symptoms merely suppressed that the damage spreads and intensifies.

He felt that many of the questions he was asking could only be answered abroad. During his extensive travels from 1976 to 1980, he studied auricular therapy with Dr Paul Nogier; the relevance of electrical measurement from Dr Reinholdt Voll; and aspects of acupuncture from Dr J Yoo. He visited China to examine classical Chinese ways of teaching acupuncture; and studied desensitization from an American colleague, Dr Tom Lambert.

He was fascinated by the connections he observed between acupuncture, homoeopathy, and clinical ecology. 'The important element, the link, is what the Chinese call "chi" – vital energy, biological energy. The force that means we're living and not dead.' He began to see the human body as affected by, and in its turn affecting, electrical phenomena. Where the body's chi was attacked, either by a damaged organ or by a substance harmful to it, the consequent normal supply of bioelectric energy would be impaired. His experience and conclusions were increasingly to influence his work and his treatment of patients.

Pre-1982 patients
On his return to England, Dr Kenyon set up in practice in Liverpool, first as a GP and later as a private specialist. Over the next few years he found that the number of his patients with illnesses caused by food or chemical allergies was growing all the time. By 1982, shortly before he left his northern practice, he estimated that these amounted to 40% of his cases. These were, however, to a considerable extent self-selected. Many suspected sensitivity already, some had been specifically diagnosed, and others came through AAA or patients' support groups. Approximately 20% were directly referred by GPs or specialists. Although some came from many different parts of the country, the majority were from within a hundred-mile radius.

Post-1982 patients
Since his move south in 1982, the pattern of his work has changed and so to some extent have his patients. He spends a larger proportion of his time in research and teaching; and his patients now come from all over the world: from Europe in particular, but also from the United States, Australia, New Zealand, and Africa. Many of them come specifically to be tested

electrically, mainly as a result of his writings (especially *Modern Techniques of Acupuncture*, Thorsons, 1983).

Electrical responses

Over the years the techniques he uses to diagnose and treat ecological illness have also changed. Initially he began by using elimination and rotation diets, but found he had problems – not least from patients' reactions. 'Some of them honestly believed that five days on lamb and pears was next door to a death sentence.'

Instead, he began to use other methods to detect allergy. As a result both of his own and other scientists' observations and experience, Dr Kenyon views the human body as 'an enormously complex piece of electrical machinery, which may have faults in different places, with each fault potentially producing many different effects'.

Not only can the body be affected by external electrical influences, but there is a field immediately surrounding it which can both detect and relate to causes within that field. 'Not only can healers who pass their hands immediately over the surface of a wound or a painful part of the body feel a sensation of warmth; so can ordinary detached observers.' Dr Kenyon believes that the body can detect a harmful substance held close to it and within its field, and will react by producing minute changes in its electrical responses. When an organ within the body is unhealthy, it is unable to maintain a normal supply of energy, and this deficiency too – with the right instruments in the hands of the right person – can be measured. These are the responses which Dr Kenyon, using different techniques, has been measuring over the past seven years.

Auricular cardiac reflex therapy

The first method he adopted was one he had learned from Dr Nogier in France: auricular cardiac reflex therapy (ACR).

Dr Kenyon explains its operation by asking the observer to imagine a sausage skin full of water. If one end is tapped repeatedly, waves are set up, which reach the other end and then bounce back. Where waves from opposite directions encounter each other, there is interference. The resultant wave will have fixed peaks and fixed troughs. This is an image of what happens within the artery. To feel the phenomenon, the observer's thumb should be placed at right angles to the radial artery.

When a substance to which an individual patient is allergic is brought close to the body in a 'sympathetic' area, the body reacts. Dr Kenyon uses small glass bottles of each suspect substance, and holds them one at a time immediately below the ear. Provided the thumb is in the correct position on the artery, the observer will detect what feels like a strengthening of the pulse beat. This is the reaction called by Dr Nogier and Dr Kenyon an auricular cardiac reflex.

This change has nothing to do with the pulse rate. What has happened is that there has been a response to the allergen by the autonomic nervous system, and as a result the whole of the standing wave has pushed, very slightly, in the direction of the patient's fingers, so that the higher amplitude of the wave is now moving beneath the observer's thumb.

'The ACR is a measurement of electro magnetic change.' If the patient is highly allergic to that substance, there may be more than thirty ACRs; if only moderately allergic, there will be between ten and thirty ACRs; if not allergic at all, possibly one and certainly not more than four.

It is possible to use this method not only to detect potential allergens but – by holding ever weaker dilutions close to the patient in the same way – to establish the correct one to provide the turn-off point, which is reached when no further positive ACR is felt.

In the first five years of his clinical ecology investigations, this was the method Dr Kenyon adopted most frequently. During this time he estimates that he diagnosed 1500 patients in this way, 80% of whom, with subsequent treatment, were significantly improved.

Responses at acupuncture points

He proceeded to test those who failed to respond to this approach with a system evolved in the 1950s by Dr Voll in Germany. It uses a piece of equipment known as the Dermatron to measure changes in electrical responses at acupuncture points.

The assumption is that the various points are connected in some way to various organs of the body. Dr Kenyon is uncertain how direct this connection is; he merely observes that the system works and gives results.

The acupuncture point, which can be anything from ⅛ to 3 inches (3-75mm) beneath the skin depending on the fleshiness of the particular area, acts as a capacitor. When the measurement probe attached to the Dermatron is moistened and pressed on to the skin at the acupuncture point, a small direct current of 8-10 amperes, at a voltage of approximately 1 volt, is applied. The ability of the point to resist this current is then measured and shown on the indicator. The power of the applied current has been calculated and adjusted so that a normal acupuncture point will be able to withstand this power, in such a way that the reading on the voltmeter should be around 50 (though in city surroundings a normal reading may be between 65 and 80).

Provided the reading is not above 80 or below 50, and stays stable, the point is healthy. But if the initial reading is above or below or if – which happens more frequently – the initial reading does not stay stable but begins to drop, this is an indication that the connected organ may be diseased: it is lacking the vital force which would enable it to resist the measured applied current. The operator can thus deduce which organs in the body may be unhealthy, indicating potential sources of the patient's problems.

Remedies

To find the appropriate remedy in such cases, Dr Kenyon uses a small independent transmitter to scan his collection of over two thousand bottles of toxins, bacilli, foods and chemicals. He continues to press the probe at the relevant acupuncture point, and watches the Dermatron indicator as he moves the transmitter over the bottles. When the indicator moves back towards the norm, he removes the remedy the transmitter has identified and checks it separately. He may find two or more remedies so indicated.

He then places the bottles containing the substances in a metal holder attached to the unit, and another bottle containing only water in another holder. He then gives the patient two metal tubes to hold and switches on the machine. After a brief pause, the water has combined the effects of the remedy or remedies.

'I know it sounds extraordinary. I have no real idea how or why it works. All I know is that it does.

'The remedies chosen are aetiological – they say something about that patient's illness. I find that these responses often indicate earlier viral infections, exposures to toxins, to dental work or drug therapy or vaccinations. Often these have happened to the patient some time in the past, even years before, yet they've caused damage which is only picked up when they are tested like this. I had one patient who was unable to walk. Part of her problem was identified, by this method, as exposure to Paraquat. When I asked her, she confirmed that she had indeed been exposed to it, but many years earlier. She hadn't thought to mention it, and hadn't connected it with her present illness. Now, with homoeopathic remedies, she's walking again.

'It may be that food and chemical sensitivities are only secondary phenomena, and perhaps earlier exposure to such episodes is the primary phenomenon. But then again it may be true only of the small percentage of patients I treat this way, and not the majority that I can sort out more easily.'

Vega testing

Dr Kenyon's third and most recently adopted system uses a Vega electrical test device, which is a version of a Wheatstone bridge. Like the ACR, it tests the electrical response of the body, through probes pressed on the finger-tips, to substances placed within the circuit. This response is then translated and measured on a dial.

In Dr Kenyon's opinion, this does no more than reproduce the same measurements that he can make using Dr Nogier's method, yet it does possess certain advantages. It is simple to learn to use; it is cheap; and because patients can see the responses for themselves they find it easier to believe that changes are actually taking place. It gives them the motivation to persevere with the management of their illness.

Unfortunately there is also one great drawback. The responses are not wholly objective: they can be influenced by the mind of the practitioner. Dr Kenyon estimates that he has taught himself to operate the Vega and translate its results with 80% accuracy, but it is difficult to make the method teachable, and the subjective element involved makes it unacceptable to orthodox medicine.

Electrical scanning

One further method, which Dr Kenyon uses only for selected and complex patients, involves testing with a segmental electrogram. This is a simple electrical scanning device which – unlike Vega testing – cannot be affected by the practitioner's subjective views. It is helpful in identifying affected organs, as it measures their function and functional inter-relationships and reproduces reactions in graphic form.

He finds this particularly useful for patients with multiple sensitivities. He now concludes that, for most of these, the underlying cause is colonic dysfunction. The majority have severe gastrointestinal symptoms. When the affected organs are identified, then all of them must be treated; normally this involves at least the pancreas and liver as well as the colon.

Reactions to chemicals

Many of the severely allergic patients – and others who are less affected – are highly sensitive to chemicals. Dr Kenyon observes that in some cases 'sensitivity' or 'intolerance' are the wrong words: his patients have been *poisoned*. He has treated twenty-two patients badly affected by pesticides; there are others where similar exposure is suspected but cannot be proved. As he points out, toxins may remain in the body fats for years, long after any initial exposure has been forgotten.

Wherever possible, the ideal first step for all such patients is removal from any further exposure, but they are often either unable or unwilling to undertake this. Among his current patients is one who lives next door to strawberry fields. She has been severely affected by the fruit-farmer's spraying; she refuses to be driven out of her home: yet there are, at present, no legal restrictions on her neighbour's right to damage her health and her surroundings.

When patients are poisoned in this way, their immune system is affected. They become additionally vulnerable to stress, illness and viral infections. It is possible to remove toxins homoeopathically but it takes time, and it is a never-ending task as long as the patient continues to be re-exposed.

Current treatment

At present Dr Kenyon see five hundred new patients a year, as does his colleague, Dr George Lewith. A recent study by medical students into two months' patients' inflow showed that 70-80% of these were completely or considerably helped. He still finds that multiple-sensitive patients present major problems, and he estimates that he can help only 50-60% of these.

Dr Kenyon will use any treatment which seems indicated by his diagnoses and tests. While he gives priority to complete avoidance of foods and chemicals, it is clear that this is often impossible. He will then prescribe neutralizing drops, homoeo-pathic remedies, vitamin or mineral supplements, depending on individual circumstances. He feels that it is also important to replace normal bacteria in the bowel, which may have been destroyed by drug therapies: using yogurt and preparations containing *E coli*.

Research into electrical phenomena

His major preoccupation remains, as it has been for several years, research into new ways to examine the electrical phenomena of illness, and new technology to detect this and make it objectively visible to others.

'Allergy is, in my view, primarily an electrical phenomenon which, if it continues long enough, may eventually produce various serological and eventually anatomical changes in the patient.'

At this stage what is urgently needed is further research into all these areas. Dr Kenyon has recently applied for a grant to enable him to design and build equipment to detect and translate into visual terms subtle electrical change in and around the body. Provided the funds can be raised, the project will be carried out at the Department of Electronics, University of Southampton. He hopes that this will help to stimulate the interest of many more scientists into what he considers will prove a very fruitful field for investigation.

Dr Kenyon has also edited or contributed to a number of specialized books on these approaches. Among them are:

Electrographic Imaging in Medicine and Biology, by Ioan Dumitrescu: Neville Spearman Publishers, 1983

The Treatment of Disease using Complex Homoeopathy, Volume 1, by Helmut Schimmel: Vega Grieshaber GmbH & Co

The Short Manual of the Vegatest Method, by J Fehrenback et al: Vega Grieshaber GmbH & Co

The Segmental Electrogram (SEG), by H W Schimmel and B Grieshaber: Vega Grieshaber GmbH & Co.

Chapter 12

Healers

**'It got really embarrassing when we were eating with friends':
Ronald Ashby, age 41**

I'm from a farming family, so we've always had good food and
plenty of milk. I was breast-fed for eleven months, and then I
went on to milk from our own cows and proper food mashed up
– just what the rest of the family had. I had a perfectly normal
healthy childhood. I did have my tonsils taken out at five, so the
doctors must have thought something was wrong, though I
gather they used to whip them out for anything then.

I got married fifteen years ago and we went to live with my in-
laws. I think my problems probably started then. We had
different milk, and tap water. Before, we had our own water
from a deep-bore well. The problems started very gradually and
built up over a period. Four or five years ago I began getting
bothered. The main thing was that I was having two or three
bowel movements every day, which I knew wasn't normal. A
friend said maybe it was the start of ulcerative colitis, which he'd
had.

I began to watch my diet. We'd always had good mixed foods
and our own vegetables, but I did drink a lot of tea – up to six
cups a day. So I thought it might be the tea, because half an hour
after I drank the first one I'd be off to the loo. I switched to coffee,
and that seemed just as bad. I wondered if it could be sweets,
because I was always fond of them, but that didn't seem to make
any difference either.

By the middle of last year it was getting to be a real nuisance.
I'd be off several times a day to the bathroom. It was getting
embarrassing, especially if we were having a meal with friends.
Half-way through I'd have to leave the table, and of course

they'd think it was their food that had caused it.

When it came to Christmas, my wife said it was time to get help. I went to my GP, who said to cut out foods with preservatives and anything that didn't agree with me. That wasn't much use, because we mostly only eat fresh foods anyway, and of course I wasn't eating anything I *knew* didn't agree with me. At the same time I didn't go into the whole history of what was happening, and he said I looked healthy enough.

My wife heard about Dr Cox through friends. I went to see him three months ago, had a full examination, and was put on the Stone Age diet. We've still got some foods to test, but so far the main one for me is definitely milk – though most mild cheese and butter is all right – followed by sweetcorn and beet sugar.

Within a few days my trips to the loo were down to once every 24 hours. I lost over a stone in one month: from 12 stone 6lbs to 11 stone 4½lbs. I do a lot of physical work, and I used to get tired very quickly. Now I don't. I'm 100% better.

'I couldn't wear back-fastening dresses any more': Sheila Wilson,* age 41

I never really had health problems when I was younger, except that I used to get bronchitis most winters: but my mother got asthma and my father had severe depressions.

Four years ago I began to get arthritic pains, starting in my shoulders and spreading down my back and across my hips. I couldn't wear back-fastening skirts or dresses – it was too much of a struggle to do them up and the fasteners pressed painfully on my spine. My GP said it was old age coming on – I was only 37! He sent me for a blood test, and prescribed aspirin and other pain-killers.

I didn't like taking the drugs. Instead I went to see Dr Cox. This was two years ago. He put me on the Stone Age diet, and we found I was allergic – though only mildly – to about thirty things, particularly to beef, cereals, onions, dairy produce, yeast, pork and tomatoes. I also reacted to a lot of inhalants.

I had desensitizing drops, which worked well. I used them for eighteen months, and now I don't need them any more. All my aches and pains have gone. There are bonuses as well. I used to get bad pre-menstrual tension, and that's gone too. I used to wake up every day with a fizzy feeling in my arms, but not any more.

I have to keep to a strict rotation diet, and I take Nalcrom occasionally to protect me when I'm eating out, but otherwise I'm absolutely fine.

Richard Wilson,* age 14

Last year, just before Christmas, I was very worried about my exams and developed asthma. In April I went with my mother to see Dr Cox. I had blood samples taken and sent to York. A month before the summer exams I left out all the things that the tests said I shouldn't have. I felt much better, I didn't have asthma, and I got higher marks. Now I keep to a rotation diet. I used to have bad hay fever before, but I don't now.

(His mother: He used to have skin problems too, but he never has spots now. That's the main reason he keeps to his diet!)

Dr Hugh Cox, MB, ChB, MRCS, LRCP, MRCGP, DRCOG, DCH, a founder member of the British Society of Clinical Ecology, qualified at Birmingham in 1951 and then worked for a year with the Birmingham teaching hospitals. He briefly entered general practice on the Isle of Wight before returning to further hospital jobs in Birmingham, Edinburgh and Warwick, ending with a stint at the Manchester group of hospitals which lasted until 1959. After a short session as Consultant Physician at the Burnley group of hospitals, he left medicine to carry out research in the pharmaceutical industry.

For the next eight years he divided his time between research (primarily into oral contraceptives and medicines acting on the reproductive system) and lecturing on allied topics world-wide. Two years later he returned to general practice in Buckinghamshire, where he has remained ever since.

Over the fifteen years in his present practice there has been a radical change in his attitude. When he started as a GP – perhaps because of his pharmaceutical background – he found himself prescribing more than the average number of drugs; and yet the patients were not 'cured'. They kept returning, with either the same or additional symptoms. Then in 1977 he attended a conference in Oxford on nutrition arranged by the McCarrison Society (page 247).

Practical steps to improved health
'It made a lot of sense. I began to look at nutrition in all sorts of ways I hadn't before. For example: I knew that in laboratory

experiments bacteria cultures in broths grew much faster if you added sugar. I wondered whether the same thing might not happen in children's mouths. I had children whose mothers kept bringing them back time and again with tonsillitis, sore throats and so on. I explained to them what might be the cause, and they agreed to keep their children away from sugary foods and drinks. I believe that this proved the main break-through in our practice.'

He estimates that the results cut his work-load by 25%. Persistently-ill children no longer reappeared in his surgery. Following from this, he began to look increasingly at the diets of his patients, and had the satisfaction of seeing improvements in health from the changes he suggested.

After the publication of Mackarness's book, in 1978 he started to use exclusion and elimination diets. The following year he attended the conference in London at which members of the US Clinical Ecology group spoke, and shortly afterwards became one of the sixteen founder members of the British Clinical Ecology group. In June 1980 he began using desensitizing techniques.

Complementary medicine
At the same time he became increasingly interested in other branches of complementary medicine. He studied acupuncture with Felix Mann in London in 1980; trained with the British Association of Manipulative Medicine from 1979 to 1981, followed by courses with the Society of Orthopaedic Medicine; and has taken numerous courses in homoeopathy since his original qualification at the Royal College of Homoeopathy in 1976.

Clinical ecology in general practice
Today, he uses the clinical ecology approach on at least 50% of his NHS patients. However, he points out that his general practice is not typical. Because of its situation, he probably sees a higher proportion of those with above-average income. It is also a *non-smoking* practice: he will not accept onto his panel anyone who continues to smoke. (He recently agreed to carry out research into bronchitis, and set aside one evening a week to examine and analyse the problems of sufferers. The research ended there. No one came: there is no bronchitis in the practice.) The general incidence of illness is low. He sees comparatively few patients in his NHS surgeries, and is rarely called out at night. He constantly stresses the importance of diet

and a complete environmental approach.

Private patients
Privately, he sees between two to three new patients a day. They come from all over the country and from abroad. Those who have travelled a distance and simply turn up he will see without references, but he insists that patients from his own local area have a letter from their own GP. He always writes follow-up letters explaining his methods.

Diagnosis and treatment
He gives each patient a complete physical examination and takes a dietary history; he sometimes also does biochemical and haematological tests, especially if the patient comes from a distance. His subsequent treatment varies, depending on his assessment of the patient and his/her problems. If he can identify potential hazards straight away, he will tackle these first. He may recommend avoidance, a trial fast, or perhaps a rotation diet; for chemicals he will where necessary use desensitization. He often uses the Stone Age diet, particularly for those for whom other methods are less readily applicable. He also holds one clinic weekly which patients can attend for both identification of allergies and desensitization.

He estimates that he can sort out 90% of his patients relatively easily; most need no desensitization. Of the rest, 5 or 6% are difficult: 4 or 5% are very difficult. He feels that in these cases he can sometimes offer only support rather than active treatment.

Bio-kinesiological techniques
While patients benefit from skin titration, Dr Cox has been trying for some time to evolve a system which would rely less heavily on the subjective evaluation of the patient; could be used to help NHS patients; and would cut costs for private patients. He believes that he is now achieving this through bio-kinesiological techniques, examining the muscle responses to allergens under the tongue, held in the hand, or placed on the skin.

He initially began experimenting along these lines 'as a bit of fun'. Because of his training in acupuncture, with its emphasis on the linking of meridians to the various organs of the body, he started testing the responses of different muscle groups. John Thie and George Goodheart in the USA had already demonstrated a connection between samples of food placed under a patient's tongue and alterations in their muscle potential. Dr Cox felt this method might cause patients' responses – consciously or unconsciously – to be affected by their food likes or dislikes. He began instead to test how muscle reactions responded to *drops* under the tongue, and matched the results with intradermal skin tests carried out in his clinic.

He discovered that they corresponded closely: a dilution of a food concentrate which on injection produced the typical flare and weal would, when placed under the same patient's tongue produce dramatically weakened muscle responses.

He found these reactions very precise, and satisfactory because they were objective, and not under the patient's conscious control. If the muscle responses remained strong, then the substance being tested was not an allergen; if they became weak, then it was. Not only was it an effective method for diagnosis; it could also identify exactly the right dilution which would desensitize the patient. (As succeeding dilutions were tested, when the correct one was reached the muscle response would return to normal.)

Dr Cox next began using these methods on his NHS patients. Since this meant that he had to pay for all the syringes and drops he used, he wondered whether it might be possible to obtain results by observing the muscle response to concentrates placed in closed phials on the skin.

He started by placing them on the navel. He got an identical response – i.e. if the patient's reaction to the allergen was positive, the muscle response was weakened. Emboldened and encouraged by this result, he went on to see whether the result would be the same if the patient merely *held* the phial containing the allergen. It was.

Double-blind tests (where his nurse handed him phials at random so that neither he nor his patient could identify the substances being tested) produced identical responses.

Weakened muscle response = allergic reaction

The method is so simple as to seem bizarre. The patient lies down on the couch and stretches out one arm in three positions: vertically upright, palm turned out; at an angle of 45° to the couch, palm turned down; and flat on the couch with the palm turned out, leaving a gap between it and the body. In each of these three positions Dr Cox, standing beside the couch, and applying pressure with one hand, attempts to push the arm down to the couch or towards the body, while the patient resists. In normal circumstances, with adult patients, it is impossible for Dr Cox (5'6" and weighing 10st.8lb) to force the arm against the patient's will.

The patient is then given a small phial to hold in the other hand containing a food or chemical concentrate diluted in either phenylated saline or plain saline. Again Dr Cox pushes. The patient resists. The result is usually stalemate: the arm stays where the patient is tensing it. On other occasions, though, the arm seems to lose all strength. Using only one finger ('Easy as taking candy from a baby!') Dr Cox can push the arm down to the couch or towards the body. Sometimes this effect is felt at each of the three positions, sometimes in two, sometimes in only one. Each reaction has its own significance. Weakness in all three positions indicates that the patient is severely allergic to the substance being tested.

'This weakness comes as a shock to a lot of people. I've had eighteen-stone lorry drivers demanding to try again and again – they just can't believe it. But when I'm able to demonstrate, by repeating the experiments, that the same results occur every time, they're convinced.

'What I believe happens is that, when the body comes into contact with an allergen, the electrical potential of the allergen interferes with the electrical firing of the motor endplate of a limb locked in position by a group of muscles. I would like to do experiments to measure electrical charges at different points of the body.'

To the best of his knowledge, he is at present the only doctor in the country – possibly in the world – to be using precisely these techniques. 'The tests are very quick. There's no hurt at all. and there's no invasion of the body by potentially harmful substances.' Although the approach is difficult to use at present for children or the elderly because of the necessity to match the physical forces involved, he feels that with experimentation variants of this technique will prove viable.

Surrogate testing

The same method can be used for what he calls 'surrogate testing'. He finds it particularly good for young children, and especially for breast-fed babies with colic. If the mother holds the baby, her muscular reactions to the potential allergens indicate what is affecting her child. When she subsequently removes the foods from her diet, the child's crying stops. Thanks to this and other diet-related investigations, 'infant colic is a thing of the past in this practice.'

Kinesiology and candidiasis

This is also an example, Dr Cox believes, of the help kinesiology can provide in arriving at a correct diagnosis. When in America (he is a member of the American Society of Clinical Ecologists) he spent some time with Orion Truss and William Crook. There, the diagnosis of candidiasis is made primarily on the patient's history, after which the patient is prescribed a course of Nystatin – possibly for as long as two or three years – and a low yeast diet. Dr Cox considers that his kinesiological method can indicate more accurately not only whether or not candidiasis is proving a problem; but can also – through the patient's altered responses – indicate the required dose and meter the continued progress. Some patients may only need to use Nystatin for as little as one month; others for two to three months; others, of course, considerably longer.

Hyperventilation
The hyperventilation syndrome should also not be neglected. This can mimic the symptoms of allergy: wheeziness, asthma, migraines, stomach upsets, and disturbed psychological problems. Women suffer from this more than men – possibly because, being more conscious of their appearance, they try to keep their stomachs flat and so breathe only from their chests; whereas, says Dr Cox, except when exercising, breathing should be primarily abdominal and not thoracic. While not encouraging self-diagnosis on this point, he suggests that a clue that someone may be hyperventilating is the observation that she or he finds it very difficult to pause and relax after exhaling; there is a compulsion to take another instant breath. Sometimes, too – though not always – there may be frequent, heavy sighing. Hyperventilation needs sympathetic medical attention and expert help in retraining breathing techniques.

Symptoms
Some patients come with specific symptoms: migraine, gastro-enteritis, colitis, asthma or arthritis. Others suffer from a general malaise. 'It's not possible to know whether what they're saying of themselves is true or not, and often they have been described as hypochondriacs: yet, when they're questioned as to the existence of other previously unmentioned symptoms, they frequently admit to having experienced them, and indeed may have been treated for them in the past. This points away from a purely psychological diagnosis.'

Case histories
Even with all his experience, Dr Cox is still astonished by the efficacy of this approach.

One patient was a man who had had colitis for seven years; he had been unable to work for five. He had regularly been back to hospital during this time, both for treatment as an in-patient and for routine testing. Finally it was recommended that he should have a colectomy. 'Mr X vacillated; he was attached to his bowel; he didn't want this done.'

He was referred to a Harley Street doctor, and then by him to Dr Cox. He was put on an elimination diet. 'When I saw him five weeks later he'd been working full-time for two weeks laying concrete slabs. He felt very well. When he went back to hospital shortly afterwards for routine tests they were amazed. In fact they suggested that he wasn't the same man! Not only did he have no colitis. He had no ulceration, and no signs of any healed ulcers.

'On his next visit to me he said that not only was he very happppy about the disappearance of the colitis – he'd also lost his permanent catarrh and his smelly feet!'

Dr Cox particularly stresses the importance of this approach for patients who are mentally ill. One of his patients was a teacher who suffered from depression, had had frequent absences from work, and had been an in-patient in a psychiatric hospital. On an elimination diet she discovered that she was allergic to milk, wheat and tap water. With these eliminated, she had no further problems.

A second was a 25-year-old woman who had been suffering from depression for ten years. She had been admitted to a psychiatric hospital on two occasions, was on drugs, and was a regular out-patient. After an elimination diet, during which she discovered she reacted to milk, wheat and potato, she rapidly improved. Three months later she was off all drugs. She was well thereafter, until her husband told her that bread was the staff of life. After eating it she swallowed all the pills in the bathroom cupboard and had to be taken to the hospital to be washed out. The hospital also assured her that she could eat anything she chose. When she came home she did. She broke every window in the house, and all the glass and crockery she could lay her hands on. Her husband phoned Dr Cox. After four days of total fast she was absolutely normal.

It gives him considerable personal satisfaction to know that taking such straightforward steps can make so much difference to people's lives. He remembers a small boy who used to have eczema: 'They don't call me "Scabby" at school any more.' He also recalls a middle-aged woman who had been suffering from severe rheumatoid disease. She had had operations on her wrists, had to use sticks to help her walk, and needed her husband's support every night to get upstairs to bed. After being sorted out through diets, she entertained her whole family to a Christmas party at her home.

Cost-effectiveness of clinical ecology
As Dr Cox points out, this approach not only saves the patients suffering, but the Health Service money. One of his patients had had ulcerative colitis for ten years, during which he had spent three weeks in hospital, had had thirty out-patient consultations, and eight years' continuous medication. Another had had rheumatoid arthritis for twenty years (positive diagnosis with high sedimentation rate): she had had constant medication, two operations on her hands, and over thirty gold injections. Following an elimination diet, both patients needed no further treatment of any kind.

Recently Dr Cox asked the Ministry of Health to look at his prescribing figures. It was found that in 1973 his prescribing costs were 48% higher than the national average. Ten years later his costs were only half of those of his local colleagues, and only 25% of the national average. Although the costs of his vitamin and mineral supplements are much higher than in other practices, he is still saving £80,000 a year in drug bills.

Healing the whole person
Every patient needs individual diagnosis. It is the overall picture which counts, the interplay between individual, family, background and environment; the links between body, mind and spirit. Doctors, however skilled, can only help. They cannot remove the symptoms of ill health without the patient's active participation.

Dr Cox regards himself primarily as a healer who will use whatever method seems most likely to benefit his patient. As a Christian, he works through Christ and with the help of Christ. Each day's clinic opens with prayers, and he will pray for guidance with complex problems. He sees the ecological approach, with its emphasis on searching for natural causes, on living in harmony with the environment, and on accepting a large degree of personal responsibility for mental and physical health, as a natural extension of his personal convictions.

'Oh dear.' That was all anyone said. 'Oh dear.': Jean Lloyd, age 34, talks about Rebecca, now age 5

Rebecca was perfectly healthy all the time she was breast-fed, but from the age of nine months she changed completely. She was never well. She got bronchitis, tonsillitis, chest and ear infections, asthma and eczema. Her eyes were continually glued shut. Though she wanted to be comforted, she didn't like being touched. She cried even when her hair was brushed or her nails were cut.

Her GP suggested she might be allergic to cow's milk, so I switched to goat's milk for a long time. It didn't make any difference. She had ever-increasing amounts of antibiotics, Ventolin and cough linctus.

The worst part was that the hospital suggested that I give her 'physiotherapy' four times a day to try to get rid of the mucus. What this meant was that I had to hold her upside down and beat her on her back and front for twenty minutes at a time. She was bruised right down her chest and back. I said to the hospital that if anyone saw it who didn't know I'd be up before the courts. They said 'Oh dear.' That was all anyone said. 'Oh dear.' It was dreadful for her and dreadful for me. It did help. It did shake the mucus free. But of course it never got at the cause of the problem.

By the time she was eighteen months old her hearing was suffering, so she had problems with talking. When she was 2½ years old she began having speech therapy.

Then, just before her third birthday, we went to see Mrs Coleman. At the consultation she wouldn't co-operate. She refused to let Mrs Coleman examine her eyes or take her pulse, and she complained all the time that her legs and arms were aching. Mrs Coleman said that her auburn hair, long lashes, aching limbs and characteristic sleeping posture – with her arms above her head – were all typical of an allergic.

She prescribed a split dose of pulsatilla 10m, and from the first of the three doses a transformation began. Mucus poured from all possible orifices! After a fortnight on a Stone Age diet Rebecca was completely better. Of course we still didn't know what had caused her trouble – Mrs Coleman still thought it might be cow's milk, especially since her cousin is lactose intolerant. But it wasn't. It was tap water. Immediately I reintroduced it she wheezed and went into a bronchial spasm, and within minutes her eyes were thick with yellow exudate. From being a happy bubbly child she was wheezy and miserable. Nothing else affected her at all.

Now she just has to remember to be careful. Her allergy's still there. Once at nursery school she got ill when her face was accidentally splashed with water. She was tested again last year.

Her eyes filled straight away with pus, but at least she didn't wheeze. She's just started at school, and she wears a big badge warning teachers of her allergy. Apart from this, Rebecca is perfectly well.

'Life-long arthritis – then last year I went on the fun run!': Nina Rutland, age 64

I've had arthritis ever since I was a child. I had rheumatic fever when I was fifteen. They gave me pain-killers and told me to rub my joints with oil. From then on I was never without it. It wasn't bad, but it bothered me on and off.

Then three years ago I began to lose the use of my legs. They were going dead. I've always been very active – folk-dancing, walking – and I couldn't do it any more. If I walked for more than ten minutes my legs went numb. I was prescribed a whole range of drugs. Some of them upset my stomach, so I was switched to others. They did help with the pain, but I got dry eyes, and my finger-nails almost vanished, they were so short and brittle.

I saw a specialist. He X-rayed my spine and said I could have an operation on it. I asked if that meant I would get less pain and if I could walk further. He said it was uncertain: I might improve 70%. That wasn't enough for me. I wanted 100%. I knew other people who'd had these operations and I wanted to be sure. Once you've had them it's done. So I said I'd like to think it over.

While I was thinking I saw a piece in the local paper about Mrs Coleman and how she'd recovered from arthritis herself. So I went to see her. That was a year ago. She put me on the Stone Age diet. With that and with vitamins I'm now very well. The headaches I've had for most of my life have gone too. My weight's gone down – it was 11 stone, and now I'm only 9½. I can walk easily for many miles.

Last year I ran a 2½ mile fun run in Hyde Park!

'No one told me I had Crohn's disease': Thea Edmonds, age 50

I had my first operation 25 years ago in Holland: the insides of my intestines were inflamed, and they took away the part where the small intestine enters the large intestine, together with my appendix.

Afterwards I got diarrhoea all the time. I thought it was a result of the operation – it never entered my head that it might be something I ate. No one else ever suggested it either. I went on taking various tablets and drugs. I was going off to the toilet sometimes five times a day. My energy was so sapped I had to rest every afternoon and go to bed early.

When we came to England seven years ago I was sent by our GP to a specialist. He said I had Crohn's disease. Apparently I'd had this for years, but although the disease was identified in 1933 this was the first time anyone had suggested that this was what was the matter with me. The consultant also said that although there was nothing malignant, I had developed a type of growth.

In 1978 I had another operation and all the large intestine was removed. It seemed to make no difference at all. I still had terrible problems, especially when I was out.

Finally two years ago I went to my local health food shop to ask if they could help. They suggested I visit Mrs Coleman. When she explained her approach, it surprised me so much that ordinary foods could be the trouble.

It's taken time to sort things out. Now I realize I must work menus out well ahead. But it's done miracles. Sometimes it's hard not to have what I like, but it's a choice between that and being ill. It's all worth it. I now have 90% control of my bowels, with only occasional disappointments. I'm so well today that I run a successful small pre-school play-group for toddlers.

'If anybody was going to help me it had to be *me*': Judith Curtis, age 46

I was a sickly child and missed a lot of school. They said my cough was due to nerves. When I started my SRN training I had to keep fighting chest infections and pneumonia. It was thought then that the touble was due to my sinuses, and I had a bilateral radical antrostomy. I qualified, married, and had two children. After the birth of my second child, I had recurrent bouts of pleurisy – *suddenly* getting awful pains and being confined to bed for three weeks at a time.

My local hospital found there was nothing much wrong with me, so my GP, who has always been very helpful and supportive, sent me to a specialist hospital. They found I had chronic obstructive airways disease – bilateral bronchitiasis. I was given Ventolin and put on steroids.

In 1977 I was diagnosed as a coeliac. In 1982 I had a hysterectomy. All this time no one seemed to see me as a whole person. When I went for check-ups and said I still felt unwell, they'd ask me questions like 'Are you happily married?' So I shut up.

After my hysterectomy I thought that if anybody was going to help me it had to be *me*. I went to Mrs Coleman's clinic, and with her help left off grains and dairy products, kept to herb teas, and generally rethought my diet.

Now I'm well and completely off drugs. I can walk upstairs and I'm still able to talk when I get to the top! When I went back to hospital for my regular check-up after stopping my drugs, I wanted to tell the consultants what had happened. It was like telling a brick wall. I was reassured that I could see my GP any time to restart them.

I've always worked full-time, though I had to take frequent periods off with my pleurisy, but now I've worked 2½ years without any time off at all. I feel better, brighter, and I've more energy than at any time I can remember.

'Within a week I was on the road to recovery': Joy Ward, age 45

As a teenager I had epilepsy. After a few years of being heavily dosed with drugs, I was able to keep it in check with a minimum dose of mysolin for the next twenty years. I went on having regular EEGs until eventually the hospital said there was no point in having any more, but that I should continue to use the mysolin when necessary – I used to get a warning 'aura' beforehand. During this time I had no further attacks.

I had three children, who are now 19, 18, and 17, and after the birth of the last I sank into a deep depression. My husband was then a pupil barrister, and for the first ten years of our marriage we lived far below the bread line. 'Bread' was the operative word. I had bread for breakfast, bread for lunch, and a 6d breast of lamb stuffed with bread for dinner, or meat minced with bread to make it go further.

Ten years ago I began to get acne, and for six solid years I was on antibiotics. I tried everything: special stuff from health shops, facial treatments and so on.

Six years ago I went to Mrs Coleman, and *literally within one week* I was on the road to recovery: I've never needed to take another antibiotic since. She discovered I was allergic to wheat, milk and sugar. She introduced me to nutrition, and I changed to raw food, fruit, nuts and vegetables, cutting out my allergic foods, all tins, colourings and flavourings, and all meats except chicken and lamb.

Within nine months of starting the diet – plus hydrotherapy and deep breathing – I was off all epilepsy pills for the first time since my teens, and have had no attacks or auras since. My skin is fine, with no hint of acne.

Mrs Coleman also discovered, through hair analysis, that I had a drastically low mineral count plus an abnormally high level of copper: in 1980 this was 45.8. Mrs Coleman began to remove the copper homoeopathically, and the last test – done in January 1984 – showed that this was now down to 6.99, while all the mineral levels bar two were up to the correct mark.

I remain perfectly well, and have more energy than I've had for years.

Pearl Coleman, a lay practioner and Born Again Christian healer, planned to become a doctor from childhood, but was withdrawn from school by her father at fifteen. She became a trainee draftswoman, and then worked for seven years on the press side of the London Stock Exchange. She left on her marriage to help in her husband's business, and later applied for admission to medical school. She was rejected as too old, so began instead to study independently aspects of health and nutrition. In 1977, at a McCarrison Society conference, she met Dr Hugh Cox, and subsequently worked as his assistant once or twice a week for four years. She studied homoeopathy at the Royal Homoeopathic Hospital, and visited Dr Mackarness. She subsequently established her own clinic for alternative medicine, with the help of four fully-qualified medical advisers.

Pearl Coleman's long interest in health and the environment, and in the contribution of alternative medicine, dates from the birth of her son in 1963.

Opposition to fluoride
Proud of his first perfect teeth, and determined to look after them, she bought fluoride toothpaste and fluoride tablets, and even planned to move to an area with fluoridated water. She was delighted when the local authorities planned to add fluoride to Surrey water, and astonished to learn that there were people who opposed this move. On pursuing the issue, however, what she discovered – by talking to scientists and reading the evidence – convinced her that fluoridation of public water was totally wrong. She began writing on this topic to papers and magazines, and in 1970 was elected Chairman of the Pure Water Preservation Society. Faced with this opposition, Surrey abandoned its fluoride plans.

In furthering her research into the effects of fluoride, Mrs

Coleman found herself admitted to universities and libraries she would never have otherwise approached. She became interested in other aspects of the environment, in lead and other forms of pollution, and started writing articles for many different magazines, taking O-levels in English language and literature to help her. Although disappointed at being turned down for medical school, her studies of books on health and nutrition, herbs and homoeopathy, led to a growing conviction that there was much that people could do to help themselves stay well; yet many of these possibilities were being ignored by conventional medicine.

Personal experiences
This belief was reinforced by her own experiences. By her early forties she was suffering badly from arthritis. She could hardly turn her head or lift a saucepan; she had progressive degeneration of the spine. She was offered pain-killers and tranquillizers and told she would have to learn to live with it. Through the help of a naturopath she completely recovered. Her only remaining problem was severe hayfever, and she later traced this to the gramineae (grains and sugar-cane) and dairy produce. By eliminating these she has remained well and free from hayfever ever since.

Thankfulness for her own recovery made her determined to help others. She was urged by Dr Blackie at the Royal Homoeo-pathic Hospital to 'use her knowledge', and was encouraged by Dr Cox and Dr Mackarness. She began to advise people locally who asked for her help, and more and more people approached her with queries. 'You've only got to get one person well in a village, and it snowballs.' She had to pay for homoeopathic remedies and equipment and eventually, in 1977, she started to charge for treatment.

Patients: diagnoses
By 1981 she was working virtually full-time, with patients coming from ever further afield. She built up her pharmacy to over a thousand remedies, and completely reorganized her clinic so that her fully-qualified medical advisers could do the smears and blood tests she was unable to carry out.

Today she sees over a hundred new patients a year, most of whom are chronically ill, having already visited many doctors and specialists. Many are local and many come from London, but others arrive from distant parts of the country and even from abroad.

Every patient has a one and a half hour initial consultation to consider mind, body and spirit, and the patient's family history. During this consultation Mrs Coleman also looks for any physical signs which, to her, indicate the possibility of allergies. These include circles under the eyes, shiny eyelids, curved eyelashes which are alternately long and short; cold sores; split lips; a split raw or red tongue; greasy or damp skin; bloated stomach, hands or feet; stooped shoulders and frequent sighing.

Clinic rules

Every patient – whether allergic or not – has to sign a paper agreeing to a set of clinic rules. They must agree to abstain completely from smoking, alcohol, tea, coffee, pork and pork products, and from all food with chemical additives. They must carry out regular hydrotherapy, and eat raw vegetables, fruit, and sprouted seeds every day. They also have to keep notebooks observing their life and health, and are expected to read extensively – Pearl Coleman keeps a lending library. 'People who come must understand what we're doing, and must accept responsibility for their own health.'

Treatment

Allergic patients are put on the Stone Age diet. She finds that many of those who come back after this have 'a sort of glow – what I call the Stone Age look. They've become beautiful. Even though they may have buck teeth or a crooked nose, they have a vitality, a presence about them.'

In 90% of cases she finds that the diet, followed by the reintroduction of foods, sorts out most of the problems. Ninety-five per cent of the patients she also takes off salt, and removes their existing salt by raising their potassium, both through homoeopathic remedies, and by prescribing potassium-rich foods such as potatoes in their skins.

Following the first two consultations, patients return for a further half-hour consultation. Some need no more than one – some not even that. Rarely does she see a patient for longer than six months. 'If I haven't restored their quality of life by then I refer them elsewhere. I refer allergic patients to a reputable allergy-testing clinic supervised by a member of the Clinical Ecology Society.'

Lead poisoning

If their symptoms have not been alleviated by the diet and other straightforward measures, Mrs Coleman next considers the possibility of lead poisoning, or a similar contamination such as aluminium. Lead attacks the brain and causes learning difficulties, hyperactivity, all kinds of mania, depression, and symptoms resembling multiple sclerosis. Among the many other symptoms are extreme sensitivity to touch or no feeling at all, restlessness, lack of sweat, foul breath and teeth-grinding. Other diagnostic signs are sunken cheeks, yellow skin, a tongue which is coated or has a red margin, and a blue lead-line around the gums. Excessive aluminium may cause arthritis, throat and bowel symptoms, irritable skin, anxiety, and an inability to coordinate: possibly only one of these symptoms, not all.

Hair analysis
Where she suspect that lead poisoning is a possibility, she uses hair analysis, but only as an adjunct to her investigation. 'I am a detective. I use a process of elimination until I track down the *causes* of illness.' She uses hair analysis mainly to establish heavy metal toxicity; she is uncertain about its value in testing minerals and is worried about the proliferation of hair-testing clinics. 'You won't get any kind of accurate reading unless you take ½" of growing hair taken close to the scalp at the base of the neck, and even where the reading may be correct it won't tell anything unless it's appreciated that it's the *ratio* of the minerals that matters.'

Mrs Coleman finds lead-poisoning, rather than allergies, to be the most common cause of hyperactivity; but, as she points out, most of the hyperactive children she sees come to her from London. One very difficult child was found to be suffering from lead-poisoning: when she questioned the parents she found the family was living above a garage in a mews, and that next door a workshop was spraying lead paint on to metal all day long. Lead-poisoning is also a common cause of arthritis, especially among plumbers.

To reduce the lead level she gives zinc supplements (preferably soluble zinc) and also prescribes zinc-rich foods such as green vegetables, nuts, wheatgerm and shellfish, and an increase in calcium intake from green vegetables, yoghurt and sesame seeds. Lead toxicity leads to low manganese levels: again green vegetables, unrefined cereals, egg yolks, bran, nuts and wheatgerm will supply this. Garlic and seaweed can be helpful in chelating lead.

Symptoms and allergens
She finds that certain symptoms are associated with certain allergens, though there are always exceptions: rheumatoid

arthritis often implicates grains and dairy products; irritable bowel syndrome (including Crohn's disease and ulcerative colitis) often has the same cause. Coeliac disease is associated with all glutens and soya products. She is particularly pleased with her successes in treating patients with Crohn's disease, an illness which orthodox medicine has done very little to treat since it was first identified fifty years ago. In 90% of her cases she has tracked down the cause and thus brought about a cure.

Schizophrenia

Schizophrenia is another illness which she feels would respond to a dietary approach. She has seen several schizophrenic teenagers. She has explained the procedure and they understand it, but they are hardly ever allowed to follow it. They go to special day-schools which will only take them if they are put on drugs. Often she finds that the mother will understand what is involved and is willing to try it, but the father objects. He can't face the results of no-drug therapy – the prospect of the noise when he comes back in the evening, the smashed furniture, the self-mutilation. Patients often feel the dietary approach is right for them, but they are trapped.

Hyperventilation and candidiasis

Mrs Coleman feels that there have recently been two vitally important breakthroughs: the understanding that both hyper-ventilation and candidiasis can have a dramatic effect on allergic reactions, and that correcting either situation in affected patients can reduce or even eliminate the allergic symptoms.

Since January 1984, with the assistance of one of her medical advisers, she has been running a candidiasis clinic. Patients are tested sublingually with bio-kinesiology, using serial one dilutions of mixed moulds, mixed yeasts, T.C.E. (trichophyton mix, candida albicans, epidermophyton sloccosum) and candida albicans. The patient's history is taken into consideration, and if a reaction is found to one or more of these, then additive-free Nystatin is prescribed orally (and vaginally for women), together with a mould-free diet. In this way the whole of the alimentary canal is tackled. Pearl Coleman also strongly recommends reading *The Yeast Connection*, by William G Crook (Professional Books, 1984.)

Single allergens

Mrs Coleman has had several cases where there was only one

allergen. One was a teenage girl who was brought to see her shortly before her O-levels depressed and crying all the time. She was on a healthy wholefood diet, but her mother had been giving her apples after most meals and three apples a day to take to school. When the apples stopped, so did her depression. Another was a woman who suffered from constipation and diarrhoea: her problem was entirely due to mince, which she loved and ate frequently.

Chemical allergens and general nutrition

Although she can do nothing directly to help where chemical allergies are concerned, she finds that often, when the burden of food allergies is lifted, then the tolerance to environmental allergens is raised. She feels that it is in this whole area of nutrition and general health that lay healers like herself can be particularly useful. At present, there are still few doctors who understand this approach; and she believes that there are many skilled lay people throughout the country who are well qualified to give immediate and practical help.

Sugar, salt, smoking

She teaches all her patients that 'the three deadly sins are sugar, salt and smoking.' Sugar is found in many prepared foods which are theoretically savoury: tinned soups, spaghetti and baked beans for example. Salt too is added in excess to many foods. It displaces oxygen in the cells so that the cells fail to pick up adequate iron, causing anaemia; it can also cause high blood pressure, oedoema, and blood problems associated with heart disease. Smoking not only causes a whole range of well-known illnesses, but forces others to be passive smokers. It burdens children and renders them sensitive to allergens which they might otherwise tolerate.

Recipe for a healthier life

Pearl Coleman's recipe for a healthier life is:

> Fresh raw vegetables and fruit daily.
> Plenty of seeds, nuts, pulses and sprouted seeds.
> Plenty of greens.
> Hydrotherapy: a warm shower followed by a short cold shower.
> Fresh air; sleep; exercise; good posture
> No fluoride toothpaste or cooking in aluminium.
> Correction of hyperventilation.
> Banishing fear.

Personal relationships

She also emphasizes the importance of personal relationships.

'People can poison you and give you stomach troubles. Bad relationships can make you ill. Jealousy can cause disease. Hatred, resentment and frustration are powerful and destructive emotions. The inability to forgive is bad for you.'

She encourages people to sort out their emotional lives, to abandon impossible situations, not to spend psychic energy accusing others. As an example of the effect of the mind upon allergies, she tells of a woman who, after treatment, remained allergic to three foods. Following a divorce from a distressing marriage she became happy and contented, and the allergies disappeared.

Though none of Pearl Coleman's family were churchgoers, she is a Born Again Christian who believes strongly that her mission is to restore health to those who are ill. She not only helps directly, by treating patients in her clinic, but indirectly, by writing extensively for health magazines. She has also recently produced a helpful practical booklet entitled *What Can I Eat?* (see page 250).

She feels privileged. 'Often those who come here have everything on a material level, but they've got nothing because they've lost their health. I'm frequently run off my feet with exhaustion, and so are my helpers in the clinic, but what could be more important than getting people well?'

Chapter 13

Foods, Chemicals and the Mind

'I tried for two years to recall my lost train of thought': Matthew James,* age 31

My obsessions started when I was eleven – after I'd left primary school. I still had a library book and a Bible that belonged to the school, and I went on worrying about these for twelve months.

I was troubled throughout my grammar school career – not so much during term-time, but very much during holidays. I'd do things like checking empty paper bags to see if I'd dropped any money inside, and I'd search the dustbins several times a week. At the same time, I was aware that other people didn't behave like this.

When I was fifteen or sixteen I was worried mainly about school subjects, but also about other things: was green really green, or could it perhaps look quite different to other people? With equations like $xy = yx$ I'd spend days at a time worrying and worrying about it – why should xy equal yx?

An infatuation with a girl precipitated the next stage. I made lists and lists of words and became totally preoccupied with them. If I forgot the sequence, I felt I'd committed the unpardonable sin. I saw a doctor. I was prescribed vitamins, which I took for two weeks, and then Librium, which I took for the next two weeks. I felt I wasn't getting anywhere, and I didn't go back.

In 1970 I went to university to study chemistry. I failed my first exam – not surprisingly. I was obsessed by my lists of words. I couldn't work. I left after failing again at the end of my second year.

In 1974 I found a job as groundsman for the local Parks Department. Then in 1977 I took a mild overdose; a combination of beer, paracetamol, and my mother's Valium.

I was referred to a psychiatrist. I had a standard interview with the usual questions, and was prescribed Tofranil. I went back a few times. It didn't make much difference. I also had one session of group therapy in which nothing much happened. We all sat around being awkward and rather embarrassed.

In 1978 things got much worse. I took two, maybe three overdoses. I ended up in a psychiatric hospital. The psychiatrist there suggested ECT. I didn't like the thought at all, so I wrote off to the Maudsley. I was finally referred there late in the summer of 1978.

I stayed in hospital for the next five months. I had all sorts of treatment: relaxation advice, social skills training, psychodrama, thought-stopping. Very little of it worked. I kept getting panic attacks. There would be a word missing on my lists, or I would worry about non-existent words.

While I was still at the Maudsley, in late 1978, I had a bad attack. I felt I'd forgotten my train of thought. I tried to recall it for two years. When this obsession finally disappeared late in 1980, the word lists – which had previously been swamped – returned.

It was then that Dr Vicky Rippere suggested that the root cause might be allergies. I was very sceptical, but I agreed to fill in her questionnaire.

As a result I eliminated certain foods: grains, milk, sugar, chicken, eggs, pork. I felt better, but I still wasn't sure that we were on the right track. When I described my feelings to Dr Rippere after a month, she raised the possibility of hypoglycaemia, and suggested a high-protein breakfast. Three weeks after I'd started on this my obsession with my word-list had disappeared. After a month it had vanished completely.

I kept on with my diet, and it wasn't until twelve months later that I tried to reintroduce foods. I experienced a bad patch late in 1983 after I'd eaten a lot of biscuits, and my obsessions came back. Since then I have switched back to a more strict diet. On a high protein breakfast with fibre I'm okay.

In October I'm going back to university again: this time to study psychology.

'I closed my eyes and wouldn't look at the scales': Gillian Lacey,* age 33

I'd already started bingeing by the time I was thirteen. I never thought of myself or my family as having allergic problems, but I always had tonsillitis all winter as a child, and my mother had migraines and my father tended to be depressive.

By the time I was married and in my late twenties I made up my mind to lose weight. I went down to 6 stone 12lbs – I'm 5'2". I stayed that way for a whole year, mainly by eating nothing but fruit. I was very scared of putting on any weight at all.

I began to get depressed. Everything was too much – my job, my home, my marriage. I began eating again, and my weight crept up until the summer of 1979. I began secretly bingeing. I'd leave work, eat two bars of chocolate on the bus on the way to the station, get off the bus, buy two more and eat them, then get off the train and buy two *more* and gobble them up on the way home. It was all done in secret. I didn't want my husband to know.

I took laxatives. I tried to make myself sick – I wasn't very successful! I got *very* depressed. I went to my GP and was sent straight to the hospital. I was diagnosed as anorexic – not so much because of my weight, which was more or less normal, but because I was taking laxatives. I had to go back every week to be weighed. I closed my eyes and wouldn't look at the scales.

I was obsessed with food. I'd eat *anything*. I was put on anti-depressants. I kept going back for a year, on drugs all the time. I was bingeing more and more, and as depressed as ever.

A lot of this time my husband had been seeing Dr Rippere. He'd had all sorts of different symptoms. She found out that it was hypoglycaemia. Eventually I told my husband about my problems. He was very supportive, and suggested I went to see Dr Rippere too. He even suggested it might be allergies, because he'd been on diets himself, but I didn't believe him.

Eventually I got a letter from my GP to see her. When she asked me about what I ate, she said I was possibly allergic to sugar and wheat. I didn't believe it at all, but I was desperate, so I tried. I cut out grains and sugar – it was an easy diet because my husband was also following it.

The effect was immediate. Within a week I felt better. I also lost weight! I'm simply not depressed now, and my husband's well too. It's so degrading to binge, to feel you have no control over what you do.

Not long ago I made a chocolate cake and ate quite a bit. I could feel the effect right away – I was all set to start bingeing again. It took four days for it to wear off. My husband said he hoped I'd learned my lesson!

Dr Vicky Rippere, BA, MA, PhD, BSc, MPhil, originally specialized in languages, graduating from Barnard College, Columbia University in 1965, magna cum laude BA, before gaining an MA from Harvard in 1966. She went to University College, London, to do a PhD, and afterwards took a BSc at Birkbeck in Psychology. In 1972 she went to the Institute of Psychiatry at the Maudsley Hospital to take an MPhil in Clinical Psychology. She returned to University College in 1974 to teach psychology to medical students, but returned to the Institute of Psychiatry in 1976. She has remained there ever since, and is now a lecturer with an honorary NHS contract as Principal Psychologist. She is a member of the British Society for Allergy and Clinical Immunology.

When Dr Rippere decided to study for a second degree in psychology, she was motivated primarily by 'wanting to move away from language and the abstract to do something that might make a practical difference to people's lives.' At the same time – though she was not to realize this until later – she was herself in need of practical changes in her own life. Over the years these two concerns converged, until today she brings a unique viewpoint and understanding to treating patients.

Personal experiences
Although she had never considered herself as in need of medical attention, throughout her childhood, teens and early adult life she had suffered from episodes of vomiting, headaches, fatigue, depression and exhaustion. By the early 1970s she was getting three migraines a week. Eventually, a registrar at the migraine clinic she was attending suggested a basic elimination diet. As a result, Dr Rippere found that she was affected by some meats, fat, chocolate, alcohol, oranges, pork and any animal protein food which had not been properly refrigerated. She became a vegetarian for the next eight years; improving considerably to begin with, but then developing a reaction to grains and milk because these had begun to feature so largely in her diet.

She developed thyroid problems and became very ill. Because her thyroid pathology failed to show up in standard tests she obtained little help from orthodox medicine (she gives details of her experience in 'Biochemical victims: false negative diagnosis through over-reliance on biochemical tests', in *Medical Hypotheses*, 10, 1983). After three years, and mostly through her own efforts, she mananged to recover a precarious health. She is now a 'reluctant carnivore', has managed to work out most of her own allergies, and provided she is scrupulously careful about her diet remains reasonably well.

Her state of calculated equilibrium is maintained at a price. She has to bring her own food to work, and take it with her if she wishes to meet friends. She dares not move away from her base unless she can rely on carrying sufficient supplies or finding 'safe' foods. Travelling, whether to teach or lecture, is a major challenge.

Yet she does not entirely regret her condition, since it enables her to empathize with many others. 'Many of these share with me the dubious advantage of starting from the right point. They're in no doubt that they have a problem. They don't waste time and effort trivializing it or dismissing it as imaginary. They have the motivation to keep trying to find a solution, while professionals too often resign from the situation.'

Her experiences also meant that when Dr Mackarness's book appeared she greeted it with an open mind. She began to read widely: the US clinical ecologists, early French allergists, and the journals of orthodox immunologists. What she discovered made her re-assess the relationship between mind and body.

Teaching and research

During these formative years she was continuing her work as a lecturer and teacher of psychology. Her principal role was – as it still is – to train students: partly through formal lecturing, but mainly through clinical teaching and research. She has ten sessions of clinical work per week, based on clinical teaching, much of which is orthodox conventional neuropsychology, behaviour therapy and counselling. She is therefore limited in the number of patients she is able to treat. Within the hospital she works for four consultants, who have different numbers of session allocations; she also sees patients from other consultants on request. She has about a hundred referrals a year, but not all of these are for treatment. She has three times the number she used to have before adopting the clinical ecology approach, and possibly five or six times as many as her colleagues have. Her total case load for treatment at present is between fifty and sixty.

It was in 1978 that she began to wonder whether some of her patients might be affected by their diets: realizing that she herself reacted with 'psychological' as well as physical symptoms to her unsafe foods, and knowing from published American work that certain foods and drinks could have an effect on the central nervous system. 'The realization that patients might actually be affected in this way dawned on me only very gradually.'

She began asking questions: and found, for example, that

some patients were drinking up to twenty cups of coffee a day. When she suggested cutting this out, they became noticeably less tense and irritable. She started to experiment by suggesting diet changes. She had previously studied psychopharmacology as a special subject in her final year at Birkbeck, and felt that the modifications she was suggesting could at least do no harm.

The first time Dr Rippere consciously adopted this approach for a patient was in 1979. He was referred to her as 'agoraphobic'. She initially tried the conventional approach – systematic desensitization and self-monitoring – but found the results made no sense. The subsequent orthodox response would be the conclusion that the patient was not ill at all, but was inventing his whole situation. She considered that this would not fit the picture either. He *looked* ill.

She started considering reactive hypoglycaemia, and asked him to keep a food diary. From this she discovered that he was existing on quantities of sugared coffee and biscuits, and that his attacks matched his diet. Having tried but failed to have him checked for hypoglycaemia, she suggested to him that he cut out his coffee and sugar and embark on a wholefood diet. 'It would have been very easy for him – he even lived opposite a health food shop – but he flatly refused to consider it. He came back eighteen months later, still agoraphobic. He wasn't a success from a treatment point of view, but I still felt I was on the right lines.'

She began to work out an inital screening questionnaire, and by late 1979 she started handing this out to patients. At first she only gave it to those she suspected might have environmental problems; later she realized that she was missing relevant evidence in others, so she began to give it to everyone as a routine practice.

Survey of patients screened for environmental problems
In 1981 Dr Rippere screened 42 patients: 23 routine referrals (with e.g. phobias, obsessions, tension), plus 19 who were already suspected as having allergy-type problems as well as psychiatric difficulties.

The responses to her questionnaire indicated that 95% of these patients probably had some type of environmental disorder: they either identified foods which they knew caused nausea, vomiting, migraines, breathing problems, bloating etc., *or* indicated foods which they would be loath to give up. Half of these also had sensitivities to chemicals. Sixty-seven per cent reported a *known* allergy: a considerably higher proportion than that expected in an average sample.

A high proportion also reported symptoms which corresponded to one or more of Mackarness's five key indices of masked allergy. On average, each patient suffered from three. Seventy-eight per cent reported persistent fatigue not helped by rest; 72% weight problems (most commonly overweight); 50% excessive sweating; 45% puffiness of face, hands, ankles or abdomen; 38% palpitations around meal-times. Over half felt 'ill all over', half suffered from insomnia, 48% from stomach problems, 48% itchy eyes or nausea, 42% itching or sudden tiredness after eating. Other common physical symptoms included binge-eating (35%), bowel disturbances, chest pain, mouth ulcers, water retention, and problems with joints, respiration and skin.

Patients also suffered from a markedly similar range of psychological symptoms: 82% from irritability, 75% from mood swings, 70% from inability to think clearly, 60% from headaches (including migraine) and panic attacks; 58% felt 'slowed down' and 55% felt 'dopey'.

Dr Rippere points out that this sample is not necessarily representative of other psychiatric patients, as those referred to her often come as a last resort. Nonetheless, she believes that the high level of positive response does at least indicate the need for far more research along these lines.

Analysis of 85 patients

At the same time that she initiated her survey, she was working on the analysis of a study carried out in 1979-80 on 85 patients who already knew they were allergic to foods and chemicals, referred either by themselves or through AAA, HCSG and the Chemical Victims Club.

Of these, 82 reported allergies to foods; 32 to food additives and contaminants; 29 to alcohol and/or coffee; 26 to petrochemical fumes; 21 to tea. Of the foods most commonly mentioned, wheat and wheat products topped the list (affecting 52), cow's milk came next (34), and cheese third (31). Among the most frequently mentioned symptoms were those generally accepted as possibly allergic in origin: migraines and headaches, respiratory and abdominal problems, and skin lesions: but 40% were those still not accepted as being allergic in origin: relating to the central nervous system, psychological functioning and behaviour.

Patients

At present Dr Rippere sees patients of all ages, and approximately equal numbers of males and females. Some have head injuries and brain tumours, but most are neurotics and recovering psychotics. They come with diagnoses of agoraphobia, claustrophobia, weight disorders and anomalies of eating, fear of social situations, depressions, obsessions, problems with living, and anxieties about specific threats, such as spiders.

She provisionally divides patients into three categories:

1.   Genuine neurotics, with apprehensions and behaviour intelligible purely from their background and history; their phobia or other problem has arisen quite reasonably from a previous psychological cause.

2.   Patients who have similar symptoms but without any reasonable explanation at all. They'll make remarks like: 'I was walking along when out of a clear blue sky I got this feeling of utter panic.' With these she now suspects an environmental origin.

3.   Patients with both true psychological causes *and* true ecological causes. They may have real psychological disorders which would respond to therapy, but are 'immersed in a matrix of ecological distress'. They are too ill (with nausea, headaches etc.) to be able to participate in, much less respond to, therapy.

She finds that she has very few group 1 patients. Most of her patients fall into groups 2 and 3: with either, she considers it is pointless to attempt other treatment before having worked out their environmental mistakes. 'It is useless to try to work on the psychological problems of someone who is living off daily cups of highly sugared tea, cola and bread and jam, with the occasional take-away and pie. Even anyone who started off perfectly healthy would develop problems on this diet before too long.'

Foods, chemicals and mental disorders
Dr Rippere finds it surprising that there is so little appreciation of the extensive part which may be played in mental disorders by chemical exposure and harmful diets, especially since organic psychiatry already recognizes the psychonoxious effects of heavy metals, alcohol dependence, recreational drug abuse, and glue sniffing.

'Recently, the American Psychiatric Association (1980) (in *Diagnostic and Statistical Manual of Mental Disorders* DSM-III, Washington DC, APA) has recognized caffein toxicity as an organic mental disorder in its own right. After the Second World War, the medical press contained numerous reports of the neurological and psychiatric sequelae of chronic or heavy exposure to the newly introduced organophosphorus and chlorinated hydrocarbon pesticides. More recently, similar effects from the herbicide Agent Orange have been reported. Cases of neurological disability resulting from exposure to paint stripper have also been published.

'Foods are made of chemicals, and may also produce chemical reactions in the brain. At present, this possibility is rarely considered, and still more rarely practically applied.'

Seven reasons to welcome clinical ecology

Dr Rippere is currently working 'on several fronts at once' to see that this awareness is extended. As she pointed out in a recent piece – as yet unpublished – there are 'Seven reasons to be nice to people doing clinical ecology'.

1. Environmental control is harmless, as opposed to the possible ill effects and overdoses from drugs. 'The risks arising from nutrient administration, elimination diets, and clean-up of the domestic chemical environment are relatively trivial.'

2. The conditions in which environmental approaches are relevant appear to be extremely common. A study of schizophrenics shows low levels of vitamins A, C, B_1, B_6, B_{12} and folic acid in the majority of sufferers. There are reported rates of reactive and relative hypoglycaemia in 31-93% of selected samples of psychiatric patients.[*]

3. Environmental treatment in patients with environmentally-induced symptoms produces rapid and effective improvement, even after many years of previous extensive and unsuccessful treatment.

4. It is cost-effective. The alternative – rounds of visits to specialists and psychiatrists, often for decades, plus expensive drugs – is extremely costly; there should also be taken into account the expense of patients who can no longer work and are supported by the state. The proper use of environmental

[*](Landmann, H R and Sutherland R L (1950). 'Incidence and significance of hypoglycaemia in unselected admissions to a psychosomatic service': *American Journal of Digestive Diseases*, 17, 105-8; Hoffman, R H and Abrahamson, E M (1949), 'Hyperinsulism – a factor in the neuroses: *American Journal of Digestive Diseases*, 16, 242-7; Salzer, H M (1966), 'Relative hypoglycaemia as a cause of neuropsychiatric illness': *Journal of the National Medical Association*, 58, 12-17; Beebe, W E and Wendel, O W (1973), 'Preliminary observations of altered carbohydrate metabolism in psychiatric patients': in D Hawkins & L Pauling (Eds): *Orthomolecular psychiatry treatment of schizophrenia*, W H Freeman, San Francisco).

therapy can free money for research into better treatment for those for whom this approach is *not* suitable.

5.   There are also financial savings in other ways. Such therapy can be administered correctly by therapists without a medical training; nutrient preparations cost much less than drugs; these methods overall take much less of the therapist's time than psychological and behavioural treatment.

6.   Environmental therapy is humane. Ineffective treatment is deeply demoralizing, especially when patients are treated as neurotic when they know that they are not.

7.   The seventh reason to be kind to environmental therapists is that continued opposition to their approach will eventually lead to the public demanding to know why these safe, relevant, non-toxic, inexpensive and non-labour-intensive environmental methods are not being employed.

Towards increased understanding
Over the past few years Dr Rippere has endeavoured to increase both lay and professional understanding of this approach. She is certainly *not* saying that all psychological patients have illnesses attributable to foods and chemicals, but she maintains that it is sensible, practicable and humane to check and, where necessary, eliminate such possibilities early on. Her screening questionnaire is now being used in the USA, Australia and widely in the UK. She is the editor of the Newsletter for the Society for Environmental Therapy, scientific adviser to the HCSG, on the editorial board of *New Health*, contributes to professional journals, and regularly attends seminars of the British Society for Clinical Ecology.

Her analysis of her 1980 study developed into a book, *The Allergy Problem* (Thorsons, 1983), which describes the lack of treatment at present available for allergic sufferers, and the professional mishandling, misunderstanding and occasionally straightforward mistreatment which they frequently encounter.

She continues to aim for more research; but meanwhile, as she says, most patients prefer to regain health unscientifically than remain ill scientifically.

Among Dr Rippere's other publications are:
'Food additives and hyperactive children: a critique of Connors';
    British Journal of Clinical Psychology, 22, 19-23. 1983.
'How long can the medical establishment go on ignoring clinical
    ecology?' in *Does Psychotherapy Really Help People?* J. Hariman
    (ed), Charles C. Thomas, Springfield, I11.

Diet-related Diseases: The Modern Epidemic, S Seely, D Freed, G Silverstone and V Rippere: Croom Helm, London.

Chapter 14

Testing

'I felt as though I were walking on cobblestones': Joan Khilkoff-Choubersky, age 63

I've always been a very healthy person, except that I used to have migraines. I got my first one on my wedding day! I went on having them for 36 years, and they gradually got worse as I got older. I started having them maybe once a month, and then more frequently. They became really incapacitating, with vomiting and so on. I've lived abroad a lot of my life, and I consulted doctors both here and in Paris. No one ever suggested that the migraines could have anything to do with anything I ate or drank. It wasn't until my daughter – who also suffered from migraines – cut out caffeine, found that she was all right, and suggested that I try too that I ever thought about it. As soon as I stopped taking caffeine I was all right. I've never had a migraine since.

Then, when I was sixty, I began getting arthritis in my hands and feet. (I had a precise clinical diagnosis of sero-negative rheumatoid arthritis.) My knuckles were so swollen that it was painful to shake hands. I had difficulty in walking – even in putting on my shoes. I felt it under the balls of my feet, as though I were walking on cobblestones. I'd get flare-ups too in my knees and elbows.

When I went to my GP I was put on drugs. I wasn't at all happy – I've never liked the thought of taking drugs for any length of time. I visited a homoeopath, but without any good results. I don't say it mightn't work for other people, but it didn't work for me.

Then Dr S D suggested that the arthritis might be due to my diet. I fasted for a week and then went on to the lamb and pears diet. I reintroduced the foods one by one and looked at what happened when I did. I had blood tests, a hair analysis and a cytotoxic test, and cut out a whole range of foods that it appeared I was allergic to. The worst were milk products, chocolate, coffee, tea, wheat, soya, crab and cinnamon. I was also put onto vitamins and mineral supplements: 2-3 gms of vitamin C per day, plus vitamins A and D, zinc, managanese, potassium, chromium, kelp, selenium and magnesium.

The result was that my arthritis improved terrifically. My doctor is delighted. I have virtually no problems. Recently I've occasionally eaten wheat – bread and so on – when I've been out to dinner, and I find my knuckles react, though not badly. Apart from that – and that's my own fault for not keeping to the diet – I feel very well indeed.

Dr S D, MA, BM, BCh, initially studied physiology and biochemistry at Oxford, then did his medical training at Westminster before returning to Oxford to qualify in 1973. After a succession of house jobs, he left for Canada in 1975, where – in partnership with his wife and a third doctor – he ran a small hospital in Newfoundland. In 1977 he returned to the UK for a short break to pursue his investigations into nutritional disease. His research into vitamins and minerals attracted so much interest that, instead of returning to Canada, he eventually set up in private practice. He has worked here ever since as a nutritionally oriented physician: treating patients, researching, writing and lecturing.

Dr D's interest in nutrition dates back to his experiences in Newfoundland. Here he assessed that a large number of illnesses were actually caused by faulty nutrition. In his first three months he took three hundred patients off psychotropic drugs and substituted his own dietary approach: in eighteen months only one patient chose to return to drug therapy.

Vitamins and minerals

He became increasingly interested in all aspects of nutrition. 'For example, I used to give patients B complex capsules to help them come off the drugs, purely as a placebo effect, or so I thought – but I was surprised to find how effective they were. They were having far more than a placebo effect. I began to look into the whole role of vitamins.'

When he returned to Britain in 1977 he found his way of thinking influenced by two major books: Henry Schroeder's *The Poisons Around Us* (Indiana University Press,) and *Trace Minerals and Human Nutrition* (Faber and Faber). Two other books which he recommends, particularly as a doctor's introduction to nutritional biochemistry, are *Nutritional Biochemistry* and *Nutritional Therapy* by Jonathan Wright (Rodale Press, 1979), and *Nutrition against Disease* by Roger Williams (Bantam Books, 1973).

At this time he was fully occupied in his research and had no intention of setting up in practice, but patients who had heard by work of mouth of a 'doctor who believed in vitamins' came to ask for his help. Initially he agreed to see them purely from a research point of view, but as he started to treat them 'the whole thing snowballed.'

He never returned to Canada. Today his time is divided between treatment of patients, further exploration into aspects nutrition, and writing and lecturing on his approach.

Patients

In order to spend more time on reading and research, Dr D has recently cut down on the number of new patients, but he still sees between eight and ten a week. Patients are increasingly directly referred by GPs: these are often their most difficult cases, so his success rate is less than 100%. Some are self-referred. He likes to have a GP's letter of reference, but this is not essential. Normally he tries to persuade patients to let him send a letter to their GP, but will not persist in the rare cases where this permission is refused. He puts those who approach him from other parts of the country in touch with sympathetic local doctors; he also sees patients from all over Europe, and from South Africa.

Almost all his patients have already been investigated. Most have been told either that there's nothing wrong; or that there *is* something wrong, but undiagnosable; or that they will have to learn to live with it. Some come to him simply because they have observed various symptoms and want to avoid invasive tests in hospital which are likely to lead to drugs they have no desire to take. A third category is those who are seeking preventive nutritional advice.

Like all doctors in this field, Dr D considers not isolated symptoms but the whole patient. The initial long history he takes – covering genetic background, environment, past illnesses, stress, emotional problems, etc. – is geared towards picking up the more obvious food and chemical sensitivities; but the tougher the case and the longer its duration, the more it justifies further investigation with all the tests at his disposal.

Hair analysis
He finds hair analysis useful as an initial screening tool, as it can pick up low zinc, calcium or magnesium deficiencies, and high toxic metal levels. Ideally, hair analysis should be confirmed by blood, serum or urine tests, but where these would be either impractical or too costly it is still possible to embark on a nutritional programme based on a combination of hair analysis and clinical indications.

Blood tests and sweat analysis
Dr D often uses immunological methods to measure the immunoglobulins in the blood; the total immunoglobulins as well as the specific ones for the food antibodies (IgE, IgM, IgG), and shortly he also hopes to be able to measure IgA. He also carries out specialized tests for gut-absorption.

Sweat analysis is extremely good for assessing magnesium and zinc status, whereas serum levels of these minerals are poor indicators of body status.

Low zinc and high lead levels
Two of the most important identifiable imbalances are low levels of zinc and high levels of lead. If either of these remains uncorrected, then work carried out to identify and eliminate allergens is often unsuccessful.

Zinc deficiency may arise from a poor intake – too few zinc-rich foods (see page 194); poor absorption, or excessive loss. Published papers show that in the UK zinc intake is frequently borderline, with many diets significantly below the recommended daily allowance: Dr D himself has treated over 250 zinc-deficiency cases. Food-allergic patients may be on a restricted diet which cuts down on zinc even further; they may also have malabsorption, and may in addition suffer from metabolic abnormalities which cause a heavy loss of zinc in the urine.

Zinc influences the whole immune system, and its importance is widely acknowledged. When Dr D asked for computer research into the number of papers linking zinc with nutrition and health, he discovered that in the past two years nearly 2,500 had been published. It affects digestion, skin integrity, hair growth and viral immunity. (He could find no published evidence of a connection between zinc and AIDS, but he is sure that one exists.)

Zinc deficiency can be a very significant aspect of food and chemical allergies. Dr D treated one woman with sore eyes, rashes on her eyelids, mouth ulcers, dandruff, wax in the ears, itches all over the body, muscle aches and pains, depression and gastro-intestinal pains: all very recognizable signs of zinc deficiency. She had also given clear indications of food allergies. Dr D prescribed large doses of zinc as an initial measure, intending thereafter to proceed to an elimination diet. However, when she returned a few weeks later she was dramatically better on all fronts. Her depression had vanished and her energy level had improved. The indications of allergy had dwindled and virtually disappeared. It was, as Dr D puts it: 'One of those happy events – a hole in one.'

Lead is also widely accepted as a hazard, but its dangers may be both more widespread and more subtle than is currently acknowledged. There may indeed by no safe threshold for lead at all, and even low level lead exposure may be a contributory factor in many illnesses.

Candida
Both zinc deficiency and iron deficiency predispose a person to candida overgrowth. For the last eighteen months Dr D has been treating candidiasis with Nystatin: 'a drug – but we have to use radical measures when candidiasis is firmly embedded in the gut.' To begin with he started only with the worst cases, then, as these responded successfully, he became more adventurous. All the time his threshold for treating these cases gets lower. It becomes more and more obvious that candidiasis is involved in an increasing number of patients.

Fatty acid deficiencies
Candidiasis also flourishes where there is a deficiency of fatty acids. Omega 3 and Omega 6 series fatty acid deficiencies produce clinical signs very similar in effect to those caused by zinc and B vitamin deficiencies.

Prostaglandin deficiencies
A new and rapidly expanding area for inquiry and research is this interaction of zinc with prostaglandin synthesis and the inter-relationships with dietary essential fatty acids – which have a vitamin-like activity, in that the body does not manufacture many of these. The whole area of prostaglandins in medicine is 'absolute dynamite, and fantastically interesting'. Food allergies interfere with prostaglandin synthesis. One interesting fact is that with evening primrose oil there is both linoleic and gammalinolenic acid; and studies made by Horrobin

demonstrate the interactions of various nutrients with the synthesis of prostaglandins.*

Total evaluation

With so many possibilities to take into consideration, it is the total evaluation that counts, particularly in difficult cases: it is the failure to consider the whole picture which leads to misdiagnosis. Dr D seldom uses *only* nutritional supplements; he usually manipulates the diet too, by – for example – eradicating sugar and refined carbohydrates, and any substances which the case history reveals as suspect. He finds that often food allergic-patients have got into a vicious circle. A food-allergic child becomes zinc-deficient, which compromises the immune system; the child is then vulnerable to recurrent infection, fails to recover completely, and thus develops further food allergies. To break the vicious circle may involve a whole range of methods.

'Multi-symptomatic patients are often labelled as hypochondriac. At this stage they begin to introvert quite heavily, and are then labelled as neurotics. They may at the same time have stresses in their environment, so it's quite understandable for a medical adviser to put all their symptoms down to this; yet it may be possible to put them right using very simple remedies.'

The middle path

Dr D ascribes the failure of medical advisers to make these observations to the tendency to divide patients into two groups: the mental and the physical. Most orthodox doctors ignore the middle path. At the same time, he points out that some nutritional and biochemical approaches are so potent that it is possible to begin to think that psychological disturbances are *all* due to these: while those who are interested primarily in psychoanalysis can see the potency of that aspect and tend to neglect the effect of nutrition. Again, it is the middle way that has the most truth.

Selection of important research papers

In order to help interested doctors, he and his colleague Dr A S have recently completed a project which he hopes will contribute to spreading the understanding of nutritional medicine. They have selected what they describe as 'The Hot Hundred' from

*Sjogren's syndrome and the sicca syndrome: the role of prostaglandin E; deficiency': D F Horrobin and A C Campbell, *Medical Hypotheses* 6, 1980: 255-232.

10,000 research papers. They have divided them into separate categories (Vitamins, Tea and Coffee, Toxic Minerals, Hypertension, Psychiatry, Gynaecology, etc.), and have reproduced appropriate parts with full references. They enclose relevant parts in patients' letters to GPs. Each week he and his colleague send out between forty and eighty letters to GPs and consultants relating to their patients who have consulted them.

Nutritional medicine
He is very sympathetic to the current problems of GPs. Most of them, he is aware, went into their difficult and demanding job to *help.* 'They are hampered in their attempts by too many patients, too much literature, and too little time.'

Dr D calls himself a nutritionally-oriented physician. Although he still has failures, he is sure that the integrated approach to disease is the right way to go. 'Failing to consider deficiencies and over-loads can give a false picture, and failing to take food sensitivities into account can also lead to a lot of heartbreak.' He is convinced that the nutritional modulation of immune dysfunction, which would include classical food allergy, is the medicine of the future. At present, he and a handful of colleagues are 'playing around with this concept with incomplete knowledge, but nonetheless producing interesting and worthwhile results.'

'Now I regret *her* feelings':
Valerie Foote, age 45, talks about Nicola, age 11

Nicola was a terrible baby from the moment I weaned her on to diluted evaporated milk. She cried a lot. She wouldn't sleep in the car like most babies do. She woke us up three or four times a night until she was four and a half. She was *such* hard work. Of course, now I realize why, and I regret *her* feelings – all those years when she wasn't calm. Still, at least we found out what was wrong before too many years had passed.

We started to get really anxious about her when she was nine. She'd always seemed bright to us, but she just wasn't making headway at school. She was getting very wound up too – very tense. She couldn't relax at all. I think now that she was on the verge of a sort of nervous breakdown.

I wondered if she might be dyslexic, so we looked for help. One of the psychologists we saw asked me if Nicola got eczema. I said: 'Not really eczema – more an itchy skin with bumps under the surface.' When I asked why she wanted to know, the psychologist said that most dyslexic children had eczema.

It seemed so odd to me. There didn't seem to be any possible connection. But then I started reading and trying to find things out for myself. Gradually I began to think that Nicola might be allergic. I'd never really considered the possibility before, though I was suspicious of milk. I'd noticed that chocolate seemed to make her hyperactive, and once, when we went on a long journey and she'd kept going on junk food and orange squash, she ended up absolutely beside herself.

I didn't know where to go. I'd read about cytotoxic testing in the States, and when I asked AAA about it – I'd joined not long before – they told me about Dr Downing's clinic.

The tests there showed that she was allergic to wheat, cream, cheese, chocolate, eggs, evaporated milk, all green vegetables – I found that astonishing – and additives.

Straight away we took all the suspect things out of her diet. We've managed well, and she's been very responsible. Our GP has been very supportive too. I hadn't gone to see him about her – I hadn't thought there was anything he could do – but I went to him to sign the referral form before we went. He was very interested.

After we put her on her diet, her remedial teacher noticed the difference right away. Nicola could sit down, she could concentrate, she could take things in. Now essays are no problem – before they were a dreadful struggle. She'll probably always be a bit dyslexic, but today she's not bad at all. She says she feels as though her head has cleared. She's a happier person altogether.

'What a waste!': Derek Foote, age 45

When I saw the change in Nicola it started me wondering whether I might perhaps be allergic too. I'd not been well for ten years, without any real reason. Not ill enough to go to a doctor, but not fit. I kept getting headaches and migraines – nothing dramatic. I just lived with it. My job took me travelling 150,000 miles a year by plane and I put it down to that, all the time changes and so on.

When my wife suggested that Nicola's difficulties might be due to dyslexia, and that that might be caused by allergies, I must admit I was sceptical. But after the testing, and after we'd seen the results, I decided to go to York myself. That was three months ago.

I found I was allergic to a whole range of foods: wheat, grapes, yeast, cheese, chocolate, pears, apples, beef, peanuts and lots of other nuts. The cheese and chocolate I'd suspected before, and the alcohol too – I hardly drink any – but some of the other things shook me rigid! I'd been eating a lot of peanuts: I'd take them with me to eat on the plane.

Well, I cut out everything on the list, and now I feel perfectly well. I never remember waking up before and thinking I'd had a good night's rest, and now that's happened to me several times. My head is absolutely clear. Always before I'd had catarrh. Now I can breathe – it's a wonderful feeling. I used to feel depressed at times, and that's completely gone. Recently I went back to houses I'd lived in. I can remember, with one we had on holiday, how very depressed I felt. What a waste! And in 3 months I've lost 2 stone. I'm self-employed now, and probably under more pressure than I've ever been before, but I feel tremendous.

Dr N P D Downing, MBBS, LicAc, was from the age of thirteen an assistant at his mother's mission hospital in Africa. On returning to England, he 'worked an apprenticeship in the Cheshire Homes.' After qualifying at Guy's Hospital in 1972, he spent six months working in a psychiatric hospital, and then took a succession of hospital jobs before working for a year in general practice. Becoming interested in acupuncture, he trained at the College of Traditional Chinese Medicine at Leamington Spa. After qualifying in 1977, he worked in the Pacific for three years to raise money to establish here his own practice as a doctor/acupuncturist. The following year he went to the States for a course organized by the American Society of Clinical Ecologists, and in 1982 set up a clinic offering alternative medicine and cytotoxic testing.

It was never part of Dr Downing's original intentions to become involved in alternative medicine. He originally intended to pursue a career in psychiatry, but found his early experiences in his psychiatric hospital unsettling, and even began to doubt the correctness of psychiatry. 'A lot of time was spent discussing and categorizing patients, but separating them into different groups didn't seem to lead anywhere or to do the patients any good.'

Acupuncture
His confidence in orthodox medicine was also affected by his wife's experience. Following her first pregnancy, she was left with a constant kidney problem. Eighteen months of antibiotics produced no results, but a course of six acupuncture treatments helped her to recover.

His subsequent training in acupuncture, in the company of interested doctors, nurses and physiotherapists, further opened his eyes. He knew that he wanted to practise a broader medicine than he had been taught.

When he first set up his clinic he obtained many good and some exciting results, often with difficult patients. Yet there were others whom he remained unable to help. Two of his patients wondered whether food allergies might be involved; so he re-read *Not All in the Mind*, took his patients through the diets, got dramatic results, and set out to learn more.

Cytotoxic testing

During his clinical ecology course in Colorado he met specialists who made use of cytotoxic testing as well as or instead of elimination diets. He visited a husband-and-wife team in St Louis who had been using and researching into this method for over twenty years: Dr W T K Bryan – an ENT doctor – and his wife, Mrs M P Bryan, a laboratory technician.

Once back in Britain it took him a year to organize and set up a laboratory and clinic offering alternative medicine and cytotoxic testing. After an initial massive response from a backlog of patients who were on the point of going to the States for the test, he now sees some six new patients with food-related problems each week. He estimates that for every three food-sensitive patients he has two affected by inhalants and one by chemicals. (This concerns only those with noticeable, short-term, large reactions, and does not take into account those to whom chemicals may be causing slow, imperceptible long-term damage.)

For the test, a small amount of blood is taken; the white cells and platelets are drawn off, re-mixed with serum and sterile water, and placed on slides in contact with extracts of suspect foods or chemicals. Over the next few hours specific reactions and changes are observed, and the foods or chemicals causing alterations or damage to the cells are placed in graded categories. The standard test covers 59 common foods, chemicals and inhalants. Additional tests are available on request for a whole range of less common foods and chemicals – including the patient's own tap water if desired.

The accuracy of cytotoxic testing varies, but averages 80%. It depends on the skill and judgment of the technician, the recent dietary history of the patient, and the effects of past and current drug therapy. Its usefulness also relies to a large extent on the interpretation of the results, and their practical application. Dr Downing observes that, as an 'off-the-street service', cytotoxic testing is not a useful tool. It needs to be considered together with a full diagnostic and dietary history.

Nonetheless, he considers that it can be a very useful guide, and that – carried out by careful technicians, and translated by a skilled medical adviser – it can attain a high degree of accuracy.

Studies of cytotoxic testing

A recent Californian study, carried out in 1981, looked at the effects of elimination diets based on the results of cytotoxic tests used by 65 patients. They were divided into two groups. All the patients were told to eat a cytotoxic positive food for several weeks; then to eliminate it for five days; then to challenge it by eating it again on the fifth day. The first group were directed to eat foods which had been genuinely identified as causing a positive reaction; the second 'control' group were in fact taking foods which had caused a negative reaction. On the fifth day, 53 out of the 55 members of the first group developed symptoms – varying from minor to severe – after the challenge. None of the control group did so. (R J Trevino, *Laryngoscope* 91, 1981 1913-1936).

A much earlier, but more extensive, survey carried out in 1960 demonstrated that when 170 patients with 133 itemized symptoms eliminated foods identified by cytotoxic testing they found 85% of their known symptoms were improved. (W T K Bryan and M P Bryan, *Laryngoscope* 70, 1960 810-824).

Patients

The majority of Dr Downing's patients are referred by GPs or clinical ecologists: 50% he sees in person, and are mainly referred by GPs; 50% send blood samples, and are mainly referred through clinical ecologists. He will not, however, refuse to see self-referred patients, though he tries – almost always successfully – to persuade them to allow him to write to their GP.

Many of those who come for testing already know that they have food allergies; a second group consists of those who have positive diagnoses such as rheumatoid arthritis, colitis or cystitis, and wish to know if allergies might be involved.

Dr Downing also considers that cytotoxic testing offers a possible solution to those who, for one reason or another, are unable to embark on elimination diets. Although he acknowledges that diets can be highly effective in detecting the causes of allergy, for some people they are in practice difficult to undertake. Other problems too can arise. For certain individuals, it can be difficult to determine safe foods; while some take longer to react than others. Unless the total diet is carefully supervised over weeks or months, it is possible for patients to become low in vitamins, leading to enzyme deficiency and thence, among other problems, to a hypersensitivity to chemicals.

For all these reasons, Dr Downing feels that cytotoxic testing offers a useful service: but *only* as part of an integrated approach. His patients are all given a full consultation, with a detailed case history and examination, and are all given a detailed booklet with full explanations of the test itself, various elimination and rotation diets, food families, and substitute foods and recipes. Dr Downing does not approve of patients' attempting elimination diets unaided, and expects either to supervise them himself or that their GP or clinical ecologist will do so. By and large, he has a good relationship with local GPs. With GPs in other areas he tends to find suspicion or caution rather than hostility.

He sees most patients four times, although some clear up after only two sessions, and some take five or six. There are also a few long-term patients who need constant support.

Enzyme potentiated densensitization
He can also offer EPD – Dr L M's treatment. Some patients come especially to be treated in this way: particularly those who have a mixture of food, chemicals and inhalant sensitivities, or who are leading the kind of life that makes it difficult to follow a diet. One such patient is a national schoolboy fencing champion. Dr Downing nursed him along for a year, but he was still facing problems. In one championship he was fencing six times during the day, yet eating nothing because it made him ill. On EPD he is doing well. Dr Downing finds it an effective long-term treatment: 'Not perfect – none is – but it gets steadily more effective as time goes by. Two years is the minimum period for successful treatment.'

Dr Downing hopes to see more research refining the use of cytotoxic testing. Meanwhile, he considers it a useful tool which enables unhappy and often confused patients, faced with a wide range of allergy-producing foods, to start by concentrating on eliminating first those which testing shows to be most hostile.

Chapter 15

Allergy and Orthodoxy

'After my wheat injections they said I looked like someone mentally ill': Joyce Yates, age 42

As a child I had constant sore throats, swollen glands and diarrhoea. I was overweight and my stomach would swell up. In my teens I got painful, swollen breasts; I suffered from terrible depression and I'd get anxiety attacks. They even thought of giving me hormonal injections, but luckily they didn't.

When I was seventeen I got engaged and went on a diet. Everything vanished – the fat and the depression. Of course I know now that as part of my diet I was giving up all those things – bread, cake, biscuits, puddings – which had been making me ill.

At 24 I got severe post-natal depression. The doctors wanted me to have ECT treatment, but luckily again I didn't. My GP told me I was a manic depressive and put me on drugs.

Then five or six years later a different doctor diagnosed me as having typical allergic symptoms. He said there was nothing he could do, and more or less told me to go away and get on with it.

Seven years ago I gave up work, took in two stressful foster children, then got pregnant again. I became really ill. I had swollen glands in my neck and my head was covered in sores. To start with I thought it was stress, and I noticed that I was always worse around my period time.

I began keeping a diary. I found that I was always very bad on Monday and Tuesday. I thought about it, and I realized that at week-ends I'd had a bit of a blow-out – eating cakes and pastries and things.

I went to see a new doctor, a woman GP. She was very sympathetic, and referred me to Dr Finn. He took it seriously, and explained everything to me. He took me into hospital three times for tests – the last time was six months ago. To start with we thought it was just a wheat allergy, but now I know I also react badly to dairy products, chocolate and oranges.

I know exactly what will happen if I eat the wrong thing. If it's wheat, for example, I'll be okay for six or eight hours. Then I get very very tired; absolutely lethargic. Two hours later I get diarrhoea. After another twelve or fourteen hours I get a pain in my stomach and it swells up, my head itches, my eyes go puffy, and I get very agitated and angry. Two to four hours after that I get a panic attack that lasts about an hour; then I feel a black depression. That lasts about three to four hours. Finally, there's a manic phase when I want to rush around doing everything at once.

I used to find it difficult to explain to people about this. I felt ashamed. I wanted to keep it quiet. I felt very alone.

But about a year ago I began to come out with it. I found that my friends and acquaintances split into three quite distinct groups. Some just cut me right out – they would *never* ask me for a meal now. Others go out of their way to do *everything* they can to help: they look on an invitation as an interesting challenge. And there's a third group who pay no attention whatever to what I say: they seem to want to pretend that everything's okay – perhaps they want to prove I'm making it up. It's difficult when I'm faced with a table on which there's virtually nothing I can eat.

Even in hospital there were nurses to start with who clearly thought it was just a funny fad, but they changed their minds when they saw the effects that injections had on me. After I'd had the wheat injections they took photos of me to show the different stages. They said I looked like someone really mentally ill. It makes me realize that lots of people in mental hospitals must be suffering in the same way; and of course the sort of food you get given there is exactly the sort of food to keep people like me really ill.

'At times I'd bang my head against the wall': Stan Alecock, age 45

I started having migraines from the age of five. By the time I was fifteen I was in hospital with third nerve paralysis: my left eye was tight shut and wouldn't open. They suspected a tumour. I had various tests, but nothing was found and I was discharged.

I kept on having migraines periodically – perhaps every two months. They began to happen more and more frequently, until when I was 28 ! had third nerve paralysis again and ended up back in hospital. The severity of the pain was killing the nerve. I had more tests, but again without any results.

Soon I was having migraines perhaps two or three times a week. I was sent to neurologists and specialists, who put me on various drugs; not ergotamine – they found I might be allergic to that – but various others including tranquillizers. They had all sorts of side effects – sickness, diarrhoea, hallucinations – but I put up with those thinking they might be doing some good. They didn't. Once a month I'd be back to the doctor.

I was married at 21 and I had two children. It was hard on my family. I was lucky: my wife was very supportive. It wasn't easy for her. I got *very* depressed. Sometimes I'd be up all night. I'd get numbness in the tongue, cheeks, even my fingers; then flashing lights in my eyes, and then the migraine proper would start. At times I'd bang my head against the wall to feel a different type of pain.

I was ready to try anything. Spiritual healing, hypnotism, acupuncture. Nothing helped.

Finally, my GP referred me to Dr Finn. He knew him personally, and he'd been discussing these ideas with him. I'm not sure he was convinced himself, but he suggested that it was worth trying.

On my first visit in September 1978 Dr Finn's opening words were: 'I'll cure you.' I didn't actually believe him, but it had a very uplifting effect.

He started me off on what he called his 3C diet: no caffeine, chocolate or cheese. After that we tried leaving out other things: meat, potatoes, alcohol, cigarettes. I saw him every couple of months, and kept a record in between. Nothing seemed to make much difference.

Dr Finn thought that because I had been suffering from migraines for so long I was probably reacting to a combination of foods and food additives. In February 1980 he took me into hospital, and I had a 'chemical diet' for ten days to clear out my system. Then I had one food at a time to build up a staple diet.

In March I went back home and tried a new food every fortnight. Dr Finn told me that we might never find the actual food or foods, but by introducing things so gradually it would give the allergy time to heal itself. Personally, I didn't mind whether we found it or not as long as I kept on being well. By this time I hadn't had a migraine for two months.

I went back to work in March. I was discharged by Dr Finn in October 1981, and I have never had a migraine since. Even now when I wake up in the morning I can still hardly believe it. The only sign I have now is that the iris of my left eye is completely dilated: it's twice the size of the other one and I have little sight in it. But that's a very small thing compared to the complete freedom from pain I enjoy.

> *Dr Ronald Finn, MB, ChB, MD, FRCP, qualified in Liverpool in 1954. After holding two junior posts in the Liverpool area, he went as a Fulbright fellow to the Johns Hopkins Hospital in New York. On his return he became a consultant physician at the Royal Southern. This later merged with several other hospitals to become the Royal Liverpool, where he has remained ever since. He is at present Consultant Physician, and is a founder member and Secretary of the British Society for Clinical Ecology. In 1981 he won the Lasker Award – the top medical award in the United States – for his contribution to the team which discovered the vaccine for Rhesus babies.*

Dr Finn has become increasingly interested in clinical ecology over the past seven years, ever since – shortly after its publication – he read what he now refers to as 'The Book'. He was fascinated, and concluded by thinking that if only a fraction of what it said was true it was of immense importance. His immediate reaction was to go and meet its writer.

'I wanted to see for myself whether he was a nutcase or not. Well, of course, you only had to talk to him for five minutes to realize that he was absolutely genuine. Indeed, I would go so far as to say, as I said once in a talk I gave to AAA, that I believe that history will come to recognize him as one of the major figures of British medicine.'

A clinical study of six cases

As a result, Dr Finn began to undertake a clinical study of patients at the Royal Southern Hospital who had not been helped by conventional investigation and treatment, and whose case histories suggested the possible involvement of foods or drinks. In all cases elimination produced positive results, and in three cases was followed up double-blind testing which confirmed the diagnosis. Patients had previously shown psychological as well as physical symptoms: depression, agoraphobia, lethargy and irritability. This study was the first of its kind in Britain.

Case No. 1: a married woman who for four years had had episodes of pain below the left breast, was terrified of a possible heart attack and suffered from acute agoraphobia, having to take a taxi to her shop two hundred yards away. X-rays and lung-scans proved negative. Her case history revealed an addiction to tea. She was double-blind tested, using a nasogastric tube (leading through the nostrils down to the stomach), for tea, coffee and tomato – interspersed with water. A pulse rate of 160 per minute, together with the symptoms she described, followed in 2½ hours after tea, coffee or tomato, but not after water. Following avoidance of her harmful foods, all her symptoms disappeared and she was able to work normally in her shop.

Case No. 2: a young married man who had had headaches for many years, suffered from acute insomnia, and had had to give up work. He went on to have bladder problems and back pain, and became virtually house-bound. Routine tests had all been normal. He had originally been assessed by a psychiatrist as suffering from anxiety over his wife's expected confinement. On subsequent investigation, it was discovered that he was drinking more than twenty cups of coffee a day. On giving this up, he lost all his symptoms and was able to start work again.

Case No. 3: a thirteen-year-old girl who had had large and painful mouth ulcers since infancy, was in constant pain, had frequently missed school, and was depressed, frustrated and difficult. All tests, including barium studies and a jejunal biopsy, had proved negative; drug therapies had all proved ineffective. On being admitted to hospital on a meat and water diet, she developed only one ulcer in three weeks. She was subsequently found to be sensitive to potato, coffee and chocolate. Without these, she remained completely ulcer-free.

Case No. 4: a young man who for three years had suffered from severe stomach pains, on one occasion being admitted to hospital for suspected renal colic. All investigations, including an intravenous pyelogram, were negative. He himself suspected a possible connection with alcohol. On being admitted to hospital he was double-blind tested on several occasions with tea and water given through a nasogastric tube. Each time tea was given he had a tachycardia with stomach pains appearing the next day. Alcohol produced a similar response. Without alcohol or tea he had no further problems.

Case No. 5: a 32-year-old woman who had suffered from nausea and vomiting since childhood, to such an extent that she rarely ate out. She was depressed, lethargic, travel-sick and irritable. Patch-tests at an allergy clinic had proved negative. On being tested with tea and water she responded thirty minutes after each dose of tea with vomiting, but never after water. After omitting tea she remained symptom-free.

Case No. 6: a middle-aged man who had been treated with a thiazide diuretic for high blood pressure, and who, after remaining symptomless for years, developed chest pain, sweating, faintness, sickness, and a general feeling of panic. Initial tests for a possible coronary thrombosis were negative. He later had ECT treatments but remained tired, anxious and suicidal. After an operation for renal-artery stenosis, his blood pressure became normal, but his psychological symptoms remained. He was on high doses of tranquillizers. A dietary investigation then revealed that he drank coffee and tea frequently. On avoiding these, he felt better within three days; subsequently all his other symptoms disappeared, and he was able to return to work.

First Lancet paper on food allergy
These investigations led to the publication, on 25 February 1978, in *The Lancet*, of a paper by Dr Finn and Dr H Newman Cohen called 'Food allergy: fact or fiction?' For the very first time, the concept of food allergy had appeared in this country in a conventional medical journal. A few months later this was followed by a leader also entitled 'Food Allergy'; and 'from this time, very gradually, food allergy became to some extent respectable.'

The Clinical Ecology Group
Shortly afterwards Dr Finn, together with a few like-minded people, combined to form a small medical society under the chairmanship of the now retired Dr George Hearn of Birmingham. The Clinical Ecology Group, as it was then called, has since grown into the British Society for Clinical Ecology, with Dr Finn as Secretary. This now numbers about 120 members, most of whom practice clinical ecology to some extent.

Patients
Dr Finn currently takes two clinics a week, in either of which food-allergic patients may appear. Most of his work is still general medicine, and most of his patients are local, but he also sees others from all over the country. All must be referred by GPs.

Most of his food-allergic patients are treated by elimination diets, with all sorts of variants depending on the case histories. Where simple elimination diets fail to produce results, he prescribes the lamb and pear diet, or other allied versions.

He estimates that this takes care of 80% of patients. The rest are treated in various ways. Some are taken into hospital and fed with chemicals: the pure constituents of food. 'It's easier for patients than a full-scale fast, and we can keep it up for longer, while the patients are supervised all the time.' Some are treated with injections and drops. Others he finally concludes are not food or chemically allergic at all.

The future of clinical ecology

He is interested in clinical ecology in its widest sense: in the overall effects of the environment – foods, chemicals, pollution in the air, soil and water – on the health of individuals. Most recently, for example, he has been researching into the relationship between salt consumption and high blood pressure ('Blood pressure and salt intake', *Lancet*, 1981).

'Where does the future of clinical ecology lie? With fringe medicine, or as part of orthodox medicine? We are now at last beginning to get grants for research. Here at the Royal Liverpool we are looking for antibodies in human blood. Dr Freed at Manchester is researching the possible connection between cereals and schizophrenia. Dr John Hunter and Dr John Soothill have both recently demonstrated a relationship between foods and symptoms.

'I feel it is vitally important to validate techniques and to have clinical ecology accepted within the NHS. Only then will we get adequate funding for research; a secure place for it as a field in which young doctors will want to specialize; and a treatment for all those who need it and not just for those who can pay.'

Chapter 16

Towards Help

You may by now be convinced that you, or members of your family, are suffering from symptoms which could be attributed to either diet, chemicals, or both.

Outlined below you'll find some possible steps to take. Which you choose, and in what order, depends on how clearly you see your problem and its solution; how much support you can expect to have; and your circumstances.

1. Consult your GP

It's important to start by consulting your GP to make sure there's no other diagnosable cause for your condition. If not, try to explain your interpretation of the situation, and seek his/her involvement. The number of doctors interested in this approach is steadily growing. Those who are already knowledgeable, or prepared to be open-minded, can offer counselling, support in handling withdrawal symptoms, and prescriptions for certain vitamin and mineral supplements.

2. Specialist help, through the NHS and privately

Your GP may refer you to an NHS allergy clinic. At the time of writing, only a handful can give any specific advice on how to cope with food or chemical allergies.

You may also be referred to one of the few doctors specializing in this approach. Where interventionary methods are involved, this at present is only obtainable privately. If you have private insurance it may be possible to claim against this. In certain limited circumstances, it may be possible for drops prescribed by a specialist to be re-prescribed by a GP and thus be obtainable through the NHS.

Some doctors will also see self-referred patients. Contact

Action Against Allergy, the National Society for Research into Allergy, or the Hyperactive Children's Support Group for advice (see page 247).

Some practitioners of alternative medicine may also be able to help. Your GP may be able and willing to refer you, or you may have a recommendation from a satisfied patient. Homoeopathic treatment, incidentally, is available through the NHS at hospitals in London, Bristol, Tunbridge Wells, Liverpool and Glasgow. (See also page 248.)

In-patient treatment is still virtually unobtainable through the NHS, and even when beds are made available the hospital conditions are not ideal for chemically sensitive patients. At the time of writing, one consultant-run private clinic has opened in the south of England, and another is due to open in the north in spring, 1985.

3. Support groups

At any stage of your progress, you're likely to welcome the presence of a local support group. Members give both emotional and practical help, through monthly or fortnightly meetings, and by being personally available in between times. Your GP, AAA, NSRA or HCSG may be able to tell you if there is one near you.

Warning Some sort of help is almost essential. Although the principle behind the treatment by elimination of allergically-caused illnesses is easy to grasp, putting this understanding into practice can be difficult; and in some cases quite impossible. This is particularly important where psychological symptoms are involved, and where it can be dangerous to attempt any kind of withdrawal without skilled and understanding support.

Self-help

Bearing all the above provisos in mind, some of the following steps are possible as a form of self-help, especially when combined with advice and support from doctors, specialists, or practitioners of alternative medicine.

Self-help is most likely to succeed where there is a well-founded suspicion as to the cause or causes of the symptoms, where it is relatively simple to avoid these, where there is strong motivation to persevere with a changed way of life, and where there is support and understanding from relatives and friends.

INVESTIGATING FOODS

1. General diet

If your former diet has been less than good (see Chapter 3), then the first step to take is a nutritional overhaul. This means switching away from refined flours, sugar, processed and packaged foods, and turning to wholemeal flours, brown rice, pulses and fresh fruit and vegetables, using limited amounts of oils, fats and dairy products; and – unless you're a vegetarian – modest helpings of meat, fish, rabbit, poultry and eggs.

Dietary supplements, in the form of vitamins and minerals, can also play an important part. Blood tests (arrangeable by your GP) can show certain deficiencies; otherwise, again, help can only be found outside the NHS.

Often the adoption of a reformed diet will – over weeks rather than days – either alleviate or remove symptoms of ill health.

2. A rotation (or rotary) diet

This is a specialized version of the 'good' diet above, in which no form of food from any one food family (see page 22) is taken more than once in every four days. This can help a seriously ill patient achieve a very basic stability, and may enable those who are less ill to be able to cope with their food allergies without taking any further steps.

3. Elimination diets

A good general diet will not, however, be enough if you're reacting to specific substances: to foods which are 'good' in themselves but 'bad' for the individual. There are different ways of tackling this problem, depending on individual circumstances.

(a) *Elimination of any one food* which has become suspect because it's taken daily and often in quantity; particularly when it's actively craved for. If a child downs a bottle of squash a day; or an adult drinks fifteen cups of tea; or a teenager gets through 3lb of cheese in a week; then it's reasonable to start by removing these specific items. The suspect food or drink should be eliminated for five days, and reintroduced on the sixth. If the response is to feel worse for the first two or three days, to feel increasingly better thereafter, and to suffer a reaction on reintroduction, then this is a clear indication that the eliminated food or drink is harmful. Complete avoidance will avoid recurrence of the symptoms.

(b) *Simple elimination of groups of foods/drinks*
Although it's possible to react only to one or two substances, it's

more common to react to several, often those in the same family. Where there's a marked finger of suspicion pointing to any one food or drink, it's advisable to eliminate one whole group – but only one group – at a time. The following three are strong candidates.

(i) *Tea/coffee*. These are not related, but because they're often drunk both frequently and impartially, it makes sense initially to treat them both together. Often it turns out that one person can drink tea but not coffee, and another coffee but not tea.

(ii) *Dairy products*: the most common group of allergens. Though some may be able to drink milk but not eat cheese, and others take cheese but not milk, again it's simpler to cut out *all* dairy products while testing. This means not only no milk, cheese or butter, but no margarine (unless kosher or one guaranteed totally milk-free), and no products containing dried milk or sweeteners, which are often processed from milk.

(iii) *Grains*: the second most common group of allergens. Again, many can eat wheat but not corn, corn but not wheat etc., but for the purpose of elimination it's easier to cut out all the grains together, and thereafter reintroduce them individually. Grains are more difficult to handle. It may prove necessary to leave them out of the diet for longer than five days; while reactions subsequent to reintroduction can take forty-eight hours or even longer to show up.

Among other foods and drinks which are likely to cause reactions are chocolate, colas, citrus fruits, eggs, pork and bacon, tap water, and foods containing additives. However, *any* food *may* cause an individual reaction.

(c) *Other elimination diets*
Other diets permit you to eliminate several groups of foods simultaneously. Of these, Dr Mackarness's (see page 23) and Dr L M's (see page 137) are both simple to follow, nutritionally sound, and lead to well-balanced meals which are good to eat. All such diets rely on using those foods which in practice have proved *less* likely to produce reactions. While most people will improve on these, some may still not do so; and further investigation will be needed. The same is true of Dr Mansfield's more fundamental lamb and pears diet. Although most patients are not allergic to either of these, some individuals will nonetheless react.

(d) *A total 5-day fast on spring water*
This is difficult for individuals to attempt on their own,

especially when working; it is not recommended unsupervised. It does, however, have the great advantage that during the fast it generally becomes clear – through remission or otherwise of the symptoms – whether or not food allergies are in fact involved.

Clearing acute reactions to foods
Where symptoms to reintroduced foods are severe, they can be relieved either by taking 2 tsp of sodium bicarbonate in ½ pint of water, or 1gm of vitamin C, also in a large glass of water. Don't take either more than twice in one day.

---

4. Reintroduction of foods
Some doctors suggest re-introducing three foods a day; others only two. All suggest bringing grains back cautiously: with only one a day, or one every two days. The foods least likely to cause trouble are brought back first, as the aim is to re-establish a nutritionally balanced diet as rapidly as possible.

The severity of any reactions can be estimated both by the reappearance of symptoms, and by pulse changes (see page 21) with the pulse taken before exposure to the food and at intervals afterwards. Symptoms and pulse changes often correspond, but either can exist independently of the other. Renewed symptoms are considered more important than pulse changes.

INVESTIGATING CHEMICALS

So far, the emphasis has been on food rather than chemical allergies, despite the observation that chemicals are at least as important, and possibly more so. This is simply because (a) nutrition is a first line of defence (a good diet makes people less vulnerable to chemicals), and because (b) we have more control over what we eat than over what chemicals we are exposed to.

The following suggestions are largely concerned with what is practicable rather than what might be ideal.

1. Chemical residues in foods
There is evidence that some react not to actual foods but to the chemicals in them. There is also evidence – from specific feeding trials rather than analytic tests – that organic foods are more nutritious. For those who are highly allergic, it is usually *essential* that they eat only organically grown foods. For others, it is a sensible precaution to prefer them whenever possible.

2. Chemical additives to foods
Avoidance of suspect foods + additives for 5 days, followed by

re-exposure, should indicate whether you are allergic to additives, and which ones to avoid. While most allergic people are well advised to steer clear of all foods containing additives, this may be a counsel of perfection – especially where children are concerned; and by using some detective work it should be possible to pin-point those which it is absolutely essential to avoid, those which it is merely preferable to avoid, and those which apparently produce no harmful effects (see p. 249).

3. Chemicals in the environment
If you suspect that you may be reacting to chemicals in your surroundings, then try to go away for at least a week – preferably a fortnight – to somewhere as pollution-free as possible. If you return much improved (and can discount the psychological benefits of a holiday), then you may have discovered that you're allergic to elements in your environment.

(a) *Chemicals in the home and garden*
This is a starting-point only because, again, here you're more likely to be in control; not because these are necessarily the chemicals most likely to affect you.

However, you can make a start straight away by cutting out *potential* sources of trouble you can easily do without, such as aerosols, chemically-impregnated strips, strongly-smelling polishes and cleaners. You should also be wary of perfumes, scented soaps and after-shaves. If you have problems with washing-powders, there are now non-petroleum derivatives available (see the Appendix).

As far as possible, stick to natural fibres for both clothes and furnishings. Beware particularly of moth-proofed carpeting, which may contain Dieldrin; foam-backed carpeting or underlays are also a possible hazard. Man-made fabrics, plastic lampshades, synthetic tops and surfaces can all provoke reactions in some people. Stainless steel or glass pans are safer than aluminium.

For some sensitive individuals gas is a potent source of trouble. Since taking gas out of your house, or moving elsewhere, can prove either expensive or plain impossible, it's important to try to establish whether or not gas really *is* a prime suspect. Although specialist doctors can help you here, the best test is that any symptoms diminish or disappear in its absence.

In the garden, use the minimum of chemical sprays: ideally none. Remember that pesticides and herbicides have a long-term effect. For advice on alternatives contact the Henry Doubleday Research Association and the Soil Association (see the Appendix).

(b) *Chemicals at work*
These represent perhaps the single largest hazard for chemically-sensitive individuals, and at the same time that most difficult to avoid. Many occupations involve the constant use of chemicals, while elsewhere workers are exposed intermittently. Even jobs not thought of as involving chemical hazards frequently do.

If your work makes you ill, the ideal solution is to change either the job itself or your place of work: in practice, of course, this is easier said than done. It may be possible, particularly if others beside you are also affected, to press for improvements in the environment: smokeless areas; improved ventilation; harmful substances to be shut away except when actually in use. If you belong to a union produce evidence and seek its support.

If such measures prove to be inadequate, then one solution is to consider desensitization (see below).

Remember also the effect of chemicals in prescribed drugs, including the Pill, and of cigarettes (see Chapter 6); and also of over-the-counter drugs. (Aspirin in particular is widely recognized as a potential allergen.) Consult with your GP.

TESTING AND TREATMENT

All the above steps involve detection through elimination and observation, and treatment thereafter primarily by avoidance. There are, however, other methods for both diagnosis and relief.

1. Tests for diagnosis (see pages 22-23)
Tests available through the NHS include radioallergosorbent tests (RAS) and skin prick tests. These will not identify delayed reactions; or those not associated with IgE antibodies; and both can give false positives and false negatives.

Other tests are available only privately. They include intradermal skin testing; cytotoxic testing (see page 218); measurements of electrical body charge (see page 171); bio-kinesiology (see page 182); and hair analysis (which is not used to detect allergens, but heavy metals or minerals). None of these can claim 100% accuracy: but the doctors who use them claim that as *part* of a diagnosis, and accompanied by detailed case histories, they can prove useful diagnostic tools.

2. Treatment following tests

(a) *Avoidance* (as above) Following the interpretation of the tests, and the complete diagnosis, total avoidance of the suspect substances may (as above) be possible; or partial avoidance combined with rotation dieting.

(b) *Neutralization/Desensitization* (see page 22)
Neutralization through drops has been used in this country since 1977, and in the States for over twenty years. Because a patient's condition is constantly changing, the actual drops prescribed need to be checked (and possibly changed) at regular intervals. Patients may also find that, after a certain period, they no longer need neutralizing.

(c) *Enzyme potentiated desensitization* (see page 138)
Dr M's method has been used here since 1973; it's also increasingly being used abroad. At the time of writing, it cannot be used for chemicals. It works slowly, over a period of time; the intervals between vaccinations gradually lengthen, until eventually it's no longer needed. If unusually severe reactions occur, the cup containing the vaccine can be removed and the reactions arrested.

(d) *Supplements*
These may consist of vitamin or mineral supplements; prescriptions for Nystatin (to counter candidiasis infection: see index); or Nalcrom, for occasional use (see page 76). Such supplements are not a specific treatment for allergy; but form part of the allergic person's return to health.

You'll find further help on aspects of diagnosis, dieting and treatment in a number of books (see the Appendix).

All the above possibilities form only part of a whole picture. Because an allergic person is responding to a total overload (see page 25), there are other steps that can be taken to reduce the burden. Among these are fresh air (as fresh as you can get – stay clear of main roads); daily exercise (just walking a mile a day will help); and a quiet mind. Don't be reluctant to seek help from someone else – whether it's a friend, relative, priest, or your social worker. There are counselling groups throughout the country (ask at your local Citizens' Advice Bureau for addresses) classes in meditation and yoga can also help.

As most of the patients in this book were lucky enough to discover, it *is* possible to take your health in your own hands; and with the help of doctors, family and friends – not necessarily in that order – to achieve a more positive and fruitful life than previously you could ever have imagined.

Chapter 17

When Today's Help is Not Enough

'Now I really am cornered': Fabienne Smith, age 62

I'm a combination of so many predisposing factors. There were allergies on both sides of the family. I'm a twin; we arrived two months premature. I weighed 4¼lbs and looked so terrible that my mother wasn't even allowed to see me for a week. My brother, who was the strong one, was breast-fed, but I wasn't until I was a week old.

My father, and an uncle living with us, were both heavy smokers, and the heating and cooking in all our homes was always gas. We used to go out for frequent excursions in the car, though I was almost always sick. I kept getting coughs and colds and flu. Headaches became part of my life. Aspirin made me unwell, but never dented the pain. I learned to handle it.

I had operations for umbilical hernia and grumbling appendicitis, because of the stomach pains. I was ill for a long time afterwards: they were both probably unnecessary.

I was always resting. When I was in my teens I'd be in bed by 8.30 – I was astonished to realize that others stayed up far later. I remember my mother taking me to the doctor and saying: 'She's always so languid,' but I knew I needed the rest.

But I had a very happy childhood: in fact nothing psychological has gone wrong in my life. I had a good and supportive relationship with my twin (I still do), and with both my parents.

When I started work I had to rest more than ever to keep going. At thirty I had my tonsils out for prolonged and severe sore throats; another unnecessary operation, after which I collapsed and haemorrhaged – probably a reaction from my first injected anaesthetic.

Interestingly, I was very well indeed during both my two

pregnancies. Dr William Frankland said that this can happen in a percentage of multiple allergic cases. Back home, though, and running the household and looking after my husband and two small boys, I became exhausted. When I attempted to cut down carbohydrates and eat more protein to lose a little weight, I reacted with asthma attacks, which became so severe that once my doctor gave me an injection. After that I thought the cure would kill me faster than the asthma!

Finding some nature cure pamphlets in a health food shop, I began a vegan diet. The results were dramatic. I lost all my symptoms and felt better than I had done in all my life. This lasted for seven years. During all this time, with only one lapse, I never had a cold or flu. My only relapse was when one nature cure practitioner told me not to be so strict and to reintroduce milk. I developed extreme weeping eczema until I gave it up again.

Then came the event which really pushed me down the slope. My husband inherited a legacy, and in 1972 we installed complete double-glazing and storage heating. Always before I'd lived in high-ceilinged draughty rooms in windswept Edinburgh.

It took three years for me to fully appreciate what was happening. Over the first year my symptoms gradually began to return, and after that they increased more and more rapidly. All the old ones came back, plus some new ones: abscesses and ulcers. I found I could control what was happening by cutting out still more foods, but I started to lose my ability to cope with protein in any form. At this point someone gave me *Not All in The Mind*. A great light dawned. I'd always known food made me ill, but I'd never read anything about it before. Now I said to my husband: 'This is what's been wrong with me all my life.'

He'd been ribbing me for years, but when he read it he said, very seriously: 'This is true.' It was the first time that I'd ever heard anything that confirmed what I thought. I'd never heard of multiple allergy before in all my life.

Over the years, I thought I'd worked out for myself that I *must* be allergic to foods, but when I'd tried to prove it I'd failed. In 1975 I'd been to a hospital allergy clinic for prick tests. I'd reacted to pollen and dust, but all the food ones were negative. They'd told me to stop thinking I was food-allergic, and I'd be perfectly well. Now, after I'd read Mackarness, I went to another hospital and asked for more tests. I showed them the book and the quoted references, but they weren't interested. I got in touch with the Ombudsman to protest that the NHS was not providing a service for allergics in my area. He found against me.

I got in touch with Dr Mackarness himself, who found me too difficult to help: I was the most extreme food allergy case he'd had. He referred me to Dr Mansfield, who discovered I was allergic to absolutely everything he tested. The drops weren't effective, though the injections were for some time – the problem was that my levels kept changing all the time.

He also told me to start by getting rid of our gas. We did. The effect was immediate. I had terrible withdrawal symptoms: very bad headaches, thudding heart, sore throat, cold symptoms and a painful abscess. I was able to eat protein again, and for the first time in my life I had a pale but natural colour. Before I'd always been pallid, with colourless lips.

Incidentally, one year later as I was visiting a friend I became extremely ill and was in bed for four days; on my next visit she apologized, and said she hadn't realized that the pilot light had blown out in a closed gas oven three rooms away.

Then I went to Dr Kingsley. He tried very hard too, with vitamin and mineral supplements.

Next I went to see Dr Grant, who sent me for an anti-pyrene liver test. My level was the highest the clinic had ever seen: they asked whether I was on drugs or an alcoholic. She was the first doctor to use the term 'universal reactor' to me.

Then I went to see Dr C W, who said I should cut out all tap water for washing as well as drinking and cooking, and not even to breathe it. I had even worse withdrawal symptoms than with the gas: violent diarrhoea, splitting headaches, sores and haemorrhoids, and eczema all over my body. Next day I nearly collapsed, and it took a week for the symptoms to die down. Afterwards I was much better, and I got on fine with one brand of spring water until I started to react to that too. Now I have different brands that I rotate. They all still give me a knock, but as long as I rotate them I can keep going.

After that I went to Dr Downing, who is very good and tries very hard too. He comes and sees me whenever he's in Edinburgh. I took a course of EPD, but I'm afraid I reacted again so badly that Dr Downing agreed that I shouldn't stay on it.

My situation now is that it seems nothing can help me. I'm in constant pain. When it goes down a notch or two I'm *so* happy. I have a permanent severe headache, bad pains in my face and ears, and great tiredness. Other symptoms come and go. I'm now completely housebound, because I can't tolerate any inhalants or the house dust in other people's houses. I reacted to one part in a thousand million when I was tested for neutralization. I have to stay in the atmosphere to which I'm acclimatized. I'm lucky that we have big rooms. That helps. I have the windows opened even when there's snow on the ground, and need to have the blower on all the time.

All foods make me ill. The only difference is some make me even worse than others. I have to eat everything with a little oil. At the moment, among the water Kristal is best – a spring water. I find carbonated water better than still.

I get up, do some very gentle exercises, and then some minimal chores. If I do too much my food reactions go haywire. I do all the cooking and the washing for Tom – my husband – but he does the shopping. I have a very little lunch, and then I go to bed and sleep. After I get up, I eat my main meal for the day at 5 pm. By this time I'm dying with hunger. At present I have a four-day rotated diet: green beans and oil every day (with the oil on a four-day rotation); and with them these extras:

Day 1: evaporated milk and some tinned cream.
Day 2: half a tin of tuna; some steamed figs.
Day 3: pork; a little unsweetened mixed peel.
Day 4: turkey; some sultanas.

I can't eat anything soft: I absorb it too quickly and get a tremendous knock. I take massive doses of vitamin C, and take sodium and potassium bicarbonate as an antidote to this. I also have regular vitamin B_{12} injections, and take large doses of the other vitamins and minerals recommended for severe multiple allergics.

In spite of this, I am not depressed. I have to cut my coat according to my cloth, and accept that things are as they are. I am lucky to have a very happy marriage, and two marvellous and supporting sons. I became a granny a fortnight ago: bliss! I read enormously. I love music. I do the *Times* crossword every day. And my hobby is finding out all I can about food and chemical allergies, and helping to break down the barriers of ignorance.

I know some people still think I'm making it up. Three different hospitals have told me foods *can't* cause headaches. There's a very long way to go.

'I was quite alone':
Sonja Rowe, age 40, talks about her son Alex

If only *one* person had agreed with me I'd have been all right. But no one did. I was quite alone.

Alex was our third child, born in August, 1976. He weighed 9lb – they were all big babies.

I knew there was something wrong from the start. He opened

his bowels before he was even born. They sent for the gynaecologist at 4am, but they never explained anything. Alex was put to the breast immediately, which was lovely, but the very next day he started crying.

He was such a large baby that when he was five days old they used him to demonstrate how to give a baby a bath. The nurse commented on how very dry his skin was. The next day all his fingers were septic.

When I took him home at a week old he started to get very bad eczema with weeping sores where his clothes rubbed. He refused to drink water. The health visitor said I should try it with rose hip syrup. The rash got worse. So I stopped, thinking it was the syrup that was causing it, but now I realize it could have been the water.

When Alex was three months old I went to see a specialist about his eczema, and also about the large lumps round his head and neck. He suggested various creams and an antihistamine, which seemed to help a little. But Alex still kept crying, day and night, so the health visitor suggested I should try Farex. It was a disaster. His lips blew up, he went quite blue and screamed for two hours, until I managed to give him some antihistamine.

Later, when I tried him on any other solid food, it would pass straight through in four hours totally undigested. It burnt little holes on his bottom, so he had awful sores. My GP saw nothing wrong until I showed him a dirty nappy, when he said Alex had 'intestinal hurry'! I was sent to a specialist, who didn't find anything wrong either.

So I stopped mixed feeding and just breast-fed him. I was exhausted. I would be up all night with Alex, and then up in the morning to take the other two boys to school. I was drinking lots of tap water to help keep lots of milk for Alex.

As he got older, he was affected by other things he came into contact with: toothpaste, my scent, cigarette smoke, even fluorescent lighting. There was a supermarket which only had fluorescent lighting at the butcher's counter, nowhere else, and he'd scream every time he got there.

He always had to lie on his back. If he was on his side, that cheek and eye would swell up so much where it touched the pillow that he couldn't even see.

Then when Alex was eleven months old I went to a doctor privately and was admitted into hospital. He was an awful man. He didn't believe a word I said. On one occasion, walking down the corridor, he said to the group following: 'And this mother says her child is allergic to potatoes!' And they all laughed.

When I showed him how, when I put a little cow's milk on Alex's cheek, it came up in a blister, he just commented that it didn't mean he would react the same inside – Alex just had a sensitive skin. He walked away saying it was time he came off the breast milk.

It was agony for me. The doctors expected me to stop the milk, just like that. I expressed milk for other babies – I got a letter from one of the mothers thanking me for saving her baby – but it seemed my milk was doing mine no good. Then when we went home I went back to giving him a night feed as he was so miserable.

I persevered with different foods. I kept experimenting all the time. Alex always seemed to know what he could and couldn't eat. If he was made to eat something he'd shown he didn't want, he'd always react in one way or another. He'd get blisters and swelling around his mouth where the food had touched; hot and cold shivers; stomach cramps or diarrhoea or character changes. I kept on and on writing lists about this and trying to work things out. A few people were helpful. A baker made special bread for him without additives, and Waitrose gave me a list of all their foods without additives or added milk. But no matter what I did Alex kept getting various symptoms.

When he was 15 months old he was admitted to another hospital, but under the same unbelieving doctor. The first day they starved him and gave him a glucose drink: no reaction. The next day they starved him again and gave him a lactose solution. He refused to drink it. They insisted – said I had to give it to him or it wouldn't be a test. I forced this dreadful stuff down him and he vomited it straight up. The nurse said they couldn't do the test and I should take him home.

He fell asleep in the car. I put him to bed. Next day he was still asleep. I rang the hospital, and I was told not to worry unless he went into a coma. I was terrified as I had no idea what the difference was between a deep sleep and a coma. He slept for two days and nights. I couldn't wake him. Then when I tried to feed him the food shot straight back as soon as it got to his tummy. *Still* I had no help from the doctors.

After that I kept him on a very strict five-day rotation diet, consisting mainly of baker's special bread, Outline, homemade jam, Marmite, honey; lamb, fish, pork or bacon; fresh vegetables but no potatoes, and the occasional half banana or raw apple. By now I had come across Dr Mackarness's books, which helped me to understand a little, but I found it very difficult to understand allergies, or to accept them.

Then I started taking Alex regularly to a specialist hospital. He was admitted a few times for tests, but in the end they sent him home saying I was managing him better than they could! So I was on my own again. I just didn't know where to turn for help.

The people at the playgroup were splendid. He'd take his own drink and biscuit, and he was treated exactly like all the others. The only time he felt different was at parties, because he couldn't eat the lovely birthday tea, but the rest of the time he felt the same as anyone else. He always had lots of friends to play with.

As he grew older the hospital kept pressing me to re-introduce foods again. I was horrified at the thought, as I felt I'd only just got him reasonably well. Where could I go for the right advice? He often slept in our bed for comfort, as he obviously had ghastly stomach aches most of the time. I remember one night he was so bad that after I'd given all the drugs I thought safe I had to call the doctor. He gave him still more, but Alex didn't sleep, just moaned all night. It was dreadful listening to him, knowing I couldn't help.

Then, just before he was four, we all went for a farmhouse holiday in Denmark. The super woman there cooked him special meals. For his fourth birthday she made a fruit mousse pudding, but without my knowing it she'd used a new artificial sweetener, instead of the one I'd supplied. The first time, he ate it without any problems. When he had it again the next day, he just couldn't cope. He was in a dreadful state. He passed out. He couldn't breathe, his throat was so swollen. He was blowing bubbles around his mouth. Next day he came out in tiny little septic spots all over his body.

The doctor we saw there said there was nothing to worry about; he'd only got tonsillitis. When we got back, I explained to the specialist what had happened. He wasn't really interested. He just said to go on introducing foods bit by bit. I was staggered. I felt lost. I was sure Alex wasn't right, yet all the doctors who saw him seemed to think there was nothing to worry about. It wasn't easy for me. He was very healthy looking, especially now the eczema had gone. I began to believe the doctors; it had to be me that was ill and not Alex.

It was November 4th. I was on the phone ordering Alex's special bread. I'd given him a raw, peeled carrot to keep him going till lunch (he'd often had them before). He was standing in front of me. I saw him take the first mouthful. He appeared to choke. I put down the phone to bang him on the back, but he was turning blue. Not choking – not even breathing. I rushed next door. She phoned for an ambulance while I tried artificial respiration. They took twenty minutes to get to us. They tried to push tubes down his throat. It was so swollen they couldn't. I gave them my adrenalin I carried for Alex, but they weren't qualified to use it.

When we got to the hospital I told them he was allergic. They said: 'To aspirin?' I said: 'No, to everything.' A doctor said: 'Take that mother away from here!' I was put in a side room and left. Two of my neighbours joined me. Then a young doctor came and said Alex was dead.

I was only allowed a few minutes with him – I've always regretted that.

Because of one particular doctor who knew what was going on, the verdict was anaphylactic shock due to multiple allergies. They found no carrot in his throat or stomach. He hadn't swallowed any at all. Finally the doctors believed me, and thought the cause must have been some chemical that had been used to grow or store the carrot. I'd bought them pre-packed from a supermarket, something I'd never done before.

It was a terrible death. Terrible for all of us. But sometimes I think . . . what sort of a life would he have had if he'd lived? In the short time he was with us he lived a *normal* life, as far as possible. He was such a super kid. Such fun to be with. But later – what sort of a life could he have had? To be seriously ill, year after year. All the ordinary places he couldn't go to . . . the pantomime, because of the puff of smoke. Buses, because of traces of cigarette smoke. Cinemas, restaurants, cafes . . . .

All the time I felt alone. People think you're neurotic, and when you know your child is ill, and when you know so much makes your child ill, and no one understands or listens to you, you do get neurotic. Once when we were at a cricket match someone gave him a sandwich, and I was so terrified about what it might do that I hit it out of his hand. Everyone looked at us.

People just kept saying: 'Oh, it's normal. Stop fussing.'

If only I could have had some support.

Physicians now began to be held in admiration, as persons who are something more than human . . . They filled their writings with an abundance of technical terms, utterly unintelligible to plain men . . . Those who understood only how to restore the sick to health, they branded with the name empirics. They introduced into the practice abundance of compound medicine, consisting of so many ingredients that it was scarcely possible for common people to know which it was that wrought the cure; abundance of exotics, neither the nature nor names of which their own countrymen understood; of chemicals, such as they neither had skill, nor fortune, nor time to prepare; yea, and of dangerous ones, such as they could not use without hazarding life, but by the advice of a physician. And thus a vast majority were utterly cut off from helping either themselves or their neighbours.

John Wesley, *Primitive Physic* (1747)

Appendix

Some Useful Sources for Further Help and Information
(Please send a stamped addressed envelope with all enquiries)

Action Against Allergy, 43 The Downs, London SW20 8HG

National Society for Research into Allergy, PO Box 45, Hinckley, Leicestershire LE10 1JY

Hyperactive Children's Support Group, 59 Meadowside, Angmering, Littlehamptom, West Sussex BN16 4BW

All the above will supply information on various aspects of allergy and on research into its causes and effects. Members receive regular newsletters, advice on helpful contacts, addresses of local support groups, and other practical assistance.

British Society for Clinical Ecology, the Burgh Wood Clinic, 34 Brighton Road, Banstead, Surrey SM7 1BS; or the Royal Liverpool Hospital, Prescot Street, Liverpool L7 8XP. Concerned to promote wider understanding of clinical ecology: full membership open only to medical practitioners.

McCarrison Society, 76 Harley Street, London W1N 1AE   Concerned to study the relationship between nutrition and health. In association with the McCarrison Society, A B Academic Publishers regularly publish the international journal *Nutrition and Health*.

Society for Environmental Therapy, 3 Atherton Road, Ipswich, Suffolk IP4 2LD   Provides a forum for medical practitioners, scientists and the lay public concerned with the environmental causes of disease. Publishes a quarterly newsletter.

British Society for Nutritional Medicine, 5 Somerhill Road, Hove, East Sussex BN3 1RP   Aims to foster a wider understanding of the role of nutrition in health and illness, and to encourage and disseminate appropriate research. Full membership is open only to medical practitioners; associate and student membership to those suitably qualified.

College of Health, 18 Victoria Park Square, London E2 9PF   Examines a wide range of health topics, publishes a quarterly magazine (Self Health), and runs a telephone information service.

British Holistic Medical Association, 179 Gloucester Place, London NW1 6DX   Founded by a group of doctors to encourage the principles and practice of holistic medicine; provides information, classes and self-help cassettes.

Sanity, 63 Cole Park Road, Twickenham, Middlesex TW1 1HT   Collates and disseminates worldwide research on nutritional and e'' vironmental factors in mental illness; can also offer some practical help.

Schizophrenia Association of Great Britain, Tyr Twr, Llanfair Hall, Caernarvon, N Wales   Promotes research into the biochemical causes of schizophrenia, and offers help and support to sufferers and relatives.

Action for Research into Multiple Sclerosis, 11 Dartmouth Street, London SW1H 9BL   Raises money and funds research into MS; offers 24-hour counselling, operates an education service, and sends out regular news letters.

Foresight, The Old Vicarage, Church Lane, Witley, Godalming, Surrey GU8 4AY   Advises on the importance for both potential parents of preconceptual care, correct nutrition, avoidance of chemicals, etc.

Homoeopathic Development Foundation, 19a Cavendish Square, London W1M 9AD   Gives information on homoeopathy and details of local homoeopaths.

British Dyslexia Association, Church Lane, Peppard, Oxon RG9 5JN.

National Eczema Society, 5-7 Tavistock Place, London WC1H 9SR

Myalgic Encephalomyelitis Association, The Moss, Third Avenue, Stanford-le-Hope, Essex SS17 8EL

Asthma Research Council, St Thomas's Hospital, Lambeth Palace Road, London SE1 7EH

MIND, 22 Harley Street, London W1

National Association for Colitis and Crohn's Disease, 98A London Road, St Albans, Herts AL1 1NX

Ash, 5-11 Mortimer Street, London W1N 7RH   Collates information about smoking, helps smokers to give up, and presses for an increase in smoke-free public areas.

Some Useful Books
(Books detailed in the text are omitted here)

Many of these books should be available in any bookshop. Wholefood (24 Paddington Street, London W1) and Junkantique (43 The Downs, London SW20 8HG) both stock a wide range dealing with all aspects of health: catalogues are available on request with sae. All those published by Thorsons can be obtained from their mail order department: Denington Estate, Wellingborough, Northants NN8 2RQ.

Robert Eagle *Eating and Allergy* (Futura, 1979: currently out of print, but should be available through libraries)

R Forman *How to Control your Allergies* (Larchmont Books, New York, 1979)

Theron G Randolph and Ralph W Moss *Allergies your Hidden Enemy* (Turnstone press, 1981)

W G Crook *Tracking Down Hidden Food Allergies* (Professional Books, 1980)

D Rapp *Allergies and the Hyperactive Child* (Cornerstone, 1980)

Belinda Barnes and Irene Colquhoun *The Hyperactive Child* (Thorsons, 1984)

B F Feingold *Why Your Child is Hyperactive* (Random House, 1975)

Amelia Nathan-Hill *Against the Unsuspected Enemy* (New Horizon, 1980)

Vicky Rippere *The Allergy Problem* (Thorsons, 1983)

Lawence D Dickey (ed.) *Clinical Ecology* (Charles C Thomas, 1976)

Joseph B Miller *Provocative Testing and Injection Therapy* (Charles C Thomas, 1972)

Gustave Hoehn *Acne Can be Cured* (Arco Books, New York, 1977)

Giraud W Campbell *A Doctor's Proven New Home Cure for Arthritis* (Thorsons, 1983)

A Hoffer *Orthomolecular Nutrition* (Keats, 1978)

Robert C Atkins *Dr Atkins' Nutrition Breakthrough* (Bantam/Perigord, 1981)

Patrick Holford *The Whole Health Manual* (Thorsons, 1983)

Miriam Polunin *The Right Way to Eat* (J M Dent/Europa, 1984)

Janet Pleshette *Health on your Plate* (Hamlyn Paperbacks, 1983)

Maurice Hanssen *E for Additives* (Thorsons, 1984)

The Organic Food Guide edited by Alan Gear (Henry Doubleday Research Association, 1983)

Practical Help

The Henry Doubleday Research Association, Convert Lane, Bocking, Braintree, Essex, and The Soil Association, Walnut Tree Manor, Stowmarket, Suffolk, both advise on all aspects of non-chemical agriculture, give advice to both amateur and professional organic growers, and have a constantly up-dated list of sources of organic produce.

Food Watch, High Acre, East Stour, Gillingham, Dorset SP8 5JR provides a mail order service supplying a wide range of additive-free basic foodstuffs.

Larkhall Laboratories, 225 Putney Bridge Road, London SW15; supplies mail order gluten-free flours and other food substitutes, also vitamins etc.

Wyeth Laboratories, Taplow, Maidenhead, Berkshire, and Cow and Gate Ltd, Trowbridge, Wiltshire, both produce soya protein infant formula foods.

What Can I Eat? (Pearl A Coleman, Clinic for Alternative Medicine, Lane End, Highlands Lane, Westfield, Woking, Surrey GU22 9PU: a booklet (£1.50 plus 8" x 5" sae) explaining the Stone Age diet, with menus, alternatives and recipes.

Shaklee International Health Foods, 15 Cotteridge Close, Stony Stratford, Milton Keynes, supply – through local dealers – vitamins, minerals and food supplements; and also a range of concentrated organic cleaners (i.e. *not* petroleum derivatives).

Brita UK Ltd, Ashley Road, Walton-on-Thames, Surrey, produce a jug water filter which removes chlorine, chalk, and traces of heavy metals: available through health food shops and chemists.

Cotton On, Bankside House, Great Plumptom, Kirkham, Lancashire, sells a wide range of cotton clothes of all kinds, though mainly for children.

Limericks, Limerick House, 117 Victoria Avenue, Southend-on-sea, Essex SS26 6EL, can supply by mail order pure cotton mattress covers, sheets and blankets.

Moulinex, Station Approach, Coulsdon, Surrey, manufacture a small mill which can grind substitutes into flour.

Chapman & Smith Ltd., Safin Works, East Hoathly, nr. Lewes BN8 6EW, have masks which protect against fumes and chemicals.

The Human Ecology Research Foundation of the South-West Inc. 12110 Webbs Chapel Road, Suite E-305, Dallas, Texas 75234, USA, can provide a cotton face mask with a charcoal filter to minimize the effects of traffic fumes.

Index